AF556469

PRESENT AND FUTURE FUELS AND ENERGY

PRESENT AND FUTURE FUELS AND ENERGY

By

Dr. Syed Aftab Iqbal
M.Sc., Ph.D., FICS
FICC, FIAEM, MNASc.
(Chief Editor & Co-author)

Mr. Rajkumar Sharma
B.Sc., M.Sc. (Chemistry)
Chief Manager
Central Laboratory
Indian Oil Corporation Ltd.
(Marketing division)
K-Oil Installation, Sewree
Mumbai - 4000 015

Dr. Ishaq Zaafarany
M.Sc., Ph.D.
Associate Professor
Dept. of Chemistry
Umm-Al-Qura University
Makkah Al-Mukarramah
Saudi-Arabia

DISCOVERY PUBLISHING HOUSE PVT. LTD.
NEW DELHI-110 002

Published by:
Tilak Wasan
DISCOVERY PUBLISHING HOUSE PVT. LTD.
4383/4B, Ansari Road, Darya Ganj
New Delhi-110 002 (India)
Phone : +91-11-23279245, 43596064-65
Fax : +91-11-23253475
E-mail : discoverypublishinghouse@gmail.com
sales@discoverypublishinggroup.com
parul.wasan@gmail.com
web : www.discoverypublishinggroup.com

***First Edition:* 2013**

ISBN: 978-93-5056-290-1

Present and Future Fuels and Energy

Printed at:
Aditi Fine Art Press
Delhi

PREFACE

Fuel is a combustible substance containing carbon as the main constituent while other elements associated in different percentages are hydrogen, nitrogen sulphur etc. Fuels on burning gives large amount of heat which can be used in a number of ways for industries and domestic purpose while the main use now-a-days is automobiles. There are variety of fuels used ancient times. Wood was the main source of fuel for cooking purpose. With the progress of the science a number of advance fuel like coke, coal, kerosene, diesel and petrol were used for various purposes especially in automobiles.

In the modern fuels LPS's mainly used for cooking. CNG, petrol, biodiesel and green petrol are being used gradually in order to have maximum energy, efficiency of the engines, cost and their combustion products with reference to the pollutants released in the atmosphere. The most modern and future fuels are hydrogen gas, solar energy, as a fuel as well as nuclear fuels which are supposed to give thousand times of energy in comparison to routine fuels like diesel and gasoline.

With the ever increasing demand of the fuels and the speed with which the fuel resources are going to be exhausted, it has become the need of the hour to carry out advance research in this field. And therefore this is the right time to float a book on the properties quality and economy of the various fuels. I am thankful to my co-authors **Dr. Ishaq Zaafarany,** Department of Chemistry, Umm Al-Qura University, Makkah Al-Mukaramah, Saudi Arabai as well as **Mr. Raj Kumar Sharma** (Chief Manager) Central Laboratory 'K' Oil Installation Sewree, Mumbai, India.

The book entitled **'Present and Future Fuels and Energy'** is up to the mark, both in respect of its contents and literary presentation. The book is equally useful for students, young researchers and teachers. All efforts have been made during the compilation of this book that its language is easy and understandable to the young scientist, teachers and students as well as for the common man.

Dr. Syed Aftab Iqbal

CONTENTS

Preface

1. **Introduction** 1

General Nature of Petroleum and Bulk Petroleum Products—Hydrocarbons—Other Types of Compounds in Petroleum—Types of Crude Oil—Bulk Petroleum Products—LPG (Liquified Petroleum Gas)—Naphtha—Motor Spirit—Kerosene—A.T.F. (Aviation Turbine Fuel)—HSD (High Speed Diesel)—LDO (Light Diesel Oil)—FO (Fuel Oil)—Bitumen—Fuel Chemistry—Molecular Size—Incomplete Combustion—Oxygen Content—Carbon Content—Avoiding Carbon Dioxide Emissions Entirely—Alternative Fuel Types—Fuel Source—Wholesale Availability—Retail Availability—Advantages—Disadvantages.

2. **Solid Fuels and Environment** 11

Introduction—Types of Solid Fuels—Coal—Types of Coal—Coal as Fuel—Refined Coal—Coal as a Traded Commodity—Cultural Usage—Charcoal—Coke—Coke Burning—Hexamine Fuel Tablets—Advantages and Disadvantages—Bagasse—Wood Pellets—Dung Cakes—Economic Aspects—Environmental Effects—Advantages—Disvantages—Conclusion—References.

3. **Liquid Fuels, Adulteration and Environmental Impact** 22

Introduction—General Properties of the Liquid Fuel—Fuel Impurities—Common Fuel Additives—Common Forms of Fuel Adulterants—Fuel Adulteration and Environmental Effect—Adulteration and Emissions—Impacts Due to Gasoline Adulteration—Impacts Due to Diesel Adulteration—Adulteration Detection—Selected Parameters for Gasoline Testing—Selected Parameters for Diesel Testing—Properties of Markers—Limitations of Marker System—Some Important Measures to Control Fuel Adulteration—Consumers Front: Anti-adulteration Tips—Green Fuel—Indian Standard Anhydrous Ethanol for Use in Automotive Fuel Specification—

Requirements—Packing and Marking—Marking—BIS Certification Marking—Quality of Reagents—1. Scope—2. Grades—3. Requirements—References.

4. Kerosene (SKO) **42**

Properties—History—Fuel Uses—Heating and Lighting—Transportation—Cooking—Entertainment—Other Uses—Toxicity—Kerosene/Superior Kerosene Oil (SKO)—Introduction—Test Methods as per IS 1459/1974 —Density: (P: 16 IS 1448 Methods of Test)—Distillation: (ASTM D 86, IP 123, P: 18 IS 1448 Methods of Test)—FlashPoint: (P 20 IS 1448 Methods of Test: ASTM D 56 & D 6450)—Viscosity : (P: 25 IS 1448 methods of test: IP 71 : ASTM D 445)—Method—Smoke Point-(IP 57 : P 31 IS 1448 Methods of Test: ASTM D 1322)—Method—Colour: (Blue dyed Kerosene) as per IS 1459 (second revision reaffirmed in 1991)—Thin Layer Chromatographic Methods for the Detection of Oil Soluble Dyes—References.

5. Diesel : Light Diesel Oil and High Speed Diesel **53**

Introduction—Test Method (Required as per IS 1460/2005 - Diesel Fuels)—Density: (P: 16 IS 1448 Methods of Test)—Distillation (ASTM D 86/IP 123, P:18 IS 1448 Methods of Test)—Flash Point (ASTM D 56 & 6450: P 20 IS 1448 Methods of Test)—Viscosity (P:25 IS 1448 Methods of Test : IP 71 : ASTM D 445)—Method—Pour Point (IP 15 : P 10 IS 1448 Methods of Test: ASTM D 97/D 2500)—Sulphur (IP 336 or P:83 or D4294)—Calculated Cetane Index (CCI)—Calculated Cetane Index (ASTM D 976-91)—Gas Liquid Chromatography for Quantitative Determination of Adulteration in Diesel with Kerosene—Equipment—Preparation of Samples—Observations and Calculations—Conclusion —Light Diesel Oil—Density: (P: 16 IS 1448 Methods of Test)—Flash P oint-Pensky-Marten Closed Cup (P:21 IS 1448 Methods of Test)—Method—Viscosity (P: 25 IS 1448 Methods of Test: IP 71: ASTM D 445)—Pour Point (IP 15: P 10 IS 1448 Methods of Test: ASTM D 977 D 2500).

6. Biodiesel **58**

Biodiesel--Engine Studies—Biodiesel and Air Pollution—Mixing and Storage of Biodiesel—Biodiesel Cost—Potential Fuel from Oil Crops—Engine Warranties—References.

7. Engine Lubricating Oil **65**

Introduction—Test Methods and Their Significance—Relative Density/Specific Gravity (P32 IS 1448 Methods of Test: ASTM D1298)—Significance—Viscosity:1 (P:25 IS 1448 methods of Test:

IP71: ASTM D 445 and 2170)—Method—Calculation—Viscosity Index (P 56 IS 1448 Methods of Test: IP 226)—Flash Point (P 20 IS 1448 Methods of Test : ASTM D56 : D 92: D 93: D 1310 and 6450)—Carbon Residue (P8 IS 1448 Methods of Test: IP 13, 14)—Neutralisation Value (P:1 IS 1448 Methods of Test: IP 177 ASTM D974/97)—Summary of Test Method—Procedure for Acid Number—Calculation—Procedure for Base Number—Calculation—Total Base Number of New and Used Lubricating Oils (Mobil Lubricants)—Reagents—Procedure—Standardisation of Acid—Total Base Number—Lubricating Greases—Introduction—Classification of Greases—Acidity and Alkalinity of Greases (P 53 IS 1448 Methods of Test)—Drop Point (ASTM D 2265 : P 52 IS 1448 Methods of Test)—Evaporation Loss (ASTM D 972 : P 61 & 68 IS 1448 Methods of Tests)—Corrosion (Copper Strip) ASTM D 4048 : P51 IS 1448 Methods of Tests—Oxidation Stability (ASTM D 942 :P 94 IS 1448 Methods of Tests)—Oil Separation from Lubricating Greases During Storage (ASTM D 1742 : P 85 IS 1448 Methods of Tests)—Thermal Stability (P 89 IS 1448 Methods of Test)—Cone Penetration (ASTM D 217 : P 60 IS 1448 Methods of Tests)—Worked Penetration—Prolonged Worked Penetration—Block Penetration—Furnace Oil/Black Oil—Test Methods and Their Significance—Relative Density/Specific Gravity—Experimental (P 32 IS 1448 Methods of Test: ASTM D1298)—Viscosity: Experimental (P: 25 IS 1448 Methods of Test: IP 71: ASTM B 445 and 2170)—Significance—Flash Point: Experimental (P20 IS 1448 Methods of Test : ASTM D56 : D 92 : D 93 : D 1310)—Significance—Carbon Residue (P8 IS 1448 Methods of Test: IP 13,14)—Significance—Water Content (IP74: P40 IS 1448 Methods of Test)—Significance—Experimental Conditions : Kerosene and Medium Boiling Hydrocarbon Solvents like Mineral Spirits, ATF, etc.—Hydrocarbon Characterization of Petroleum Hydrocarbon Solvents by GC-DHA—References.

8. Petroleum 79

Introduction—Basic Refinery Process : Description and History—Basics of Crude Oil —Basics of Hydrocarbon Chemistry—Non-hydrocarbons—Major Refinery Products—Common Refinery Chemicals—Petroleum Refining Operations—Introduction—Refining Operations—Description of Petroleum Refining Processes and Related Health and Safety

Considerations—Cude Oil Pretreatment (Desalting)—Description—Health and Safety Consideration—Crude Oil Distillation (Fractionation)—Atmospheric Distillation Tower—Health and Safety Considerations—Solvent Extraction and Dewaxing—Health and Safety Considerations—Thermal Cracking—Health and Safety Considerations—Catalytic Cracking—Fluid Catalytic Cracking—Health and Safety Considerations—Hydrocarcking—Hydrocracking Process—Health and Safety Considerations—Catalytic Reforming—Health and Safety Considerations—Catalytic Hydrotreating—Other Hydrotreating Processes—Health and Safety Considerations—Isomerization—Safety and Health Considerations—Polymerization—Safety and Health Considerations—Alkylation—Sulphuric Acid Alkylation Process—Health and Safety Considerations—Sweetening and Treating Processes—Health and Safety Considerations—Unsaturated Gas Plants—Health and Safety Considerations—Amine Plants—Health and Safety Considerations—Saturate Gas Plants—Health and Safety Considerations—Asphalt Production—Health and Safety Considerations—Hydrogen Production—Health and Safety Considerations—Blending—Health and Safety Considerations—Lubricant, Wax and Grease Manufacturing Processes—Health and Safety Considerations—Other Refinery Operations—Heat Exchangers, Coolers and Process Heaters—Health and Safety Considerations—Steam Generation—Heater Fuel—Feedwater—Health and Safety Considerations—Pressure-Relief and Flare Systems—Pressure Relief Health and Safety Considerations—Wastewater Treatment—Health and Safety Considerations—Cooling Towers—Health and Safety Considerations—Electrical Power—Health and Safety Considerations—Gas and Air Compressors—Health and Safety Considerations—Marine, Tank Car and Tank Truck Loading and Unloading—Health and Safety Considerations—Turbines—Health and Safety Considerations—Pumps, Piping and Valves—Health and Safety Considerations—Tank Storage—Health and Safety Considerations.

9. Ethanol **131**

Introduction—Ethanol as a Fuel—Ethanol World-wide—The Gazette of India: Extraordinary [Part I- Sec. I] Ministry of Petroleum and Natural Gas Resolution New Delhi, 3rd September, 2002 No. P-45018/28/2000-C.C.—Process-of-manufacture—Molecular-sieve-dehydration—I. Dehydration-with-Molecular-Sieve-Process—Molecular Sieve Ethanol Dehydration Technology for Fuel Ethanol—Process-description—Advantages of the System (Molecular Sieves)—Demand Supply for Ethanol—Anhydrous Ethanol Potential for Gasoline Blending—A Sugar Industry Perspective and Ethanol Production—Availability—Cost—Conclusion—Why Ethanol Blended Petrol—Ethanol and Your Car—Exhaust *Versus* Evaporative Emissions—Ethanol and Health.

10. Advantages of Ethanol Fuel 146

Ethanol Fuel as Organic Fuel—Ethanol Fuel as a Source of Renewable Energy—Ethanol Fuel Ease of Access—Ethanol Fuel Advantage of Independency—Ethanol Fuel Advantage of Employability—Ethanol Fuel is Cost-Effective—Ethanol Fuel Reduces GHG Gases—Ethanol Fuel is Environment Friendly—Ethanol Fuel Promotes Agriculture—Ethanol Fuel is Hydrogen Producer—Ethanol Challenges in a Current Scenario and Technical Tips—What are the Key Issues Related ter E10 Ethanol Use?—E10 Performance Issues Fuel Properties—Deposits—Additive Compatibility—Corrosion—Fuel Economy—E10 Blending and Handling Issues—Equipment Compatibility—Tech Tips—Bioethonal—Introduction—What is Bioethanol?—What are the Benefits of Bioethanol?—Bioethanol Production—Concentrated Acid Hydrolysis Process—Dilute Acid Hydrolysis—Enzymatic Hydrolysis—Wet Milling Processes—Dry Milling Process—Sugar Fermentation Process—Fractional Distillation Process.

11. Bioethanol from Lignocellulose 156

Bioethanol—Ethanol as Fuel—Environmental Impact—The Market—Lignocellulosic Materials—Hydrolysis—Dilute-acid Hydrolysis—By-products of Dilute-acid Hydrolysis—Organic Acids—Phenolic Compounds—Furan Compounds.

12. Solar Fuel 170

The Sun—Using Sunlight—An Introduction to Solar Energy—About Solar Power Applications—Solar Power Systems—Grid-Tied (On Grid)—Solar Power Systems—Grid-Tied with Battery Backup—Solar Power Systems—Off-Grid—Solar Power System—Direct DC—Hybrid Power Systems—Advantages of Solar Power—Advantage—Disadvantages—Relation Between Environment—Solar Energy and the Environment.

13. Solar Power 183

Introduction—Solar Water Pump for Irrigation—New Models of Solar Pumps—Photovoltaic Technology--Product and Services—Our Specialization is in Providing DC Application Solutions for—How It Works—1. Solar Cells—2. Solar Water Heating—3. Solar Furnace—Advantages—Disadvantages—Renewable and Non-Renewable—Industry and the Environment Renewable Energy—Hydrogen as Fuel—Fuel Source—Wholesale Availability—Retail Availability—Advantages—Disadvantages.

14. Nuclear Fuels 198

An Introduction to Nuclear Energy—Nuclear Fission and Nuclear Fusion—Uranium : The Nuclear Fuel—Using Nuclear Energy to Generate Electricity—Nuclear Energy and the Environment—How Does Nuclear Energy Work?—The Benefits of Using Nuclear Power—The Future of Nuclear Power—Nuclear Power Technology Development Section—Highlights and Events—New Leadership for Nuclear Power Technology Development—Non-Electric Applications of Nuclear Energy—IAEA Nuclear Power Newsletter : September 2011—Applications of Nuclear Energy—Benefits of Nuclear Energy—Limitations of Nuclear Energy—Nuclear Energy at Work—Uses of Nuclear Energy—Reasons to Use Nuclear Energy—Environmental Safety—Clean Water—Reliable—Reduces the Dependence on Fossil Fuels—Peaceful Uses—Food and Agriculture—Human Health—Advantages and Disadvantages of Nuclear Energy—What are the Advantages of Nuclear Energy?—What are the Disadvantages of Nuclear Energy?—How Does Nuclear Energy Affect the Environment?—Introduction—Carbon Dioxide--Low Level Radiation—Radioacative Waste—Cooling Water System—Nuclear Power Plant Accidents and Terrorism—Conclusion—MKVI Spareswww.gasturbinecontrols.com—Environmental Impact of Nuclear Power—Waste Streams—Radioactive Waste—High-level Waste—Other Waste—Power Plant Emissions—Radioactive Gases and Effluents—Tritium—Uranium Mining—Risk of Cancer—Comparison to Coal-fired Generation—Waste Heat.

15. Glossary : Refinery-related Terms 215

Index 221

Introduction

General Nature of Petroleum and Bulk Petroleum Products

Petroleum is the name given, to an oily liquid, which exists at various places in the earth's crust. In some places it is found at the surface in the form of seepages, in others it occurs trapped at greater or lesser depths in rocky formations. It is usually a dark coloured or black liquid with a characteristic odour imparted by small quantities of compounds such as those containing sulphur or nitrogen.

It is common to find gas associated with liquid petroleum, and in some cases wells are drilled solely for the production of this Natural Gas, which is classified as one of the forms of petroleum found in nature. There are cases where seepages and oil wells exist side by side; for example, in Southern California, the Los Angeles basin contains oilfields in which liquid crude petroleum and natural gas are produced alongside the famous La Brea asphalt pits, which contain a sticky, thick liquid form of asphaltic bitumen.

Hydrocarbons

Petroleum consists of mixtures of hydrocarbons, which is the name given to those compounds in which the molecules consist solely of atoms of carbon and hydrogen. There exist a great variety of these hydrocarbons, depending upon the number of carbon and hydrogen atoms in each molecule and the way in which the various atoms are linked one with the other. Fortunately, as we shall see, they fall into several distinct groups or series, which helps greatly in studying them.

***(a)* Saturated Hydrocarbons:** The hydrocarbon methane consists of carbon with all its valencies combined with separate hydrogen atoms. This type of compound is known as a 'Saturated' compound, since there are no possibilities of further combination of the molecule with anything else. A series of these saturated hydrocarbons exists in which chains of carbon atoms are linked together with hydrogen occupying the remaining carbon valencies. At each end of the chain will be CH_3 groups. Thus one can write:

Propane $CH_3—CH_2—CH_3$

or Butane $CH_3—CH_2—CH_2—CH_3$

The whole series of such hydrocarbons is known as the 'paraffin' series, and when the carbon atoms form a straight chain, so to speak (as above), the series is known as the 'normal paraffin' series.

(*b*) Unsaturated Hydrocarbons: In addition to the hydrocarbons in which every valency or bond is satisfied by a separate atom, there are hydrocarbons in which carbon is linked to carbon by two or more of the valencies. In this case the number of hydrogen atoms that can be linked to the carbon atoms is reduced. For example, in the hydrocarbon C_2H_4 or $H_2C{=}CH_2$ the carbon atoms are linked together by two bonds, and only two additional hydrogen atoms can then be linked to each carbon atom. It will be noticed that each carbon atom still has four valencies, but they are not all used up in separate combination with other atoms. Such a hydrocarbon is called an 'unsaturated' hydrocarbon, and the one referred to above is known as ethylene.

Hydrocarbons of this class, known as 'olefins', are not found in natural crude petroleum, but they are formed in the cracking process. Being unsaturated they can readily take part in chemical reactions and can combine with each other (polymerize), both of which facts form significant bases for some of the processes which will be discussed in later chapters.

(*c*) Ring Hydrocarbons: The hydrocarbons so far discussed have been all of the 'chain' variety. There are however, other series of hydrocarbons in which carbon atoms form closed rings. Two of the principal series found in petroleum are:

(*i*) the naphthenes or cycloparaffins;

(*ii*) the aromatics.

(*i*) *Naphthenes or Cycloparaffins*: These compounds are hydrocarbons in which the carbon atoms forming a ring are fully saturated. This means that, in addition to the bonds connecting the carbon atoms with each other, the remaining two bonds on each carbon atom are linked to separate atoms of hydrogen or an equivalent group. The ring may contain various numbers of carbon atoms, though those most frequently found in petroleum contain 5.6 or 7.

(*ii*) The second important series of ring hydrocarbons is the series whose simplest member is benzene. This is a six-carbon ring hydro-carbon in which each carbon atom in the ring has only one hydrogen atom attached.

Other Types of Compounds in Petroleum

At the outset it was pointed out that petroleum consists predominantly of hydrocarbons. In addition all natural crudes contain small quantities of compounds containing sulphur, nitrogen or other elements. Some crudes also contain appreciable quantities of complicated organic compounds containing certain metals in the molecules.

Of particular interest are sulphur compounds, which due to their bad odour, corrosive and other objectionable characteristics, make it essential to adopt processes in the refinery for their removal. Chief of these sulphur compounds is a series known as mercaptans. These compounds can be considered as hydrocarbons in which a hydrogen atom has been replaced by a grouping of an atom of sulphur and an atom of hydrogen, this:

$$\underset{\text{ethane}}{CH_3CH_3} \longrightarrow \underset{\text{ethyl mercaptan}}{CH_3CH_2SH}$$

Such compounds can react with many metals as do acids, and are therefore corrosive to such metals.

Types of Crude Oil

Although all crude oils consist mainly of hydrocarbons of the various series discussed above, oils from various sources differ widely in the proportion of the different hydrocarbon series which they contain. Thus, one type of crude oil may contain more of the paraffins, including the solid paraffin waxes, while another may contain more of the naphthenes. The products that are worth producing will therefore vary from crude to crude, and economic factors, such as market demand and accessibility, often have a determining influence on the products made. Thus, from some crude oils useful yields of lubricating oils and waxes may be obtained, while others may yield insignificant quantities of wax but may contain asphaltic bitumen together with lubricating oil of a different character due to different chemical nature. Other again may contain little lubricating oil but provide excellent stock for cracking.

In a very general way, crude oils may be divided into three classes:

(*a*) Paraffin Base Crudes: Which contain paraffin wax but little or no asphaltic matter. Such crude oils consist mainly of paraffin hydrocarbons and usually yield gasoline of low octane value and gas oil of high cetane value. They usually give good yields of paraffin wax and high grade lubricating oils.

(*b*) Asphaltic Base Crudes: Which contain little or no paraffin wax but usually asphaltic matter, often in quite large proportions. The hydrocarbons consist mainly of the naphthene series, and these crude oils yield lubricating oils.

(c) Mixed Base Crudes: Which contain both paraffin wax and asphaltic matter in quantity. Both paraffin and naphthenic hydrocarbons are present together with a certain proportion of aromatic hydrocarbons.

The above classification of crude oils is a rough and ready division into types and should not be used too strictly. There is considerable overlapping between the types in the case of most crude oils.

Bulk Petroleum Products

Crude oil consists of a very complex range of different hydrocarbons. These form precursors for a variety of specially products and the entire host of petrochemical products and the entire host of petrochemical products, apart from the bulk petroleum products. The bulk petroleum products, however, are mainly the following:

- Liquified Petroleum Gas (L.P.G.)
- Naphtha
- Motor Spirit (M.S.)
- Kerosene
- Aviation Turbine Fuel (A.T.F.)
- High Speed Diesel oil (H.S.D.)
- Light Diesel Oil (L.D.O.)
- Furnace Oil (P.O.)
- Bitumen

Some of the end-uses of the above bulk petroleum products are described below.

LPG (Liquified Petroleum Gas)

This is generally a mixture of propane and butane. At atmospheric temperature and pressure it is gas. It has therefore to be stored under pressure to keep it liquified; hence the name LPG.

LPG is used largely as a domestic fuel. It is also invaluable for use as a fuel in certain industries such as glass manufacture due to its being a clean and a convenient fuel.

LPG is alsc a good feedstock for the manufacture of various petrochemicals.

Naphtha

The most important usage of Naphtha is in the production of Motor Spirit. It is partly blended direct into M.S. and partly processed in a catalytic reforming unit to produce high octane number reformate. Reformate is then blended into the M.S. pool, Naphtha is also an important feedstock for fertilizer manufacture.

Steam cracking of Naphtha produces a large variety of olefins including ethylene and propylene which are the precursors for various petrochemicals.

Motor Spirit

This is a blend of a variety of light hydrocarbons such as straight run naphtha, reformate, cracked gasoline from crackers, alkylates etc. Octane rating of M.S. is an important anti-knock property which makes the modern high compression ratio internal combustion engines possible for automotive purpose.

Kerosene

While in India, kerosene is largely used for illumination, elsewhere it is used for heating purposes. A special cut of kerosene can be processed for the manufacture of Linear Alkyl Benzene used as a detergent.

A.T.F. (Aviation Turbine Fuel)

Aviation turbine fuel also called the jet fuel is becoming an increasingly important fuel with the development of aviation industry and with the phasing out of the earlier piston type of aero-engines. This is a kind of a kerosene cut with certain important specifications such as the freezing point of ATF should be below 47°C.

HSD (High Speed Diesel)

This is an important petroleum product used for automotive purposes in compression ignition engines. It is an important fuel used for road, rail and marine transport systems.

LDO (Light Diesel Oil)

This is an inferior kind of a gas oil used as fuel in low speed engines largely used in lift irrigation sector in India.

FO (Fuel Oil)

This is used in a variety of industrial applications as fuel in furnaces.

Bitumen

The bulk grades of bitumen are used for road making.

Source: *The above report has been extracted from the book 'Technology in Indian Petroleum Refining Industry by Department of Scientific and Industrial Research'.*

Fuel Chemistry

This page shows the chemical structure of various alternative fuels, and discusses why the following aspects of different fuels have an effect on their tailpipe emissions:

- Molecular size

- Oxygen content
- Carbon content

Molecular Size

Alternative fuels tend to be made up of small, fairly simple molecules; for example, here are schematic chemical diagrams (*C* denotes a carbon atom, *H* is hydrogen, and *O* is oxygen) of

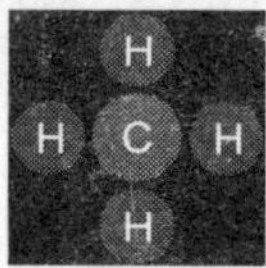

methane (CH_4), the primary constituent of liquified or compressed natural gas, and

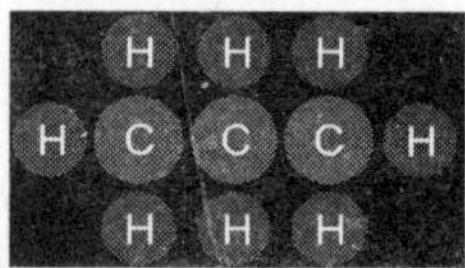

propane (C_3H_8), the primary constituent of *liquified petroleum gas.*

Petroleum fuels are blends of lots of different chemical species; in general, the molecules of a liquid petroleum fuel are pretty big and complex. Here is

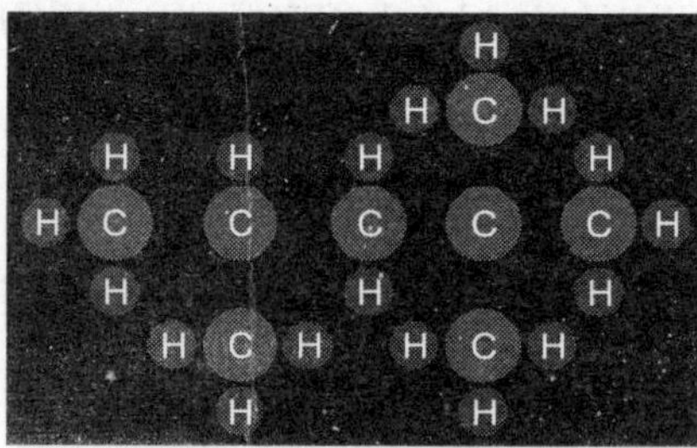

isooctane (C_8H_{18}), typical of the molecules found in gasoline (I had to spread out the structure a bit to get all the hydrogen atoms to fit in the picture—all of these molecules are, of course, three-dimensional, but some squish into a plane better than others!), and

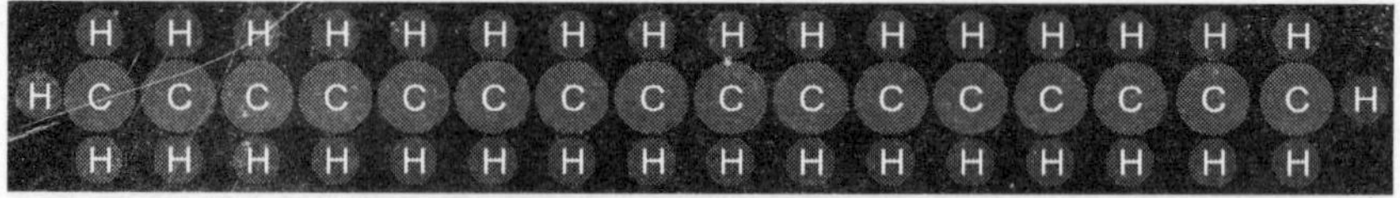

this monster is cetane, or n-hexadecane ($C_{16}H_{34}$), typical of diesel fuel.

Incomplete Combustion

When a hydrocarbon fuel (that is, one that is made up of hydrogen and carbon) burns completely, the oxygen in the air combines with the hydrogen to form water (H_2O) and with the carbon to form carbon dioxide (CO_2). If the burning is not complete, then some of the carbon atoms only combine with one oxygen atom rather than two, to form carbon monoxide (CO), a highly poisonous gas.

Some of the carbon atoms may remain stuck together with each other and with some of the hydrogen atoms as well, so that unburned hydrocarbon molecules (mostly smaller than the ones in the original fuel) can also come out the tailpipe. These unburned hydrocarbons (plus any fuel hydrocarbons that evaporate from the fuel system before getting into the engine to be burned at all) react with nitrogen oxides (another pollutant from combustion) in the presence of sunlight to form ozone, which is a lung irritant (the 'ozone layer' in the stratosphere is a shield against the sun's ultraviolet light, but at ground level ozone is the main component of 'photochemical smog'). Carbon atoms can also remain stuck to one another with few or no hydrogen atoms attached, especially during incomplete combustion of diesel fuel, producing soot.

This is one of the reasons alternative fuels are less polluting than gasoline and diesel their simpler, molecules are easier to burn more completely in an engine : so that less carbon monoxide, spot, and unburned hydrocarbons come out the tailpipe. In addition, any unburned hydrocarbons that are produced are less reactive than those that come from incomplete burning of gasoline or diesel fuel, and so they produce less ground-level ozone; methane in particular is almost incapable of forming smog.

Oxygen Content

Some alternative fuels are not hydrocarbons; alcohols and *biodiesel* contain oxygen atoms as well as carbon and hydrogen. Here are the chemical structures of the common alcohol fuels:

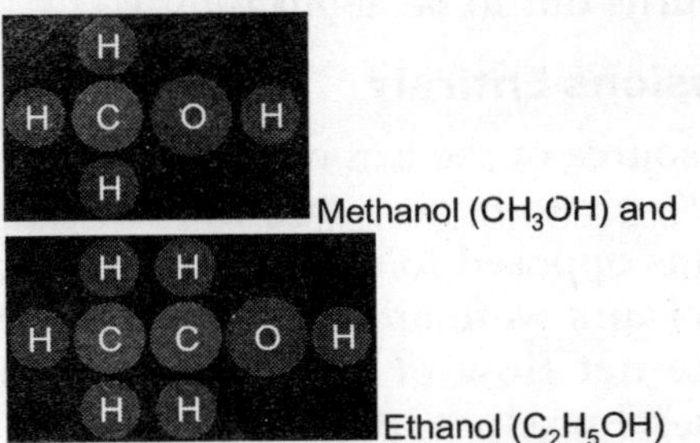

Methanol (CH_3OH) and

Ethanol (C_2H_5OH)

(Biodiesel molecules are 'monoalkyl esters', but I haven't been able to trace down anything more specific. The 'ester' part of that name, however, indicates that the molecules include oxygen atoms.)

In many parts of the USA, gasoline is 'oxygenated' during at least part of the year; this means that oxygen-bearing compounds are added to the fuel mixture. The reason for doing this is that having some oxygen as part of the fuel molecules to start with promotes more complete combustion, so that less carbon monoxide, soot, and unburned hydrocarbons come out the tailpipe, as described *above*. Alcohol fuels and biodiesel carry this one step further, in that the oxygen-bearing compound is not an additive at the 5 to 10 per cent level, but a major constituent of the fuel, which increases the benefits of oxygenation.

Carbon Content

Even if, with the aid of electronic engine controls and efficient catalytic converters, a hydrocarbon fuel is burned completely to water and carbon dioxide, there is now growing concern about carbon dioxide as a greenhouse gas. Measures to cut back on production of carbon dioxide by automobiles without sacrificing performance can focus on efficiency, *i.e.*, getting as much useful propulsive power out of a given amount of fuel as possible, which typically involves replacing the traditional drivetrain of a piston engine driving the wheels through a gearbox with a *more efficient design*.

However, some fuels inherently produce less carbon dioxide when burned completely than gasoline or diesel fuel. For example, counting the numbers of oxygen atoms it takes to burn up an isooctane molecule and a methane molecule (typical of gasoline and natural gas respectively), one can calculate that 100 oxygen atoms will combine with four isooctane molecules to produce 32 carbon dioxide molecules and 36 water molecules, while the same number of oxygen atoms will combine with 25 methane molecules to produce 25 carbon dioxide molecules and 50 water molecules. That is, a given amount of air (oxygen) will produce about 25 per cent less carbon dioxide if used to burn natural gas than if used to burn gasoline. (Of course, this advantage will be reduced if you have to open the throttle wider and burn an additional amount of air with natural gas to get the same amount of power, but in the real world the 25 per cent figure turns out to be about right.)

Avoiding Carbon Dioxide Emissions Entirely

The other thing to consider is the source of the carbon in the fuel; if it came from the carbon dioxide in today's air to begin with, like an alcohol fuel produced by fermenting biomass (as opposed to a fossil fuel, whose carbon came out of the air when the dinosaurs were around), then returning it to the air now adds nothing to the net flow of carbon dioxide into the atmosphere. Alcohol fuels or biodiesel produced from plants, when burned, just return to the air the carbon dioxide that those plants took out of the air while growing.

Finally, there's one fuel that, in itself, produces no carbon dioxide at all when burned, namely.

HH *Hydrogen*; there's no carbon there to produce carbon dioxide! Of course, since free hydrogen molecules don't occur in nature, it is typically produced by 'reforming' a hydrocarbon or alcohol fuel or by using electricity to split water into hydrogen and oxygen. Then the size of the contribution of hydrogen fuel to carbon dioxide emissions depends on the source of the hydrocarbon fuel that was reformed or the source of the electricity used to split the water.

If a fossil fuel was the ultimate source of the energy that is, in effect, stored in the hydrogen, then you can still gain a large improvement in carbon-dioxide production if the hydrogen is used in an *efficient drivetrain*, as noted above; the same is true for the electrical energy stored in a battery-powered *electric* vehicle. In order to obtain the full benefits of reduction of carbon dioxide (or of ordinary air pollutants like carbon monoxide), of course, the energy used to split the hydrogen or charge the battery can be obtained from a renewable source like wind power or photovoltaics.

The nice thing about hydrogen—or battery-powered vehicles is that they can run on whatever is available—efficient natural-gas-burning powerplants today, with an increasing contribution from renewable energy as time goes on and the price of photovoltaic cells (solar cells) and other renewable energy sources continues to decline. As renewable energy becomes an ever larger part of the power generation mix over the next few decades, hydrogen—and battery-powered vehicles can switch over to the new power sources without a hiccup—it's all electricity to them!

Alternative Fuel Types

These days, you can drive a variety of cars and trucks off the dealer showroom floor that use something besides gasoline or diesel fuel for a power source. The pages linked to the list below discuss some of the alternative fuels that are available today. There are no commercially-available hydrogen-powered vehicles (yet!), but vehicles that use all of the other fuels are available in at least part of the United States.

- Liquified Petroleum Gas (LPG, commonly known as propane)
- Compressed Natural Gas (CNG)
- Liquified Natural Gas (LNG)
- Methanol (M85)
- Ethanol (E85)
- Biodiesel (B20)
- Electricity
- Hydrogen

For each fuel type, the page discusses the following points:

Fuel Source

Where does the fuel come from?

Wholesale Availability

Is there a national distribution network already in place, as there is for petroleum fuels, and...

Retail Availability

...is it a lot harder to tap into it than it is to drive to your corner gasoline station? (There's a very good list of publicly-accessible refueling stations for several fuel types at the *Alternative Fuels Data Center*.)

Advantages

Vehicles running on any of the alternative fuels listed will emit less pollution than petroleum fuels, so I won't harp on that, but there are additional advantages particular to each fuel, including advantages relative to other alternative fuels.

Disadvantages

There are, of course, disadvantages to these fuels too, or else our transportation system wouldn't still be almost 100 per cent dependent on petroleum products!

2

Solid Fuels and Environment

Introduction

Fuel is a combustible substance, containing carbon as main constituent, which on proper burning gives large amount of heat, which can be used economically for domestic and industrial purposes. Wood, charcoal, coal, kerosene, petrol, diesel, producer gas, oil gas, etc.

Solid fuels are termed as fuels which are in solid state it includes wood, charcoal, peat, coal, hexamine fuel tablets and pellets made from wood, corn, wheat, rye and other grains. Solid fuel rocket technology also uses solid fuel.

Solid fuels have long been used by humanity to create fire. Coal was the fuel source which enabled the industrial revolution, from firing furnaces, to running steam engines. Wood was also extensively used to run steam locomotives. Both peat and coal are still used in electricity generation today.

TYPES OF SOLID FUELS

Coal

Coal is a readily combustible black or brownish-black sedimentary rock normally occurring in rock strata in layers or veins called coal beds. The harder forms, such as anthracite coal, can be regarded as metamorphic rock because of later exposure to elevated temperature and pressure. It is composed primarily of carbon along with variable quantities of other elements, chiefly sulphur, hydrogen, oxygen and nitrogen.

Coal was formed from layer upon layer of annual plant remains accumulating slowly that were protected from biodegradation by usually acidic covering waters that gave a natural anti-septic effect combating microorganisms and then later mud deposits protecting against oxidization in the widespread shallow seas—mainly during the Carboniferous period—thus trapping atmospheric carbon in the ground in immense peat bags that eventually were covered over and deeply buried by sediments under which they metamorphosed into coal. In this manner, over time, the chemical and physical properties of the plant remains (believed to mainly have been fern-like species antedating more modern plant and tree species) were changed by geological action to create a solid material.

Coal, a fossil fuel, is the largest source of energy for the generation of electricity worldwide, as well as one of the largest worldwide anthropogenic sources of carbon dioxide emissions. Gross carbon dioxide emissions from coal usage are slightly more than those from petroleum and about double the amount from natural gas. Coal is extracted from the ground by mining, either underground or in open pits.

Types of Coal

Believed approximate position of the proto-continents toward the end of the Carboniferous period; the light blue represents shallow seas where many of today's coal deposits are found, as opposed to deeper waters which gave rise to oil bearing rocks derived from marine species. The ice caps were known to be very large, lowering sea levels extensively by locking up oceanic waters into solid ice, though how large the ice caps became is a matter of debate. The position of most continental foundations in lower latitudes definitely created a series of successive shallow swamplike seas we burn for today's coal sourced electricity.

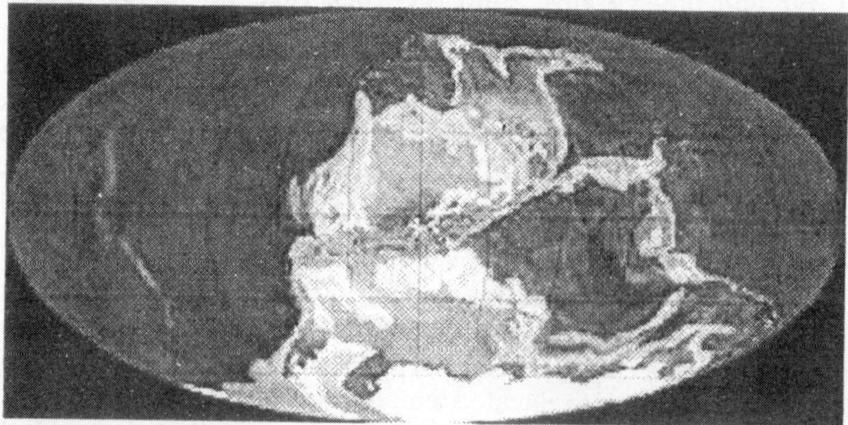

As geological processes apply pressure to dead biotic matter over time, under suitable conditions it is transformed successively into:

- Peat, considered to be a precursor of coal, has industrial importance as a fuel in some regions, for example, Ireland and Finland.

- Lignite, also referred to as brown coal, is the lowest rank of coal and used almost exclusively as fuel for electric power generation. Jet is a compact form of lignite that is sometimes polished and has been used as an ornamental stone since the Iron Age.
- Sub-bituminous coal, whose properties range from those of lignite to those of bituminous coal are used primarily as fuel for steam-electric power generation. Additionally, it is an important source of light aromatic hydrocarbons for the chemical synthesis industry.
- Bituminous coal, dense mineral, black but sometimes dark brown, often with well-defined bands of bright and dull material, used primarily as fuel in steam-electric power generation, with substantial quantities also used for heat and power applications in manufacturing and to make coke.
- Anthracite, the highest rank; a harder, glossy, black coal used primarily for residential and commercial space heating. It may be divided further into metamorphically altered bituminous coal and petrified oil, as from the deposits in Pennsylvania.
- Graphite, technically the highest rank, but difficult to ignite and is not so commonly used as fuel: it is mostly used in pencils and, when powdered, as a lubricant.

The Classification of coal is generally based on the content of volatiles. However, the exact classification varies between countries. According to the German classification, coal is classified as follows :

Name	Volatiles %	C Carbon %	H Hydrogen %	O Oxygen %	S Sulphur %	Heat content kJ/kg
Braunkohle (Lignite)	45-65	60.0-75.0	6.0-5.8	34-17	0.5-3	<28470
Flammkohle (Flame coal)	40-45	75.0-82.0	6.0-5.8	>9.8	~1	<32870
Gasflammkohle (Gas flame coal)	35-40	82.0-85.0	5.8-5.6	9.8-7.3	~1	<33910
Gaskohle (Gas coal)	28-35	85.0-87.5	5.6-5.0	7.3-4.5	~1	<34960
Fettkohle (Fat coal)	19-28	87.5-89.5	5.0-4.5	4.5-3.2	~1	35380
Esskohle (Forge coal)	14-19	89.5-90.5	4.5-4.0	3.2-2.8	~1	<35380
Magerkohle (Non-baking coal)	10-14	90.5-91.5	4.0-3.75	2.8-3.5	~1	35380
Anthrazit (Anthracite)	7-12	>91.5	<3.75	<2.5	~1	<35300

The middle six grades in the table represent a progressive transition from the English-language sub-bituminous to coal, while the last class is an approximate equivalent to anthracite, but more inclusive (the U.S. anthracite has <6% volatiles).

Cannel coal (sometimes called 'candle coal'), is a variety of fine-grained, high-rank coal with a large amount of hydrogen. It consists primarily of 'exinite' macerals, now termed 'liptinite'.

Coal rail cars in Ashtabula, Ohio

Coal as Fuel

Coal is primarily used as a solid fuel to produce electricity and heat through combustion. World coal consumption was about 6,743,786,000 short tons in 2006 and is expected to increase 48 per cent to 9.98 billion short tons by 2030. China produced 2.38 billion tons in 2006. India produced about 447.3 million tons in 2006. 68.7 per cent of China's electricity comes from coal. The USA consumes about 14 per cent of the world total, using 90 per cent of it for generation of electricity.

When coal is used for electricity generation, it is usually pulverized and then burned in a furnace with a boiler. The furnace heat converts boiler water to steam, which is then used to spin turbines which turn generators and create electricity. The thermodynamic efficiency of this process has been improved over time. 'Standard' steam turbines have topped out with some of the most advanced reaching about 35 per cent thermodynamic efficiency for the entire process, although newer combined cycle plants can reach efficiencies as high as 58 per cent. Increasing the combustion temperature can boost this efficiency even further. Old coal power plants, especially "grandfathered" plants, are significantly less efficient and produce higher levels of waste heat. About 40 per cent of the world's electricity comes from coal, and approximately 49 per cent of the United States electricity comes from coal.

The emergence of the supercritical turbine concept envisions running a boiler at extremely high temperatures and pressures with projected efficiencies of 46 per cent, with further theorized increases in temperature and pressure perhaps resulting in even higher efficiencies.

Other efficient ways to use coal are combined cycle power plants, combined heat and power cogeneration, and an MHD topping cycle.

Approximately 40 per cent of the world electricity production uses coal. The total known deposits recoverable by current technologies, including highly polluting, low energy content types of coal (*i.e.*, lignite, bituminous), is sufficient for many years. However, consumption is increasing and maximal production could be reached within decades.

A more energy-efficient way of using coal for electricity production would be via solid-oxide fuel cells or molten-carbonate fuel cells (or any oxygen ion transport based fuel cells that do not discriminate between fuels, as long as they consume oxygen), which would be able to get 60 per cent-85 per cent combined efficiency (direct electricity + waste heat steam turbine). Currently these fuel cell technologies can only process gaseous fuels, and they are also sensitive to sulphur poisoning, issues which would first have to be worked out before large-scale commercial success is possible with coal. As far as gaseous fuels go, one idea is pulverized coal in a gas carrier, such as nitrogen. Another option is coal gasification with water, which may lower fuel cell voltage by introducing oxygen to the fuel side of the electrolyte, but may also greatly simplify carbon sequestration. However, this technology has been criticised as being inefficient, slow, risky and costly, while doing nothing about total emissions from mining, processing and combustion. Another efficient and clean way of coal combustion in a form of coal-water slurry fuel (CWS) was well developed in Russia (since the Soviet Union time). CWS significantly reduces emissions saving the heating value of coal.

Petroleum coke is the solid residue obtained in oil refining, which resembles coke but contains too many impurities to be useful in metallurgical applications.

Refined Coal

Refined coal is the product of a coal upgrading technology that removes moisture and certain pollutants from lower-rank coals such as sub-bituminous and lignite (brown) coals. It is one form of several pre-combustion treatments and processes for coal that alter coal's characteristics before it is burned. The goals of pre-combustion coal technologies are to increase efficiency and reduce emissions when the coal is burned. Depending on the situation, pre-combustion technology can be used in place of or as a supplement to post-combustion technologies to control emissions from coal-fueled boilers.

Coal as a Traded Commodity

The price of coal has gone up from around $30 per short ton in 2000 to around $150.00 per short ton as of September 26, 2008. As of October 31, 2008, the price per short ton has declined to $111.50.

In North America, a Central Appalachian coal futures contracts are currently traded on the New York Mercantile Exchange (trading symbol QL). The trading unit is 1,550 short tons (1,410 t) per contract, and is quoted in U.S. dollars and cents per ton. Since coal is the principal fuel for generating electricity in the United States, coal futures contracts provide coal producers and the electric power industry an important tool for hedging and risk management.

In addition to the NYMEX contract, the Inter-continental Exchange (ICE) has European (Rotterdam) and South African (Richards Bay) coal futures available for trading. The trading unit for these contracts is 5,000 tonnes (5,500 short tons), and are also quoted in U.S. dollars and cents per ton.

Cultural Usage

Coal is the official state mineral of Kentucky and the official state rock of Utah. Both U.S. states have a historic link to coal mining.

Some cultures uphold that children who misbehave will receive only a lump of coal from Santa Claus for Christmas in their stockings instead of presents.

It is also customary and lucky in Scotland to give coal as a gift on New Year's Day. It happens as part of First-Footing and represents warmth for the year to come.

Charcoal

Charcoal is the blackish residue consisting of impure carbon obtained by removing water and other volatile constituents from animal and vegetation substances. Charcoal is usually produced by slow pyrolysis, the heating of wood, sugar, bone char, or other substances in the absence of oxygen (see pyrolysis, char and biochar). The resulting soft, brittle, lightweight, black, porous material resembles coal and is 85 per cent to 98 per cent carbon with the remainder consisting of volatile chemicals and ash.

The first part of the word is of obscure origin, but the first use of the term 'coal' in English was as a reference to charcoal. In this compound term, the prefix 'chare-' meant 'turn', with the literal meaning being 'to turn to coal'. The independent use of 'char', meaning to scorch, to reduce to carbon, is comparatively recent and is assumed to be a back-formation from the earlier charcoal. It may be a use of the word charren or chum, meaning to turn; *i.e.* wood changed or turned to coal, or it may be from the French charbon. A person who manufactured charcoal was formerly known as a collier (also as a wood collier). The word 'collier' was also used for those who mined or dealt in coal, and for the ships that transported it.

Coke

Coke Burning

Coke is a solid carbonaceous residue derived from low-ash, low-sulphur bituminous coal from which the volatile constituents are driven off by baking in an oven without oxygen at temperatures as high as 1,000°C (1,832°F) so that the fixed carbon and residual ash are fused together. Metallurgical coke is used as a fuel and as a reducing agent in smelting iron ore in a blast furnace. The product is too rich in dissolved carbon, and must be treated further to make steel. The coke must be strong enough to resist the weight of overburden in the blast furnace, which is why coking coal is so important in making steel by the conventional route. However, the alternative route to is direct reduced iron, where any carbonaceous fuel can be used to make sponge or pelletised iron. Coke from coal is grey, hard, and porous and has a heating value of 24.8 million Btu/ton (29.6 MJ/kg). Some cokemaking processes produce valuable by-products that include coal tar, ammonia, light oils, and 'coal gas'.

Hexamine Fuel Tablets

A hexamine fuel tablet is a form of solid fuel in tablet form. The tablets burn smokelessly, have a high energy density, do not liquify while burning and leave no ashes. Invented in Murrhardt, Germany, in 1932, the main component is hexamine.

A number of alternative names are in use, including heat tablet and Esbit. Esbit (which stands for Erich Schumms Brennstoff in Tablettenform or Erich Schumm's Fuel in Tablets) is a genericized trademark as it is used to refer to similar products made by other companies. The tablets are used for cooking by campers, the military and relief organizations. They are often used with disposable metal stoves that are included with field ration packs. Backpackers concerned with ultra light gear tend to buy or make their own much lighter stove. An Esbit beverage-can stove can be made by cutting off the bottom of an aluminum soft drink can, and turning it upside down to support the fuel tablet. A pot can be supported above this with a circle of poultry netting or metal tent pegs. The burning tablets are sensitive to wind, so a simple windscreen should be used; such as a strip of aluminum foil, curved in a circle around the pot and stove. Although not ideal, the fuel tablet can be placed on a rock or on the dirt, with a pot supported above it.

Advantages and Disadvantages

Fuel tablets are simple, ultra-lightweight compared to other stove options, and compact; the entire stove system and fuel can be stored inside a small 850 ml cooking pot. However, the heat given off cannot be easily adjusted, so water can be boiled, but cooking requiring simmering is more difficult. Tablets are not a particularly powerful stove fuel, and are sensitive to wind. They are expensive and less widely available than alternatives such as alcohol or petrol.

The solid form is completely safe to handle or even ingest (it is "is not compromised by any known toxicity" according to one study. When burned, however, the chemical oxidation of the fuel yields noxious fumes, requiring foods being cooked to be contained in a receptacle such as a pot or pan, and burned tabs will leave a sticky dark residue on the bottom of pots.

Bagasse

Bagasse is the fibrous residue remaining after sugarcane or sorghum stalks are crushed to extract their juice and is currently used as a renewable resource in the manufacture of pulp and paper products and building materials. Bagasse is often used as a primary fuel source for sugar mills; when burned in quantity, it produces sufficient heat energy to supply all the needs of a typical sugar mill, with energy to spare. To this end, a secondary use for this waste product is in cogeneration, the use of a fuel source to provide both heat energy, used in the mill, and electricity, which is typically sold on to the consumer electricity grid.

Wood Pellets

Wood pellets are used on specially designed stoves. Pellets are typically made from timber waste from sawmills. The wood goes through a fairly lengthy process of transformation before it is finally extruded as hard pellets.

In spite of the processing, the fuel is still carbon neutral and so is less harmful to the environment than other fossil fuels. For commercial undertakings, as with any wood fuel, wood pellets do not attract climate change levy tax.

Dung Cakes

Some animal feces, especially those of the camel, bison and cow, is used as fuel when dried out Animal dung Cow dung is the waste of bovine animal species.... In many parts of the developing world, cow dung is used as a fertilizer and fuel. But these are mostly used in rural areas.

Economic Aspects

Coal liquefaction is one of the backstop technologies that could potentially limit escalation of oil prices and mitigate the effects of transportation energy shortage that will occur under peak oil. This is contingent on liquefaction production capacity becoming large enough to satiate the very large and growing demand for petroleum. Estimates of the cost of producing liquid fuels from coal suggest that domestic U.S. production of fuel from coal becomes cost-competitive with oil priced at around 35 USD per barrel, (break-even cost). With oil prices back at around USD 40 per barrel in the U.S. as of December 15, 2008, liquid coal has currently lost much of its economic allure in that country.

Among commercially mature technologies, advantage for indirect coal liquefaction over direct coal liquefaction are reported by Williams and Larson (2003).

Intensive research and project developments have been implemented from 2001. The World CTL Award is granted to personalities having brought eminent contribution to the understanding and development of Coal liquefaction. The 2009 presentation ceremony will take place in Washington DC (USA) at the World CTL 2009 Conference (25-27 March, 2009).

Environmental Effects

There are a number of adverse environmental effects of coal mining and burning, specially in power stations.

These effects include:

- Release of carbon dioxide, a greenhouse gas, which causes climate change and global warming according to the IPCC. Coal is the largest contributor to the human-made increase of CO_2 in the air.
- Generation of hundred of millions of tons of waste products, including fly ash, bottom ash, flue gas desulphurization sludge, that contain mercury, uranium, thorium, arsenic, and other heavy metals.
- Acid rain from high sulfur coal.
- Interference with groundwater and water table levels.

- Contamination of land and waterways and destruction of homes from fly ash spills such as Kingston Fossil Plant coal fly ash slurry spill.
- Impact of water use on flows of rivers and consequential impact on other land-uses.
- Dust nuisance.
- Subsidence above tunnels, sometimes damaging infrastructured.
- Coal-fired power plants without effective fly ash capture are one of the largest sources of human-caused background radiation exposure.
- Coal-fired power plants shorten nearly 24,000 lives a year in the United States, including 2,800 from lung cancer.
- Coal-fired power plant releases emissions including mercury, selenium, and arsenic which are harmful to human health and the environment.

Advantages

- They are easy to transport.
- They are convenient to store without any risk of spontaneous explosion.
- Their cost of production is low.
- They possess moderate ignition temperatures.

Disvantages

- Their ash content is high.
- Their large proportions of heat are wasted during combustion. In other words, their thermal efficiency is low.
- They burns with clinker formation.
- Their combustion cannot be controlled easily.
- Their cost of handling is high.
- Their calorific value is lower as compared to that of liquid fuels.
- For complete combustion they require excess of air.
- They cannot be used as 1C engine fuel.

Conclusion

We had seen solid fuel is good in transportation handling and maintenance but bad in when we talk about efficiency heat content and environmental point of view. As solid fuel burns with large amount of smoke accompanied by clinker and soot formation and left behind considerable amount of carbon residue which results in an extra cost for its disposal. Smoke produced by solid fuels contains high amount of carbon dioxide and carbon mono oxide. These gasses are responsible for GREEN HOUSE EFFECT which results in global warming which is one of the major problem world is facing today. The use of some solid fuels (*e.g.* coal) is restricted or prohibited in some urban areas, due to unsafe levels of toxic emissions. The use of other solid fuels such as wood is increasing as heating technology and the availability of good quality fuel improves. In some areas, smokeless coal is often the only solid fuel used. In spite of above facts due to is cheapness and availability in abundance solid fuels are most widely used fuels in Industries, power plants and in rural areas.

- Engineering Chemistry by Jain & Jain.
- Engineering Chemistry by S.S. Dara.
- Wikipedia, Google.
- Images from Google Image Search.

3

Liquid Fuels, Adulteration and Environmental Impact

Introduction

Liquid fuels are those combustible or energy-generating molecules that can be utilize to create mechanical energy, usually producing kinetic energy they also must take the shape of their container. Most liquid fuels, in widespread use, are or derived from fossil fuels; however, there are several types, such as hydrogen fuel (for automotive uses), which are also categorized as a liquid fuel. It is the fumes of Liquid fuels that are flammable instead of the fluid.

Since the birth of automotives in the 19th century, diesel and gasoline are used as the primary source of energy for the vehicles, though many alternate fuels like CNG, LPG, alcohol, dimethylether, biodiesel, methanol, etc. are emerging in the market. The conventional fuels are basically derived from crude oil, where crude oil is fractioned by continuous distillation into several fractions: Petrol (gasoline), kerosene (kerosene, paraffin oil), gas oil (heavy oil), vacuum gas oil, naphtha, lubricating oil and residue.

1. **Fossil fules** — 1.1 Gasolene, 1.2 Diesel, 1.3 Kerosene
2. **Biodiesel**
3. **Alcohols—3.1** Methanol, 3.2 Ethanol, 3.3 Butanol
4. **Hydrogen**

Fossil fuel: Fossil fuels are also generally liquid fuels. The most notable of these is gasolene. Although unproven, it is generally accepted that they formed from the fossilized remains of dead plants and animals by exposure to heat and pressure in the Earth's crust.

Gasoline: Gasoline is the most widely used liquid fuel. Gasoline, as it is known in United States and Canada, or petrol in India, Britain, Australia,

New Zealand, South Africa and many English-speaking countries, is made of hydrocarbon molecules forming aliphatic compounds, or chains of carbons with hydrogen atoms attached. However, many aromatic compounds (carbon chains forming rings) such as benzene are found naturally in gasoline and cause the health risks associated with prolonged exposure to the fuel.

Production of gasoline is achieved by distillation of crude oil. The desirable liquid is separated from the crude oil in refineries. Crude oil is extracted from the ground in several processes, the most commonly seen may be beam pumps. To create gasoline, petroleum must first be removed from crude oil. Gasoline itself is actually not burned, but the fumes it creates ignite, causing the remaining liquid to evaporate. Gasoline is extremely volatile and easily combusts, making any leakage extremely dangerous. Gasoline for sale in most countries carries an octane rating. Octane is a measure of the resistance of gasoline to combusting prematurely, known as knocking. The higher the octane rating, the harder it is to burn the fuel, which allows for a higher compression ratio. Engines with a higher compression ratio produce more power (such as in race car engines). However, such engines actually *require* a higher octane fuel.

Diesel: Conventional diesel is similar to gasoline in that it is a mixture of aliphatic hydrocarbons extracted from petroleum. Diesel may cost more or less than gasoline, but generally costs less to produce because the extraction processes used are simpler. After distillation, the diesel fraction is normally processed to reduce the amount of sulphur in the fuel. Sulphur causes corrosion in vehicles, acid rain and higher emissions of soot from the tail pipe.

Kerosene: Kerosene once used in kerosene lamps as an alternative to whale oil, is today mainly used in fuel for jet engines (more technically Avtur, Jet A, Jet A-l, Jet B, JP-4, JP-5, JP-7 or JP-8). One form of the fuel known as RP-1 is burned with liquid oxygen as rocket fuel. These fuel grade kerosenes meet specifications for smoke points and freeze points. Kerosene is sometimes used as an additive in diesel fuel to prevent gelling or waxing in cold temperatures, sometimes it is used in some cars so that it will manage well than a petrolum used in some cars.

Biodiesel: Biodiesel is similar to diesel, but has differences akin to those between petrol and ethanol. For instance, biodiesel has a higher cetane rating (45-60 compared to 45-50 for crude-oil-derived diesel) and it acts as a cleaning agent to get rid of dirt and deposits. This does however depend on locality, economic situation, a host of other factors—and it has been proven to be viable at much lower costs in some countries. Also, it gives about 10 per cent less energy than ordinary diesel : As with alcohols and petrol engines, taking advantage of biodiesel's high cetane rating potentially overcomes the energy deficit compared to ordinary number 2 diesel.

Alcohols: Generally, the term alcohol refers to ethanol, the first organic chemical produced by humans but any alcohol can be burned as a fuel. Ethanol and methanol are the most common, being sufficiently inexpensive to be useful.

Methanol: Methanol is the lightest and simplest alcohol, produced from the natural gas component methane. Its application is limited due to its toxicity (similar to gasoline). Small amounts are used in some gasolines to increase the octane rating. Methanol-based fuels are used in some race cars and model airplanes. Methanol is also called *methyl alcohol* or *wood alcohol,* the latter because it was formerly produced from the distillation of wood. It is also known by the name *methyl hydrate.*

Ethanol: Ethanol, also known as grain alcohol or ethyl alcohol, is most commonly used in alcoholic beverages. However, it may also be used as a fuel, most often in combination with gasoline. For the most part, it is used in a 9:1 ratio of gasoline to ethanol to reduce the negative environmental effects of gasoline. There is increasing interest in the use of a blend of 85 per cent fuel ethanol blended with 15 per cent gasoline. This fuel blend called E85, has a higher fuel octane than most premium gasolines. When used in a modem Flexible fuel vehicle, it delivers more performance to the gasoline it replaces.

Butanol: Butanol is an alcohol which can be used as a fuel in most gasoline internal combustion engines without engine modification. It is typically a product of the fermentation of biomass by the bacterium *Clostridium acetobutylicum* (also known as the Weizmann organism). This process was first delineated by Chaim Weizmann (1916) for the production of acetone from starch for making cordite, a smokeless gunpowder.

Hydrogen: Liquified hydrogen is the liquid state of element hydrogen. It is a common liquid rocket fuel for rocket applications and can be used as a fuel in an internal combustion engine or fuel cell. Various concept hydrogen vehicles have been lower volumetric energy, the hydrogen volumes needed for combustion are large. Hydrogen was liquefied for the first time by James Dewarin (1898).

General Properties of the Liquid Fuel

This section presents basic information about petroleum-based fuels in general and some of the many physical and chemical properties they share.

Petroleum fuels ignite and burn readily, and produce a great deal of heat and power in relation to their weight. The one composition requirement common to all petroleum fuels is that they consist entirely of hydrocarbon molecules (hydrogen and carbon) except for small amounts of impurities and/or additives.

The refining of crude oil, also known as fractional distillation, produces a range of petroleum compounds that are primarily characterized by their boiling points and molecular weights. Short chain, single ring, or 'light' hydrocarbons, are more volatile, less viscous, and have lower boiling points than long chain, multiple ring, or 'heavy' hydrocarbons. Denoting the number of carbon atoms (CX) in a hydrocarbon molecule is a way to describe its weight relative to other hydrocarbon molecules. Natural gas is composed primarily of the light hydrocarbons methane (C_1), ethane (C_2), propane (C_3), and butane (C_4). Gasoline typically contains hydrocarbons in the C_4-C_{10} range.

Most petroleum fuels are mixtures of hundreds of different hydrocarbon compounds. The exact number and proportions of these compounds in a particular fuel may vary; therefore, most fuels are formulated to meet general property limits, rather than a specified chemical composition.

For a particular fuel product, governing standards may limit upper and lower percentage composition of certain hydrocarbons as required to meet performance criteria.

Propulsion system demands, such as fluidity, combustion properties, corrosion protection, and impurity limits, are the primary determinants of standardized fuel formulations.

Volatility is a property of fuels that affects its ability to vapourize and form a combustible mixture with air. This property results in a quantifiable characteristic called vapour pressure. Vapour pressure and volatility are important properties to be considered by designers of fuel storage and delivery systems because they can lead to unwanted evaporative fuel losses or 'fugitive' vapours. Lighter fuels such as gasoline and aviation fuel tend to be more volatile and have higher vapour pressures than heavier fuels such as diesel and heating oil at the same temperature and pressure. (*See Table 3.1 on Next Page*)

Fuel Impurities

Refined petroleum fuels can contain a variety of undesirable impurities that originate from the crude oil, develop during the refining process, or are introduced during shipment or storage. The most common fuel impurities are discussed below.

Gums are high molecular weight compounds containing hydrogen, carbon, oxygen, and usually sulfur and nitrogen. They are formed when the hydrocarbon molecules in stored fuels are oxidized or polymerized after exposure to air, sunlight, and/or elevated temperatures. When gums precipitate from the fuel, they can clog and form deposits on vital engine components such as filters and injectors, causing mild to severe engine performance problems. Anti-oxidant fuel additives can prevent the formation of gums.

Metals formed during certain refining processes can oxidize and contribute to the formation of filter clogging gums in any type of fuel. This problem is addressed by using a metal deactivator additive.

Table 3.1

	Gasoline	Diesel	Biodiesel
Chemical Structure	C_4 to C_{12}	C_8 to C_{25}	Methyl esters of C_{12} to C_{22} fatty acids
Cetane Number	N/A	40-55 (a)	48-65 (a)
Pump Octane			
Number [1]	84-93 (c)	N/A	N/A
Main Fuel Source	Crude Oil	Crude Oil	Fats and oils from sources such as soy beans, waste cooling oil, animal fats, and rapeseed
Energy Content	116,090	128,450 Btu/gal	119,550 Btu/gal for B100 (g)
(Lower Heating Value)	Btu/gal (g)	(g)	
Energy Content	124,340	137,380 Btu/gal	127,960 Btu/gal for B100 (g)
(Higher Heating Value)	Btu/gal (g)	(g)	
Energy comparison (per cent of gasoline 100% energy)	100%	100%	B100 has 103% the energy of gasoline or 93% or diesel. B20 has 109% of gasoline or 99% of diesel
Physical State	Liquid	Liquid	Liquid

Microbial contamination occurs after fuels leave the refinery since the refining process sterilizes fuel. Microbes, including algae, bacteria, and fungi feed on the fuel and use the water in the fuel for their oxygen supply. They can multiply and plug fuel filters with an odorous slime. Some of the microbes can also produce corrosive acid byproducts. Minimizing water content and treating with a biocide additive will control microbial growth in fuel.

Sediment is a common contaminant of fuels and usually consists of rust, mineral scale, sand, dirt, and other insoluble impurities. To address this problem, fuels are filtered upon delivery into bulk and operating storage systems to remove as much sediment as possible before the fuel is delivered to the end user.

Sulphur compounds can be corrosive to metals in fuel systems and are controlled by the total sulphur content limits found in the fuel specification.

Water is a very common fuel impurity. Fuel can become contaminated with water during shipping and storage. Water can condense from the fuel itself, may leak into fuel containers from the outside, or it may be present in containers before they are filled with fuel. Water in fuel may also contain other impurities that can cause corrosion problems and damage filters, pumps, and injectors. Water is denser than fuel and can be removed as it collects at the bottom of a storage container.

Common Fuel Additives

Fuel additives are intended to help improve fuel economy, lower maintenance costs, reduce impurities and harmful deposits, reduce exhaust emissions, and improve the overall performance and reliability of the fuel. Different fuels may be formulated with different 'packages' of fuel additives. Additives may also be added to fuels during storage or at the time of fueling. Often, the precise chemical composition of many fuel additives and additive packages is proprietary to the manufacturer. Particular combinations and per cent content of additives may be specified in a fuel's governing standard. Where additives are approved for use or required by American Society for Testing and Materials (ASTM) standards or military standards, the chemical composition of the additive may be more readily available. Common fuel additives include:

Alkyl lead was a common gasoline additive until the late 1960s used to obtain higher octane ratings and reduce engine 'knock.' Lead additives have been reduced or entirely phased out of most automotive gasoline formulations due to the environmental hazards associated with lead-containing exhaust emissions. As lead additives have been phased out of gasoline formulations, other oxygenating additives are now used to boost octane ratings and control knock, as well as reduce harmful exhaust emissions. Leaded automotive gasoline typically contained one or more grams per liter (> 1,000 parts per million [ppm]) of alkyl lead. Today, unleaded automotive gasoline contains only a few ppm of lead. Aviation gasoline (Avgas) continues to contain significant concentrations of alkyl lead, typically at levels greater than 1,000 ppm.

Anti-oxidants are primarily used to prevent gum formation in gasolines and aviation fuels.

Biocides may be added to any type of fuel to kill microbes when their growth becomes a recurring problem.

Conductivity additives increase the electrical conductivity of gasolines, aviation, and diesel fuels, thereby reducing the buildup of static charges during mixing, transfer, and shipment.

Corrosion inhibitors protect against corrosion during pipeline transfer and storage of fuels. They have also been found to improve the lubricity, or capacity to reduce friction of fuels. Corrosion inhibitors are used primarily in gasolines, aviation fuels, and diesel fuels.

Detergent additives prevent the buildup of gum deposits in engines and extend fuel injector life. They also help keep fuel filters clean. Detergent additives are primarily found in diesel fuels and automotive gasolines.

Icing inhibitors are used primarily in aviation fuels to prevent the formation of ice crystals from entrapped water in the fuel at freezing temperatures encountered during high altitude flight. Icing inhibitors have also been found to be an effective barrier to microbiological growth. Diethylene glycol monomethyl ether is specified for most military aviation fuels as an icing inhibitor.

Metal deactivators prevent metal contaminants in any type of fuel from oxidizing with hydrocarbons and other compounds to form gums or precipitates.

Oxygenates are oxygen-containing hydrocarbons that are added to automotive gasoline to boost the octane rating, reduce the smog-forming tendencies of exhaust gases, and suppress engine knock. The increased oxygen content promotes more complete combustion, thereby reducing tailpipe emissions. Common oxygenating additives are methyl tertiary butyl ether (MTBE) and ethanol.

Thermal stability additives reduce fuel fouling of critical jet engine components. Thermal stability refers to the ability of the fuel to be used in a system without degradation. Thermal stress results in fuel breakdown that can cause carbon build-up on engine nozzles, afterburner spray assemblies, and manifolds. In some instances, fuel degradation changes the spray pattern in the combuster or afterburner, which leads to damage of engine components, flameouts, and augmentor anomalies.

Gasoline additives increase gasoline's octane rating or act as corrosion inhibitors or lubricators, thus allowing the use of higher compression ratios for greater efficiency and power, however some carry heavy environmental risks. Types of additives include metal deactivators, corrosion inhibitors, oxygenates and antioxidants.

Common Forms of Fuel Adulterants

Blending or mixing of adulterants into the base transport fuels exists in various forms and both the type and quantity of adulterants vary from place to place. Moreover, profitability, availability and blendability are the prominent factors governing the choice of adulterants.

Specific Types of Adulteration may be Broadly Classified as Follows:

- Blending relatively small amount of distillate fuels like diesel or kerosene into automotive gasoline.
- Blending variable amount (as much as 30%) of the gasoline boiling range hydrocarbons such as industrial solvents into automotive gasoline.
- Blending small amounts of spent waste industrial solvent such as used lubricants, which would be costly to dispose of an environmentally approved manner—into gasoline and diesel.
- Blending kerosene into diesel, often as much as 20-30 per cent.
- Blending small amount of heavier fuel oils into diesel.

There are several petroleum products in our country or abroad, which are close substitutes of petrol (Motor Spirit or MS) and high-speed diesel (HSD), and are available at considerably lower prices. The consequence is that these products are widely used as adulterants. Some of the possible adulterants available in Indian markets are listed in Table 3.2 and 3.3.

Table 3.2 : Potential Adulterants for Gasoline (MS)

Sl.No.	Solvent/Chemical	Source
1.	Naphtha	Refineries
2.	SBP	BPCL
3.	GAIL Solvents	Bijalpur
4.	GAIL Solvents	Pata
5.	Pentane	GAIL
6.	Cixon	IPCL
7.	Solvent-90	IOC
8.	Hexane	Refineries
9.	Resol	Reliance
10.	Raffinate/Slop	Refineries
11.	C6-C9 Raffinate	Petrochemicals
12.	Naphtha/NGL	GAIL/ONGC
13.	PDS Kerosene	Government
14.	Free Kerosene	Parallel Marketers
15.	MTO	Refineries
16.	Pyrolysis Gasoline	Naphtha Crack
17.	Oxygenates	Refineries
18.	Food grd. Hexane	Refineries
19.	Benzene	Koyali
20.	Toluene Koyali	

Source: *Report of MoPNG Task Force to examine the use of solvent, raffinate and slop in automobile.*

Table 3.3 : Potential Adulterants for Diesel (HSD)

Sl.No.	Solvent/Chemical	Source
1.	Aromex	Digboi
2.	Lomex	NA
3.	C9 Raffinate	Ptrochmcls
4.	MTO	Refineries
5.	PDS Kerosene	Government
6.	Free Kerosene Parallel Markets	

Source: *Report of MoPNG Task Force to examine the use of solvent, raffinate and slop in automobile fuel.*

Fuel Adulteration and Environmental Effect

Adulteration of transport fuel, which is currently a very flourishing business in our country, can lead to economic losses, increased emissions and deterioration of performance and parts of engines using the adulterated fuels. Some of the effects of adulteration are outlined below:

- Mal-functioning of the engine, failure of components, safety problems etc. The problem gets further magnified for high performance modern engines.
- Increased tailpipe emissions of hydrocarbons (HC), carbon monoxide (CO), oxides of nitrogen (NOx), particulate matter (PM) and can also cause increased emissions of air toxin substances.
- Adulteration of fuel can cause health problems directly in the form of increased tailpipe emissions of harmful and sometimes carcinogenic pollutants. While indirectly in the form of diversion of PDS kerosene to the diesel sector for adulteration, thus prompting the use of biomass as domestic fuel which in turn leads to health problems of various types due to indoor air pollution. It may be noted that all forms of adulteration are not harmful to public health. Some adulterants increase emission of harmful pollutants significantly, whereas others have little or no effect on air quality.
- Significant loss of tax revenue: Various estimates have been made of the extent of financial loss to the national wealth as well as the oil companies as a result of diversion of PDS kerosene, use of off-spec, low value, hydrocarbons mixed with petrol and diesel, evasion of sales tax etc. Although these estimates vary over a wide range, it is safe to assume that the nation is losing at least Rs. 10,000 crores annually as a result of adulteration of fuel.

Adulteration and Emissions

Fuel adulteration causes marked effect on the tailpipe emissions of vehicles, as adulterants alter the chemistry of the base fuel rendering its quality inferior to the required commensurate fuel quality for the vehicles. This in turn affects the combustion dynamics inside the combustion chamber of vehicles increasing the emissions of harmful pollutants significantly. In some cases effects of adulteration are indirect—for example, large scale diversion of rationed kerosene subsidized for household use to the diesel sectorfor mixing with diesel not only hamper engine performance of diesel vehicles, but also deprives the poor of kerosene which can otherwise be used for cooking and as a consequence of lack of availability of subsidized kerosene force the poor to continue to use biomass which expose them to high levels of indoor pollution.

In general fuel adulteration can increase the tailpipe emissions of hydrocarbons (HC), carbon monoxide (CO), Oxides of nitrogen (NOx) and particulate matter (PM). Adulteration of fuels can also cause emissions of air toxins like benzene and polyaromatic hydrocarbons (PAHs) both well-known carcinogens.

Impacts Due to Gasoline Adulteration

Adulterating gasoline with kerosene causes increase in emissions, as kerosene is more difficult to burn than gasoline and this results in higher levels of HC,

CO and PM. High sulphur contents of the kerosene can deactivate the catalyst and lower conversion of engine out pollutants. Kerosene addition may also cause fall in octane quality, which can lead to engine knocking. When gasoline is adulterated with diesel fuels, the same effects occurs but usually at lower levels of added diesel fuel. Both diesel and kerosene added to gasoline will increase engine deposit formation.

Gasoline may also be adulterated with gasoline boiling range solvent like toluene, xylene and other aromatics. With the 'judicious' adulteration, the gasoline would not exhibit drivability problems in motor vehicles. Larger amounts of toluene and /or mixed with xylene cause some increase in HC, CO, NOx emissions, and significant increase in the level of air toxins—especially benzene—in the tailpipe exhaust. The adulterated gasoline itself could have increased potential human toxicity if frequent skin contact is allowed.

Extremely high levels of toluene (45% or higher) could cause premature failure of neoprene, styrene butadiene rubber and butyl rubber components in the fuel system. This has caused vehicle fires in some cases, especially in older vehicles.

Adulteration of gasoline by waste industrial solvents is especially problematic as the adulterants are so varied in composition. They will cause increased emissions, may even cause vehicle breakdown. Even low levels of these adulterants can be injurious and costly to vehicle operation.

For gasoline, any adulterant that changes its volatility can effect drivability. High volatility (resulting from addition of light hydrocarbons) in hot weathers can cause vapour lock and stalling. Low volatility in cold weather can cause starting problems and poor warm-up.

Impacts Due to Diesel Adulteration

The blending of kerosene with automotive diesel is generally practiced by oil industry worldwide as a means of adjusting the low temperature operability of the fuel. This practice is not harmful or detrimental to tailpipe emissions, provided the resulting fuel continues to meet engine manufacturer's specifications (especially for viscosity and cetane number). However, high-level adulteration of low sulphur diesel fuel with higher-level sulphur kerosene can cause the fuel to exceed the sulphur maximum. The addition of heavier fuel oils to diesel is usually easy to detect because the resultant fuel will be darker than normal. Depending on the nature of these heavier fuel oils and the possible presence of additional PAHs, there could be some increase in both exhaust PM and PAH (Poly Aromatic Hydrocarbons) emissions.

Adulteration Detection

A number of analytical techniques are available to detect adulteration. In all cases described below, it is important to have good sampling technique and access to a good petroleum analytical laboratory. For the majority of the tests, accurate data and analysis of original or uncontaminated fuel are also pre-requisite. Some of the approaches for detecting adulteration are outlined below:

***(i)* Full specification tests of the standards :** This may be quite time consuming and many parameters may be well within the requirements even if the fuel is adulterated. In fact fuel standards or specifications are framed to ensure that the fuel corresponds to certain level of quality commensurate to technology requirements of the vehicles. Parameters in the fuel standards may not necessarily stand as checkpoint for any sort of fuel adulteration.

***(ii)* Testing selected parameters:** This asks for testing some critical parameters, which are likely to be affected or altered by adulteration and adversely affect engine performance and emissions and can be evaluated. Lists of such parameters are given below. In general, many of the selected parameters may already be included in the full specification standards. However, dosage of multifunctional additive and cetane improver are intended for following the adulterants by dilution. However, convenient methodology for determination at refinery and outlet levels are yet to be lined up in the country.

Selected Parameters for Gasoline Testing

1. Density
2. Distillation
3. Hydrocarbon Composition
   Aromatic, Vo1%
   Olefms,Vo1%
   Benzene, Vo1%
   Sulphur, ppm
4. Stability
   Existing gum
   Potential gum
5. Octane Number
   Research
   Motor
6. Multifunctional additives-dosage

Selected Parameters for Diesel Testing

1. Flash Point
2. Density
3. Distillation
4. Sulphur

5. Fob/cyclic aromatics (+2 rings)
6. Total sediment
7. Cetane number
8. Cetane index
9. Multifunctional additives-dosage
10. Cetaneimprover-presence.

Dosage: For diesel fuel without cetane improver, cetane index can be utilized. If dosage can be determined, it may be used for detection of adulteration based on depletion from original dosage.

(*iii*) Testing methods: There can be several alternate approaches, some prominent approaches are:

- Use of conventional manual petroleum testing methods.
- Utilization of automated instruments for conventional petroleum testing. For example- gas chromatographic method is used for simulated distillation. A number of instrumental analysis methods have been developed for establishment of parameters of fuels.

(*iv*) Emerging instruments for fuel surveillance: Several new instruments are available which claimed to carry out instrumental analysis for the estimation of key parameters of transport fuel. For example the following may be noted :

(*a*) Accurate and comprehensive fuel analyzer. The portable FOxFTIR fuel analyzer is claimed to be ideal for the analysis of commercial fuels.

(*b*) ZeltexZXlOlCC Portable Octane analyzer.

(*v*) Use of marker : Various markers can be used to identify adulteration, such as kerosene in gasoline. Earlier kerosene was used as major adulterant for adulteration in gasoline and diesel fuel. For detection of adulteration of fuels with kerosene a blue dye and furfural were used. However, where visible dyes have been applied in South Asia, they have not been effective. It is believed that presently the range of adulterants has widened. Various chemical/biochemical markers are available in market *e.g.* Spectrace marker by Mortan international, petro markers by M/S GFI, Biocode markers by M/S Biocode ltd., etc. The marker is added in trace level with the fuel and whenever the product is to be tested, the marked chemical is detected and measured by specific instruments/ immunoassay. This detection test can also be easily carried out in field with equal accuracy as laboratory tests.

Properties of Markers

- They should be miscible with fuels
- Detectable by simple test procedures
- Difficult to remove from marked fuels

- Non-reactive with other fuel additives
- No interaction with material of construction and fuel impurities; and
- Should be cost effective

Limitations of Marker System

- Relatively a high cost option
- Difficult to maintain a constant dosage at low concentration
- May be leached out by water in the product tanks
- May interact with materials and fuel impurities

Some Important Measures to Control Fuel Adulteration

Some important measures to control fuel adulteration are listed below:

- An important step in tackling fuel adulteration is reducing incentives and opportunities for adulteration. Though it is generally recognized that eliminating pricing differential is the most effective method of controlling adulteration, it will be difficult to eliminate differences among such a wide variety of fuels and solvents meant for different usages.
- Checking adulteration requires a credible monitoring and surveillance system. To ensure that the engine can give the desired performance including low emissions, it is necessary to ensure the fuel quality at the consumer end, which can be achieved by appropriate surveillance programmes.
- Any anti-adulteration programme should be backed up by sound financial and legal framework. The fiscal framework should take into account-associated costs like monitoring and testing infrastructure. Policy for imposing severe penalty and exemplary punishment to the adulterators needs to be imbibed into legal framework tb discourage adulteration.
- The manner in which retail fuels are distributed has an important bearing on fuel adulteration. For example, having large numbers of small, independent transport trucks operators moving fuels from terminals to the point of sale creates an environment conducive to adulteration. One effective 'market based' approach is the practice in many industrialized countries whereby oil companies market at retail and assume responsibility throughout the supply chain to guarantee fuel quality in order to protect their public image and market share.
- One of the acceptable internationally accepted method for detecting and thereby preventing adulteration of fuels is the use of markers. A number of chemical and biochemical markers are available in the international market. Some of them are dyes, one of which is already

being used in India to mark SKO (Superior Kerosene Oil) used for PDS (Public Distribution System).

- The Standard fuel test method being used today when properly executed should be able to give acceptable results. Precision and repeatability could be improved by setting up programmes for cross checking inter-laboratory variability.
- In Industrial countries, practices of adulteration are expected to be less or rare today; in part because public pressure has led most oil companies to take public image seriously and socially responsible behaviour is considered as integral part of good business. Thus a culture of 'Good Business' needs to be developed within the concerned industry to eradicate adulteration via awareness raising by Government organizations, NGOs, and citizens groups; independent checks by universities and research institutes to 'name and shame' those who are not in compliance; efforts by trade associations to identify those retailers that comply in order to 'upgrade' the market; international pressure on large oil companies operating in developing countries; and greater effort by governments to monitor and enforce regulations.
- Use of alternative fuels which are less prone to adulteration, can play a positive role in minimizing adulteration. Thus, promoting use of cleaner fuels like CNG, LPG etc can prove effective in dealing with adulteration.
- Taking and maintaining samples for checking fuel quality is not easy. Finding proper sample containers and not being personally harassed at retail outlets while sampling are just two of the very real operational problems to be resolved

Consumers Front: Anti-adulteration Tips

Consumers are the sufferers of this malpractice. Any quality conscious consumer has the right to be assured of the quality of the products and if he desires he can get his sample checked for adulteration. Some easy and important checks can be conducted at the retail outlet for MS/HSD:

Filter Paper Test: For MS. First the mouth of nozzle is cleaned to remove stains. Then, a drop of petrol is put on the filter paper from the nozzle. The petrol dropped on the filter paper is allowed to evaporate for 2 minutes. The petrol should evaporate without leaving any stain on the filter paper. If the colour left on the paper is pinkish, it is the colour of MS and not a stain. Dealers are expected to provide filter paper to customers on demand.

Density test: This is a very simple test for both MS and HSD. This test takes approximately 5 to 10 minutes. Product is taken in a glass jar and then a Hydrometer (separate Hydrometers for MS and HSD) available with the dealer is immersed in the product. A Thermometer is also immersed into the product jar simultaneously without touching the walls of the jar. The readings of Thermometer and Hydrometer are taken. Then, with the help of a conversion chart, the density is converted to 150C and this is compared with the recorded density/reference density, which can be seen from the density register maintained by the dealer. If the variation between the observed density and recorded/ reference density is within + 0.0030, then the product density can be considered to be correct. If the difference is more than + 0.0030, then it indicates possibility of adulteration.

Water contamination checks: For both MS and HSD can be done with the help of a dip rod and water finding paste, available with the dealer.

In case of lubricants: the customer must check the seal of container, date of manufacture and name of the manufacturer. For convenience of 2/3 wheelers, Retail Outlets provide 2-T dispensers/2-T mix dispensing units and also keep tamper proof 2-T pouches.

Green Fuel

Any solid, liquid, or gaseous fuel produced from organic (once living) matter, either directly from plants or indirectly from industrial, commercial, domestic, or agricultural wastes.

There are three main methods for the development of biofuels:

(*i*) The burning of dry organic wastes (such as household refuse, industrial and agricultural wastes, straw, wood, and peat);

(*ii*) The fermentation of wet wastes (such as animal dung) in the absence of oxygen to produce biogas (containing up to 60% methane),

(*iii*) The fermentation of sugar cane or maize to produce alcohol and esters; and energy forestry (producing fast-growing wood for fuel).

Fermentation produces *two main types of biofuels: alcohols and esters*. These could theoretically be used in place of fossil fuels but, because major alterations to engines would be required, biofuels are usually mixed with fossil fuels. The EU allows 5 per cent ethanol, derived from wheat, beet, potatoes, or maize, to be added to fossil fuels. In Brazil ethanol from sugar cane is used in cars run either on ethanol, or gasohol (a blend of petrol and ethanol), or on both ('dual-fuel' engines). Ethanol replaces 40 per cent of the petrol that the country would use for motor transport.

Green fuel, also known as biofuel, is a type of fuel distilled from plants and animal materials, believed by some to be more environmentally friendly than the widely-used fossil fuels that power most of the world. In the desperate search for alternative energy sources, green fuel has evolved as a possible fueling option as the world drains its fossil fuel resources. Detractors suggest that the term 'green fuel ' is a misnomer, as the processing of crops into biofuel actually creates a considerable amount of pollution that may be just as damaging to the environment as current practices.

In creating basic forms of biofuel, crops are broken down into two types: sugar producing and oil producing. Sugar and starch producing crops, such as sugar cane or corn, are put through a fermentation process to create ethanol. Oil producing plants, like those used in vegetable oils, can be used much like fossil sources of oil; they create diesel that can be burned by cars or further processed to become biodiesel.

Recent technological innovations have created the fields of advanced biofuels, which focus on non-food sources and waster renewal as energy. By converting landfill material, as well as wood and inedible plant parts, into green fuel, we not only cut down on the use of fossil fuels but also effectively recycle enormous amounts of waste. These biofuels help quell the debate on whether growing crops for fuel will result in fewer available food crops.

A new form of fuel can literally called *green,* as it derives from green algae. Algae, often seen growing on bodies of water, is a tiny plant with a rapid growth rate. Its usefulness as fuel derives from the fact that it has an extremely high oil content that can be processed like other oil-producing crops. Many countries are now doing extensive research on algae, which is easy to cultivate and grows extremely quickly. According to some estimates by start-up algae oil companies, one acre of algae can produce 200 times as much oil as one acre of corn.

Some detractors warn against the assumption that green fuel is free from pollution-causing attributes. The processing of sugar and starch plants into ethanol has come under heavy criticism in recent years; not only do these plants take away food-growing space, the fermentation process releases considerable pollution into the air. Moreover, green fuel does not necessarily burn clean, and may emit formaldehyde, ozone, and other carcinogenic substances when used.

It is not yet clear whether the green fuel currently available is the wave of the future or merely an interim step on the journey away from fossil fuel use. Governments around the world are devoting enormous resources to the research of clean, sustainable fuels to replace the pollutant and quickly disappearing oil reserves used today. Green fuel may not be a perfect solution to the problems of oil need and global protection, but it remains an important innovation that may pave the way to a better future.

INDIAN STANDARD

Anhydrous Ethanol for Use in Automotive Fuel-Specification

Scope: This standard prescribes requirements, methods of sampling and test for anhydrous ethanol, which is used either as such or more usually in admixture with petrol and diesel as a fuel for automobile engines.

All standards are subject to revision and parties to agreements based on this standard are encouraged to investigate the possibility of applying the, most recent editions of the standard indicated below:

Table 3.4

IS No.	Title
2 : 1960	Rules for rounding off numerical values *(revised)*
196 : 1966	Atmospheric conditions for testing *(revised)*
264 : 1976	Nitric acid *(second revision)* 264 : 1993 Hydrochloric acid *(fourth revision)*
323 : 1959	Rectified spirit *(revised)*
1070 : 1992	Reagent grade water *(third revision)*
1448	Methods of lest for petroleum and its products:
[P:26] : 1960	Knock characteristics of motor fuels by motor method
[P:27] : 1960	Knock characteristics of motor fuels by research method
2302 : 1989	Tables for alcoholometry by .hydrometer method *(first revision)*
2362 : 1993	Determination of water by Karl Fischer method—Test method; *(second revision)*

Terminology: For the purposes of this standard, the following definitions shall apply.

Ethyl Alcohol (Absolute Alcohol): Ethyl alcohol (Absolute alcohol) is a clear, colourless and homogeneous liquid, consisting essentially of ethanol admixed with not more than 0.5 per cent by volume of water.

Anhydrous Ethanol: Anhydrous ethanol is essentially ethyl alcohol, which is denatured and is meant for use as fuel in automobile engines.

Denaturant: Denaturant is a substance completely miscible in ethyl alcohol and of such a character that while its addition makes the material or any aqueous dilution of it unpleasant and unwholesome for potable purposes, its presence does not render anhydrous ethanol, either as such or blended with petrol or diesel, unsuitable for use in automobile engines.

Standard Atmospheric Conditions: Standard atmospheric conditions for testing shall comprise a relative humidity of 65±2 per cent and a temperature of 27±2 °C provided that, in a given series of experiments, the temperature does not vary by more than 1°C.

Requirements

Description: Anhydrous ethanol shall be a clear, colourless and homogeneous liquid, free from matter in suspension.

Denaturant: The denaturant to be admixed with ethyl alcohol and the proportion in which it is to be used shall be as prescribed by law from time to time.

Prohibited Denaturants: Specific mention must be made of some materials that have extremely adverse effects on fuel stability, automotive engines and fuel systems. These materials shall not be used as denaturants, for anhydrous ethanol for use in automobile fuels, under any circumstances.

They are as follows: methanol, pyrroles, turpentine, ketones and tars (high-molecular weight pyrolysis products of fossil or non-fossil vegetable matter). Unless a denaturant, such as a higher aliphatic alcohol or ether, is known to have no adverse effect on a gasoline-ethanol blend or on automotive engines or fuel systems, it shall not be used.

Acidity: The material shall be neutral or acidic in reaction to phenolphthalein and when tested as prescribed in Annex D, the acidity, other than due to dissolved carbon dioxide shall not exceed the sacified value.

Packing and Marking

Packing: The material shall be packed in such containers and packages as agreed to between the purchaser and the vendor, subject to the provisions of law in force from time to time.

All containers in which the material is packed shall be dry, clean, free from substances soluble in anhydrous ethanol, and leak-proof.

Necessary safeguards against the risk arising from the storage and handling of large volume of flammable liquids shall be provided and all due precautions shall be taken at all times to prevent accidents or explosions.

Except when they are opened for the purpose of cleaning and rendering them free from alcohol vapour, all empty tanks or other containers shall be kept securely closed unless they have been thoroughly cleansed and freed from alcohol vapour.

Marking

Each container shall be marked legibly and indelibly with the following information:

(*a*) Name of the material;

(*b*) Manufacturer's name;

(*c*) Net, gross and tare weight;

(*d*) Recognized trade-mark, if any;

(*e*) Date of packing;

(*f*) Only for automotive use;

(*g*) Highly flammable; and

(*h*) Hazardous chemical and injurious to health.

BIS Certification Marking

The container may also be marked with the Standard Mark.

The use of the Standard Mark is governed by the provisions of *Bureau of Indian Standard Act,* 1986 and the Rules and Regulations made thereunder. The details of conditions under which the licence for the use of the Standard Mark may be granted to manufacturers or producers may be obtained from the Bureau of Indian Standards.

Quality of Reagents

Unless specified otherwise, pure chemicals and distilled water (*see* IS 1070) shall be employed in tests.

Note: *'Pure chemicals' shall mean chemicals that do not contain impurities, which affect the results of analysis.*

Table 3.5 : Requirements of Anhydrous Ethanol for Use in Automotive Fuel (Clauses 4.3, 4.5, 4.6 and 7.1)

Sl. No.	Characteristics	Requirement	Method of Test, Ref. to Annex
(*i*)	Relative density at 15.6 /15.6 °C, Max	0.7961	A
(*ii*)	Ethanol content per cent by volume at 15.6/15.6°C, Min (excluding denaturant)	99.50	B
(*iii*)	Miscibility with water	Miscible	C
(*iv*)	Alkalinity	Nil	D
(*v*)	Acidity (as CH_3COOH) Mg/l, Max	30	D
(*vi*)	Residue on evaporation per cent by mass, Max	0.005	E
(*vii*)	Aldehyde content (as CH_3CHO) Mg/l, Max	60	F
(*viii*)	Copper, mg/kg, Max	0.1	G
(*ix*)	Conductivity, µS/m, Max	300	H
(*x*)	Methyl alcohol, mg/litre, Max	300	J
(*xi*)	Appearance	Clear and bright	Visual

1. Scope

This standard prescribes the requirements and the methods of sampling and test for absolute alcohol. The material is intended for use as a raw material, regent and solvent in the chemical and pharmaceutical industries and for the production of power alcohol for which purpose it is partially or completely denatured.

2. Grades

The material shall be of three grades, namely:

(*a*) *Special Crude* to meet special requirements, such as for Defence purposes;

(*b*) *Grade 1* for pharmaceutical and medicinal purposes; and

(*c*) *Grade* 2 for general purposes.

3. Requirements

Description: The material shall be clear, colourless and homogeneous liquid free from suspended matter and consisting essentially of ethanol (CH_3CH_2OH).

REFERENCES

1. Central Pollution Control Board Publication, PROBES/78/2000-2001, “Transport Fuel Quality 2005”.
2. The World Bank Publication, South Asia Urban Air Quality Management Briefing note No. 7, “Catching Gasoline and Diesel Adulteration”.
3. The World Bank Publications, September 2001, Note No. 237, “Abuses in Fuel Market”.
4. Report from MoPNG on “Steps Undertaken to Control Adulteration of Fuel in India”.
5. Website of Anti-adulteration Cell, www.antiadulterationcell.com.
6. Government of India, “Report of the Expert Committee on Auto Fuel Policy.”
7. The World Bank Publications, Pollution Management in Focus, Discussion Note No. 11, December 2001, “Transport Fuel Taxes and Urban Air Quality”.
8. Centre for Science and Environment, New Delhi, February 2002. “A Report on the Independent Inspection of Fuel Quality at the Fuel Dispensing Stations, Oil Depots and Tank Lorries” and its Website www.cseindia.org.
9. Government of India, Ministry of Petroleum and Natural Gas, “The Indian Hydrocarbon Sector Spreads Its Wings”.
10. Website of The Hindu, www. hinduonnet.com. and Business Line, www.blonet.com
11. Website of The World Bank Group, www.rru.worldbank.org, Rapid Response, Topic Regulating Fuel Market for Cleaner Air.”
12. Report by Indian Oil Corporation Limited, R & D Centre, “Monitoring Fuel Adulteration.”
13. “http://en:wikipedia.org/wiki/Liquid_fuels”
14. “http://cpcbenvis.nic.in
15. http://en.wikipedia.org/wiki/E85

Kerosene (SKO)

Kerosenes are distillate fractions of crude oil in the boiling range of 150-250°C. They are treated mainly for reducing aromatic content to increase their smoke point (height of a smokeless flame) and hydrofining to reduce sulphur content and to improve odour, colour and burning qualities (char value).

Kerosene is used as a domestic fuel for heating/lighting and also for manufacture of insecticides/herbicides/fungicides to control pest, weeds and fungi. Since kerosene is less volatile than gasoline, increase in its evaporation rate in domestic burners is achieved by increasing surface area of the oil to be burned and by increasing its temperature. The two types of burners which achieve this fall into two categories namely vapourisers and atomisers.

The Indian Standard governing the properties of kerosene is IS 1459:1974 (2nd Rev).

Properties

Kerosene, a thin, clear liquid formed from hydrocarbons, with a *density* of 0.78-0.81 g/cm^3, is obtained from the *fractional distillation* of *petroleum* between 150°C and 275°C, resulting in a mixture of carbon chains that typically contain between six and 16 *carbon atoms* per molecule.

The *flash point* of kerosene is between 37 and 65°C (100 and 150°F), and its *autoignition temperature* is 220°C (428°F).

Heat of combustion of kerosene is similar to that of diesel; its *lower heating value* is around 18,500 Btu/lb, or 43.1 MJ/kg, and its *higher heating value* is 46.2 MJ/kg.

Kerosene is *immiscible* in water (cold or hot), but miscible in petroleum solvents.

Kerosene contains a mixture of Hydrocarbon liquids ranging from $C_{12}H_{26}$ to $C_{15}H_{32}$. The combustion reaction of Kerosene will depend upon the components of the mixture. However, as a hydrocarbon, the reaction will produce mainly, CO_2 gas and H_2O vapour but, as Kerosene is a fairly oily substance, the liquid must first be atomised (formed into a fine mist) in order for it to completely vapourise and then mixed with sufficient air to give complete combustion, otherwise some Carbon (as soot) and some Carbon Monoxide (CO) will also form.

History

The process of distilling crude oil/petroleum into kerosene, as well as other hydrocarbon compounds, was first written about in the mid-800s by the *Persian* scholar *Razi* (or Rhazes). In his *Kitab al-Asrar (Book of Secrets)*, the physician and chemist Razi described two methods for the production of kerosene, termed *naft abyad* ('white naphtha'), using an apparatus called an *alembic*. One method involved using *clay* as an *absorbent*, whereas the other method involved using *ammonium chloride (sal ammoniac)*. The distillation process was to be repeated until the final product was perfectly clear and 'safe to light', *i.e.* volatile hydrocarbon fractions had been mostly removed. Kerosene was also produced during the same period from *oil shale* and *bitumen* by heating the rock to extract the oil, which was then distilled.

In 1846, Canadian geologist *Abraham Gesner* gave a public demonstration in *Charlottetown, Prince Edward Island* of a new process he had discovered. He heated coal in a *retort* and distilled from it a clear, thin fluid which he showed made an excellent lamp fuel. He coined the name 'Kerosene' for his fuel, a contraction of *keroselaion*, meaning *wax-oil*. The cost of extracting kerosene from coal was high. Fortunately, Gesner recalled from his extensive knowledge of New Brunswick's geology a naturally occurring *asphaltum* called *albertite*. He was blocked from using it by the New Brunswick coal conglomerate because they had coal extraction rights for the province, and he lost a court case when their experts claimed albertite was a form of Gesner subsequently moved to *Newtown Creek, Long Island*, New York, in 1854, where he secured the backing of a group of businessmen. They formed the North American Gas Light Company, to which he assigned his patents. Despite clear priority of discovery, Gesner did not obtain his first kerosene patent until 1854, two years after *James Young's* US patent. Gesner's method of purifying the distillation products appears to have been superior to Young's, resulting in a cleaner and better-smelling fuel. Manufacture of kerosene under the Gesner patents began in New York in 1854, and later in *Boston*, being distilled from *bituminous coal* and oil shale.

In 1848, Scottish chemist James Young experimented with oil discovered seeping in a coal mine as a source of lubricating oil and illuminating fuel. When the seep became exhausted, he experimented with the dry distillation of coal, especially the resinous 'boghead coal' (torbanite). He extracted a number of useful liquids from it, one of which he named 'paraffine oil', because at low temperatures, it congealed into a substance 'resembling paraffin wax. Young took out a patent on his process and the resulting products in 1850, and built the first truly commercial oil-works in the world at *Bathgate* in 1851, using oil extracted from locally mined torbanite, shale, and bituminous coal. In 1852, he took out a US patent for the same invention. These patents were subsequently upheld in both countries in a series of lawsuits, and other producers were obliged to pay him royalties. (*See also coal oil.*)

In 1851, *Samuel Martin Kier* began selling kerosene to local miners, under the name 'Carbon Oil'. He distilled this by a process of his own invention from *crude oil.* He also invented a new lamp to burn his product. He has been dubbed the *Grandfather of the American Oil Industry* by historians. Since the 1840s, Kier's *salt wells* were becoming fouled with *petroleum.* At first, Kier simply dumped the useless oil into the nearby *Pennsylvania Main Line Canal,* but later he began experimenting with several distillates of the crude oil, along with a chemist from eastern Pennsylvania.

Ignacy Lukasiewicz, a *Polish* pharmacist residing in *Lvov,* had been experimenting with different kerosene distillation techniques, trying to improve on Gesner's process, using local *seep* oil. Many people knew of his work, but paid little attention to it. On the night of July 31, 1853, doctors at the local hospital needed to perform an emergency operation, virtually impossible by candlelight. They therefore sent a messenger for Lukasiewicz and his new lamps. The lamp burned so brightly and cleanly that the hospital officials ordered several lamps plus a large supply of fuel. Lukasiewicz realized the potential of his work and quit the pharmacy to find a business partner, and then travelled to *Vienna* to register his technique with the government. Lukasiewicz moved to the *Gorlice* region of Poland in 1854, and sank several wells across southern Poland over the following decade, setting up a refinery near *Jaslo* in 1859.

The widespread availability of cheaper kerosene was the principal factor in the precipitous decline in the *whaling* industry in the mid-to-late 19th century, as the leading product of whaling was oil for lamps.

FUEL USES

Heating and Lighting

At one time, the fuel was widely used in *kerosene lamps* and lanterns. Although it replaced *whale oil,* the 1873 edition *of Elements of Chemistry* said, "The vapour of this substance [kerosene] mixed with air is as explosive as gunpowder. This may have been due to the common practice of adulterating kerosene with other, more volatile hydrocarbons, such as the cheaper benzene.

Kerosene was also a fire risk; in 1880, nearly two of every five New York City fires were caused by defective kerosene lamps.

These were superseded by the electric light bulb and *flashlights* powered by *dry cell* batteries, which are still used to this day.

Its use as a *cooking* fuel is mostly restricted to some *portable stoves* for *backpackers* and to *less-developed countries,* where it is usually less refined and contains impurities and even debris.

As a heating fuel, it is often used in portable stoves, and is sold in some *filling stations.* It is sometimes used as a heat source during power failures. The use of portable kerosene heaters is not recommended for closed indoor areas without a *chimney* due to the danger of buildup of *carbon monoxide* gas.

Kerosene is widely used in Japan as a home heating fuel for portable and installed kerosene heaters. In Japan, kerosene can be readily bought at any filling station or be delivered to *homes.*

In the United Kingdom and *Ireland,* kerosene is often used as a heating fuel in areas not connected to a gas pipeline network. It is used less for cooking, which has more commonly been *LPG* for some decades now, wing to its (LPG's) easier lighting. Kerosene is still often the fuel of choice for range cookers such as Rayburn.

The *Amish,* who abstain from the use of electricity, rely on kerosene for lighting at night.

More ubiquitous in the late 19th and early 20th centuries, *kerosene space heaters* were often built into kitchen ranges, and kept many farm and fishing families warm and dry through the winter. At one time, citrus growers used a *smudge pot* fueled by kerosene to create a pall of thick smoke over a grove in an effort to prevent freezing temperatures from damaging crops. *'Salamanders'* are kerosene space heaters used on construction sites to dry out building materials and to warm workers. Before the days of blinking electrically lighted road barriers, highway construction zones were marked at night by kerosene fired, pot-bellied torches. Most of these uses of kerosene created thick black smoke because of the low temperature of combustion.

A notable exception, discovered in the early 19th century, is the use of a *gas mantle* above the wick on a kerosene lamp. Looking like a delicate woven bag above the woven cotton wick, the mantle is a residue of mineral materials (mostly *thorium dioxide)* which is heated to *incandescence* by the flame produced by the wick. The *thorium* and *cerium* oxide combination produces both a whiter light and a greater fraction of the energy in the form of visible light than a *black body* at the same temperature would. These types of lamps are still in use today in areas of the world without electricity, because they give a much better light than a simple wick-type lamp does.

Transportation

In the mid-20th century, kerosene or *tractor vapourising oil* (TVO) was used as a cheap fuel for tractors. The engine would start on gasoline, then switch over to kerosene once the engine warmed up. A heat valve on the manifold would route the exhaust gases around the intake pipe, heating the kerosene to the point where it was vapourized and could be ignited by an *electric spark.*

In Europe following the Second World War, automobiles were modified similarly to turn to run on kerosene from the gasoline which would have to be imported and was heavily taxed. Besides additional piping and the switch between fuels, the head gasket was replaced by a much thicker one to diminish the compression ratio (making the engine less powerful and less efficient, but able to run on kerosene). The necessary equipment was sold under the trademark 'Econom'.

During the fuel crisis of the 1970s, Saab-Valmet developed and series-produced the *Saab 99* Petro that ran on kerosene, *turpentine* or gasoline. The project, codenamed 'Project Lapponia', was headed by Simo Vuorinen, and towards the end of the 1970s, a working prototype was produced based on the Saab 99GL. The car was designed to run on two fuels. Gasoline was used for cold starts and when extra power was needed, but normally it ran on kerosene or turpentine. The idea was that the gasoline could be made from peat using the *Fischer-Tropsch process.* Between 1980 and 1984, 3756 Saab 99 Petros and 2385 *Talbot Horizons* (a version of the Chrysler Horizon that integrated many Saab components) were made.

Kerosene is used to fuel smaller-horsepower outboard motors built by Yamaha Motors, Suzuki Marine, and Tohatsu. Primarily used on small fishing craft, these are dual-fuel engines that start on gasoline and then transition to kerosene once the engine reaches optimum operating temperature. Multiple fuel Evinrude and Mercury Racing engines also burn kerosene, as well as jet fuel.

Today, kerosene is mainly used in *fuel for jet engines* (more technically Avtur, *Jet A and Jet A-l, Jet B. JP-4, JP-5, JP-7* or *JP-8*). One form of the fuel known as *RP-1* is burned with *liquid oxygen* as rocket fuel. These fuel grade kerosenes meet specifications for *smoke points* and *freeze points.* The combustion reaction can be approximated as follows, with the molecular formula $C_{12}H_{26}$ (dodecane):

$$C_{12}H_{26}(l) + {}^{37}/_{2}\ O_2(g) \rightarrow 12\ CO_2(g) + 13\ H_2O(g);\ \Delta H^\circ = -7513\ \text{kJ}$$

In the initial phase of liftoff, the *Saturn V* launch vehicle was powered by the reaction of liquid oxygen with RP-1. For the five 6.4 meganewton sea-level thrust *F-1* rocket engines of the Saturn V, burning together, the reaction generated roughly 1.62×10^{11} *watts* (J/s) (162 gigawatt) or 217 million horsepower.

Kerosene is sometimes used as an additive in diesel fuel to prevent gelling or waxing in cold temperatures.

Ultra-low sulphur kerosene is a custom-blended fuel used by the *New York City Transit* to power its bus fleet. The transit agency started using this fuel in 2004, prior to the widespread adoption of *ultra-low sulphur diesel,* which has since become the standard. In 2008, the suppliers of the custom fuel failed to tender for a renewal of the transit agency's contract, leading to a negotiated contract at a significantly increased cost.

Cooking

In countries such as India, kerosene is the main fuel used for cooking, especially by the poor, and kerosene stoves have replaced traditional wood-based cooking appliances. As such, increase in the price of kerosene can have a major political and environmental consequence. The Indian government subsidizes the fuel to keep the price very low, to around 15 cents per litre as of February 2007, as lower prices discourage dismantling of forests for cooking fuel.

Kerosene is used as a fuel in *portable stoves,* especially in *Primus stoves* invented in *1892.* Portable kerosene stoves earn a reputation of reliable and durable stove in everyday use, and perform especially well under adverse conditions. In outdoor activities and mountaineering, a decisive advantage of *pressurized kerosene stoves* over *gas cartridge stoves* is their particularly high thermal output and their ability to operate at very low temperature in winter or at high altitude.

Entertainment

Kerosene is often used in the entertainment industry for fire performances, such as *fire breathing, fire juggling or poi,* and *fire dancing.* Because of its low flame temperature when burnt in free air, the risk is lower should the performer come in contact with the flame. Kerosene is not usually used as fuel for indoor fire dancing, as it produces an unpleasant odour, which becomes poisonous in sufficient concentration. *Methanol* was sometimes used instead, but the flames it produces look less impressive, and its lower *flash point* poses a high risk. Moreover, methanol is highly *toxic* for the *optic nerves,* and can cause *blindness* when swallowed.

Other Uses

- Liquid pesticides have traditionally used kerosene or some other petroleum distillate as a carrier, though water has recently begun to replace kerosene.
- Kerosene has also been found effective in killing bed bugs upon direct spray.

- Kerosene has been used to treat pools of standing water to prevent *mosquitoes* from breeding, notably in the *yellow fever* outbreak of 1905 in *New Orleans*.
- It can be used to remove *lice* from hair, but this practice is painful and potentially very dangerous. Also, this practice removes all natural oils and fats from the scalp.
- Since kerosene is chemically stable, it is used to store substances with *redox* tendencies within to prevent unwanted reactions, such as *alkali metals*.
- In *X-ray crystallography,* kerosene can be used to store crystals. When a *hydrated* crystal is left in air, *dehydration* may occur slowly. This makes the colour of the crystal become dull. Kerosene can keep air from the crystal.
- It is sometimes used as a solvent.
    - Kerosene can be applied topically to hard-to-remove mucilage or adhesive left by stickers on a glass surface (such as in show windows of stores).
    - Kerosene can be used to remove candle wax that has dripped onto a glass surface; the excess wax should be scraped off prior to applying kerosene via a soaked cloth or tissue paper.
    - Kerosene can be used to clean bicycle and motorcycle chains of old lubricant before relubrication.
- It can be used in conjunction with *cutting oil* as a thread cutting and reaming *lubricant*. When machining aluminium and its alloys, kerosene on its own is an excellent cutting lubricant.
- In military applications, kerosene is a primary component in the explosive *ANFO,* which also has widespread use in the mining and agricultural industries.
- Kerosene-based *diluent* is commonly used as a component of the organic solvent in *SX/EW copper* refining.
- Hydrotreated kerosene can be used as a starting material to produce high-purity, linear paraffins, which are subsequently dehydrogenated to linear olefins, and when the latter are reacted with benzene in the presence of a catalyst, the result is *linear alkyl benzene*.
- Kerosene is used as a lubricant for glass cutting. It prevents chipping of the glass as the cutting tool is drawn along the surface, and it prevents the surface of the glass from resealing along the scored line, which would cause an uneven and jagged cut.
- Kerosene was used in lava lamps from the 1970s to the early 2000s.

Toxicity

Ingestion of kerosene is harmful or fatal. Kerosene should never be used to get rid of hair lice as it can cause burns and serious illness. A kerosene shampoo can even be fatal if fumes are inhaled.

KEROSENE/SUPERIOR KEROSENE OIL (SKO)

Introduction

Fuel oils are complex mixtures of compounds of Carbon and Hydrogen, they cannot be classified rigidly or defined exactly by chemical formulae or definite physical properties. Two broad classifications are generally recognized:

1. 'distillate fuel oils' and 2. 'Residual fuel oils'... The latter are often referred to as heavy fuel oils and may contain cutter stock or distillates, *e.g.*, furnace oil. Distillate fuel oils are Petroleum fractions that have been vapourizd and condensed. They are produced by distillation process in which petroleum is separated into fractions according to their boiling range. Distillate fuel oils may be produced not only from 'straight run' crude oils but also from subsequent refinery process such as thermal or catalytic cracking. Kerosene and Diesel (gas oil) are typical examples of distillate fuels. Kerosene normally boils in the range of 150°C - 250°C (max: 300°C) and consists of C_{11} - C_{18} hydrocarbons. Kerosene is a blend of Paraffins, Naphthenes and Aromatics wherein Paraffins and Napthenes as major components and aromatics as minor components. The most important charactristics governed by *IS 1459/1974 (reaffirmed 1996)* are distillation; colour, flash point, smoke point and burning quality.

Two types of Kerosene are normally available commercially:

- Kerosene (colourless)
- Regular Blue dyed Kerosene for Public Distribution Supply (PDS)

(Blue dye is Di-alkyl amino anthraquinone)

Test Methods as per IS 1459/1974

Density: (P: 16 IS 1448 Methods of Test)

Methods are same as described in Petrol. This parameter is hot included in Bureau of Indian Standard Specifications. A typical Standard Kerosene is having density (gm/cm^3) at 15°C 0.78 – 0.82.

Distillation: (ASTM D 86, IP 123, P: 18 IS 1448 Methods of test)

It gives an idea of volatility characteristics of the fuel. It can be determined by:

- Non-fractionating type ASTM — Manual
- Non-fractionating type ASTM — Automatic

Procedure is similar to that of Petrol. The entire sample should distill below 300°C.

FlashPoint: (P 20 IS 1448 Methods of Test ASTM D 56 & D 6450)

Test method is similar as mentioned above.

Viscosity : (P : 25 IS 1448 methods of test : IP 71 ASTM D 445)

The Viscosity is the property of its resistance to flow. Different units of viscosity are in use, based on a number of seconds taken for a specific and measured quantity of oil to flow in a standard apparatus at a fixed temperature.

The universally accepted method is Kinematic Viscosity and is a measure of resistance to gravity flow of fluid, the pressure head being proportional to density. For the determination of Kinematic Viscosity, the time liquid flow under gravity, through a standard capillary of a calibrated viscometer at a closely controlled temperature. The Kinematic Viscosity is the product of time in seconds and calibration constant of the viscometer and is measured in centistokes at 40°C for Kerosene and Diesel.

- Canon Penske Viscometer — routine
- BS/IP U tube or any equivalent calibrated Viscometer .

Method

The sample is put in a viscometer and kept in a viscosity bath to attain the temperature. Sample is sucked with the help of rubber sucker (bellow) and time of flow is noted. The time of flow in seconds multiplying-with the constant of viseometer will give viscosity in cst.

Smoke Point-(IP 57 : P 31 IS 1448 Methods of Test ASTM D 1322)

It is the maximum height in mm at which Kerosene will burn without smoke in a smoke point lamp. It is an indication of degree of refinement. Higher the smoke point the larger will be smoke free flame therefore better illumination and degree of refinement of kerosene. Paraffins have the highest smoke point, aromatics the lowest and naphthenes the intermediate.

Method

Smoke point is an indicator of the combustion qualities of Aviation Turbine Fuels and Kerosene. The fuel sample is burned in the Smoke Point, lamp and the maximum flame height obtainable without smoking is measured.

The Smoke point of atypical standard Kerosene is *18 mm to 22 mm.*

Colour: (Blue dyed Kerosene) as per IS 1459 (second revision reaffirmed in 1991)

- *Visual:* Note down the colour of the sample visually
- *UV-Visible Spectrophotometry:* Note down the wavelength for maximum absorption for *BLUE* using visible spectrophotometer.

Equipment	:	Spectrophotometer
Method	:	Scan-ordinate mode
Scan Speed	:	120 nm / min
Lamp	:	Tungston (Visible region)
Wavelength	:	600 nm – 700 nm
Peak threshold	:	0.02
Oil Blue dye	:	λ_{max}-645 nm - 655 nm (Di alkyl amino anthroquinone dye is normally used for colouring PDS kerosene)

Thin Layer Chromatographic Methods for the Detection of Oil Soluble Dyes

The standard Kerosene sample (2 µl), reference standard dyes namely oil blue in solvent ether (2 µl) each were spotted on TLC (Silica Gel 60 G) plates or Silica Gel (60 F 254) Alumina pre-coated plates along with case samples. The plates were developed in the saturated chambers containing *Hexane: Toluerie: Acetic Acid [50 : 50 : 2]* as solvent systems and run the plate upto 10 cm distance and remove the plate from the chamber and dry it.

Detection: Blue dye from Kerosene (Standard) sample shows one blue colour-spot at Rf around 0.4. This blue dye was found to-be oil blue dye used for colouring Kerosene. *(PDS-Kerosene).*

REFERENCES

1. Webster's New World College Dictionary, '*kerosene*'.
2. Asbury, Herbert (1942). *The Golden Flood: An Informal History of America's First Oil Field.* Alfred A. Knopf, p. 35.
3. Oxford Eglish Dictionary, 'Kerosene'.
4. Chris Collins (2007), 'Implementing Phytoremediation of Petroleum Hydrocarbons, *Methods in Biotechnology* 23:99—108. Humana Press. ISBN 1-58829-541-9.
5. 'Kerosene'. Retrieved 2009-06-10.
6. Annamalai, Kalyan; Ishwar Kanwar Puri (2006). *Combustion Science and Engineering.* CRC Press. p. 851. ISBN 978-0849320712.
7. Bilkadi, Zayn. 'The Oil Weapos'. *Saudi Aramco World* 46 (1) : 20-27.
8. Russell, Loris S. (2003). *A Heritage of Light: Lamps and Lighting in the Early Canadian Home.* University of Toronto Press. ISBN 0802037658.
9. Black, Harry (1997). *Canadian Scientists and Inventors.* Pembroke Publishers. ISBN 1551380811.

10. World, American Manufacturer and Iron (1901). *Greater Pittsburgh and Allegheny County, Past, Present, Future; The Pioneer Oil Refiner.* The American Manufacturer and Iron World.
11. McInnis, Karen. "Kier, Samuel Martin-Bio". *Biography.* The Pennsylvania State University. Retrieved 2008-12.
12. Harper, J.A. (1995). "Samuel Kier-Medicine Man and Refiner". *Pennsylvania Geology* (Oil Region Alliance of Business, Industry and Tourism) 26 (1). Retrieved 2008-12-12.
13. Steil, Tim; Luning, Jim (2002). *Fantastic Filling Station.* MBI Publishing. pp. 19-20. ISBN 0760310645.
14. Cooley, Le Roy Clark (1873). *Elements of Chemistry: For Common and High Schools.* Scribner, Armstong, p. 98.
15. Crew, Benjamin Johnson; Ashburner, Charles Albert (1887). *A Practical Treatise on Petroleum.* Baird, p. 395.
16. Bettmann, Otto (1974). *The Good Old Days and Ndash; They Were Terrible!.* Random House, p. 34. ISBN 9780394709413.
17. Popular Science December 1951, p. 193.
18. Bakrutan: 'Saab 99 Petro' by Petri Tyrkos, No. 4, 2008
19. Banse, Timothy (7 July 2010). "Kerosene Outboards: An Alternative Fuel?". *Marine Engine Digest.*
20. Ebbing, D.D.; Gammon, S.D. (2005). *General Chemistry* (8th ed). New York: Houghton Mifflin.
21. Kerosene blending, (pdf from EPA).
22. How a Plan for Bus Fuel Grew Expensive, The New York Times, 2008-09-25.
23. Bradsher, Keith (28 July 2008). "Fuel Subsidies Overseas Take a Toll on U.S.". *New York Times.*
24. http:// www.meab-mx.se/en/sx/_principles.htm
25. Levine, Michael D; Gresham, Chip, III (30 April 2009). 'Toxicity, Hydrocarbons'. *Emedicine.* Retrieved 1 December 2009.
26. Mahdi, Awad Hassan (1988). "Kerosene Poisoning in Children in Riyadh". *Journal of Tropical Paediatrics* (Oxford University Press) 34 (6): 316-318. doi:10.1093/tropej/34.6.316. PMID 3221417. Retrieved 1 December 2009. "Radiological signs of pneumonia were shown in nine out of 27 patients who had chest X-rays. There was one death.".

5 Diesel

Light Diesel Oil and High Speed Diesel

Introduction

Diesel and non-aviation gas turbine fuels were originally straight run products obtained from the distillation of crude oil. Today with the various refinery-cracking processes, these fuels may contain varying amounts of selected cracked distillates. This permits an increase in the volume of available fuel at a minimum cost. The boiling range of distillate fuel (Diesel) is approximately 150°C to 400°C. It consists of C_{18} to C_{28} hydrocarbons. It is a blend of Saturates and aromatics (mainly polyaromatics). The relative merits of the fuel types to be considered will depend upon the refining practices employed, the nature of crude oils from which they are produced, and the additive package if (any) used. The broad definition of fuels for land and marine diesel engines and non-aviation gas turbines covers many possible combinations of volatility, ignition quality, Viscosity, gravity, stability and other properties. The most important characteristics governed by IS 1460/2005 are density at 15°C, Flash Point, Pour Point, distillation and Kinematic Viscosity at 40°C, Cetane No, Cetane Index and Sulphur. Two types of Diesel namely Light Diesel Oil (LDO) and High Speed Diesel Oil. (HSD) are normally referred for analysis.

Test Method (Required as per IS 1460/2005—Diesel Fuels)

Density: (P: 16 IS 1448 Methods of Test)

Methods are same as described in Petrol. A typical Standard HSD is having density (Kg/m^3) at 15°C 820-845

Note:
- Increase in density (above 845 Kg/M^3) indicates the presence of possible adulterants like Hi-Flash Heavy Aromatic Naphtha, light viscous oil, etc.
- Decrease in density (below 820 Kg/M^3)/indicates the presence of possible adulterants like Kerosene and middle distillates.

Distillation (ASTM D 86/IP 123, P:18 IS 1448 Methods of Test)

It gives an idea of volatility characteristics of the fuel. It can be determined by:

- Non-fractionating type ASTM-Manual
- Non-fractionating type ASTM-Automatic

Procedure is similar to that of Petrol. The entire sample should distill below 400°C. 95 per cent volume recovery should be below 360°C. The distillation range of typical standard Diesel is *150°C to 380°C.*

Flash Point (ASTM D 56 & 6450: P 20 IS 1448 Methods of Test)

Test method is similar as mentioned in Section. 3, The flashpoint of typical standard Diesel is *35°C – 40°C.*

Viscosity (P:25 IS 1448 methods of test : IP 71 : ASTM D 445)

The Viscosity is the property of its resistance to flow. Different units of viscosity are in use, based on a number of seconds taken for a specific and measured quantity of oil to flow in a standard apparatus at a fixed temperature.

The universally accepted method is Kinematic Viscosity and is a measure of resistance to gravity flow of fluid; the pressure head being proportional to density. For the determination of Kinematic Viscosity, the time is measured in seconds for a fixed volume of liquid flow under gravity through a standard capillary of a calibrated viscometer at a closely controlled temperature. The Kinematic Viscosity is the product of time in seconds and calibration constant of the viscometer and is measured in centistokes at 40°C for Kerosene and Diesel.

- Canon Penske Viscometer - routine
- BS/IP U tube or any equivalent calibrated Viscometer

Method

Already discussed in 4.2.5.

Constant temperature Kinematic Viscosity bath can be utilized to maintain at a specified temperature. (KV Bath)

Note:
- Decrease in Kinematic Viscosity indicates the presence of possible adulterants like Kerosene and Heavy aromatic Naphtha.
- Increase in Kinematic Viscosity indicates the presence of possible adulterant like low viscosity grade oil.

Pour Point (IP 15 : P 10 IS 1448 Methods of Test ASTM D 97/D 2500)

Petroleum oils do not have any freezing points as they contain compounds of large molecular size and configuration. They become only semi/plastic solid when cooled to sufficient low temperature under standard conditions. Pour point is the lowest temperature which is multiple of 3°C at which the oil ceased to flow under prescribed conditions and is reported 3°C higher than it. Manual/Automatic Pour point Apparatus can be used.

Note: • Adulteration with low viscous oil will raise the Pour Point and some times this parameter becomes not characteristic.

Although different methods have been incorporated in BIS, the methods mentioned below will be very authentic and effective in analysing any type of Diesel adulteration.

Sulphur (IP 336 or P:83 or D4294)

Calculated Cetane Index (CCI)

It is an indicative of ignition quality and can be calculated from density and distillation data. ASTM D 86 using ASTM D 4737 Method given below:

A correlation in SI units has been established between the ASTM cetane number and density and 10 per cent, 50 per cent and 90 per cent recovery temperatures of the fuel. The relationship is given by the following equations:

$$
\begin{aligned}
CCI = {} & 45.2 \\
& +(0.0892)\ (T_{10N}) \\
& +(0.131 + (0.901)(B))\ (T_{50\ N}) \\
& +(0.0523 - (0.420)(B))\ (T_{90N})^2 \\
& +(0.00049)(T_{10N})^2 - (T_{90N})^2) \\
& +(107)(B) + (60)\ (B)^2
\end{aligned}
$$

Where :

CCI = Calculated Cetane Index by four variable equation

D = Density at 15°C, determined test method D 1298

DN = D-0.85

$B = (e^{(-3.5)(DN)}) - 1$

T_{10} = 10% recovery temperature, °C, determined by test method D 86 and corrected to Standard barometric pressure

$T_{10N} = T_{10} - 215$

T_{50} = 50% recovery temperature, °C, determined by test method 86 and corrected to Standard barometric pressure

$T_{50N} = T_{50} - 260$

T_{90} = 90% recovery temperature, °C, determined by test method 86 and corrected to Standard barometric pressure

$T_{90N} = T_{90} - 310$

Calculated Cetane Index (ASTM D 976-91)

CCI = 454.74 – 1641.416 D + 774.74 D^2 – 0.554 B + 97.803 $(LogB)^2$

Where D = Density at 15°C g/ml and B = Mid-boiling Temperature °C

Gas Liquid Chromatography for Quantitative Determination of Adulteration in Diesel with Kerosene

Equipment

Gas Chromatograph with FID and temperature programmer.

Operating Conditions:

- Column: Dual columns of 15% Apizeon on CHW Aw, $^1/_4$ inch OD, 8′ length SS, max. temp. 300°C.
- Nitrogen : 60ml/min Hydrogen/air: 40 ml/min
- Sensitivity range: back off: 10^{-9}A
- Attenuation : 2
- Sample for injection : 0.3 to 0.4 µl
- 10% solutions of Diesel (D), Kerosene (K) and different admixtures (D-K) derived from D and Kin moisture free solvent ether.
- Programming : Isothermal at 90°C for 3 min then continued at 10°C/ min between 90°C to 230°C and isothermal at 230°C for 8 min.

Preparation of Samples

Pure Diesel, Kerosene and various admixtures (9D: 1K, 8D:2K, 7D:3K....) were prepared in moisture free solvent ether. About 0.5 µl was injected and the chromatograms were compared.

Observations and Calculations

A characteristic pattern of chromatogram for diesel samples indicate less amplitudes of earlier peaks (between 100C and 180C) and more amplitudes of later peaks (between 180C and 230C including 8 min final isothermal hold). The reverse is true for Kerosene samples similarly experimental admixtures. The area of the earlier peaks, between the cut off points 1 to 2 (100C to 180C) was recorded as A and the area of the later peaks between the cut off points 2 to 3 [between 180C and 230C including 8 min final isothermal hold] was recorded as B. log (10X A/B) values were calculated for different D—K compositions in all the samples. A simple ratio of A/B *Vs* D—K composition would give a non-linear curve: Hence, with a view to have a linear plot log of this ratio was found to be necessary. Any adulteration of Diesel with Kerosene, will charige this value within the limits of standards.

Conclusion

Kerosene adulterant can easily be detected by Pour Point determination and also Instrumental technique like GC and HPLC.

Light Diesel Oil

As per IS 1450, the analysis of light diesel oil involves measurement of density, flash point, distillation, pour point, Kinematic viscosity at 40°C.

Density: (P: 16 IS 1448 Methods of Test)

Methods are same as described in Petrol. A typical Standard LDO is having density (gm/cm^3) at 15°C *0.850 – 0.890.*

Flash Point-Pensky-Marten Closed Cup (P:21 IS 1448 Methods of Test)

The Fen sky-Martens closed cup (PMC) is used for the measurement of flash point of light diesel oil. In general, the flash Point of LDO is 66°C (minimum).

Method

Clean and dry all parts of cup arid its accessories before starting the test. Fill the cup with the sample to be tested to the level indicated by the filling mark place the lid on the cup. Insert the thermometer in the sample cup, Light the test, flameplaced on the top of cup and adjust it to 4.0 mm diameter. Heat the Pensky—marten apparatus with Bunsen burner and keep the rate of heating *as 5°C to 6°C per* minute. Turn the stirrer in the apparatus at the rate of 90 to 120 rev/min. Stirring in downward direction measure the flash point with the help of test flame and measure the flash point of LDO.

Viscosity (P: 25 IS 1448 Methods of Test IP 71: ASTM D 445)

Test method is similar to HSD, Kerosene. The experimental procedure is identical to that for measurement of Kinematic Viscosity in High Speed Diesel and Kerosene.

Pour Point (IP 15: P 10 IS 1448 Methods of Test ASTM D 977/D 2500)

Experimental procedures and methods are similar to that of HSD. The values are recorded. The minimum value of pour point for summer is +12 and for winter +21.

6

Biodiesel

Biodiesel could be an excellent renewable fuel for diesel engines. It is derived from vegetable oils that are chemically converted into biodiesel. As the name implies, it is similar to diesel fuel except that it is produced from crops commonly grown in North Dakota, including canola, soybean, sunflower and safflower. These crops are all capable of producing several gallons of fuel per acre that can power an unmodified diesel engine, Vegetable oil is Converted into biodiesel through a chemical process that produces methyl or ethyl ester; After washing and filtering to meet American Society for Testing and Materials (ASTM) standards, it is usable as an alternate renewable fuel.

Biodiesel

Biodiesel is composed of long-chain fatty acids with ani alcohol attached, often derived from vegetable oils. It is produced through the reaction of a vegetable oil with methyl alcohol of ethyl alcohol in the presence of a catalyst Animal fats are another potential source. Commonly used catalysts are potassium hydroxide (NaOH). The chemical process is called transesterification which produces biodiesel and glycerin. Chemically, biodiesel is called a methyl ester if the alcohol used is methanol. If ethanol is used, it is called an ethyl ester. They are similar and currently; methyl ester is cheaper due to the lower cost for rnethanol. Biodiesel can be used in the pure form or blended in any amount with diesel fuel for use in compression ignition engines. Figure 6.1 shows basic transesterification technology.

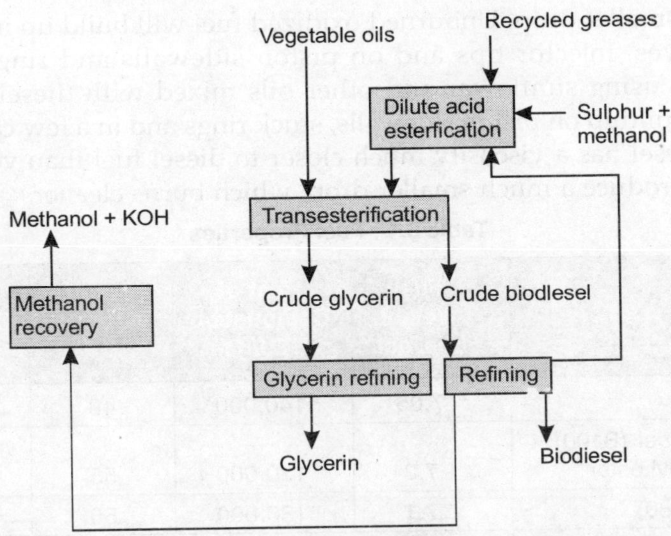

Fig. 6.1 : Basic transesterification technology

The transesterification process of converting vegetable oils to biodiesel is shown in Fig. 6.2. The *'R'* groups are the fatty acids, which are usually 12 to 22 carbons in length. The large vegetable oil molecule is reduced to about 1/3 its original size, lowering the viscosity making it similar to diesel fuel the resulting fuel operates similar to diesel fuel in an engine. The reaction produces three molecules of an ester fuel from one molecule of vegetable oil.

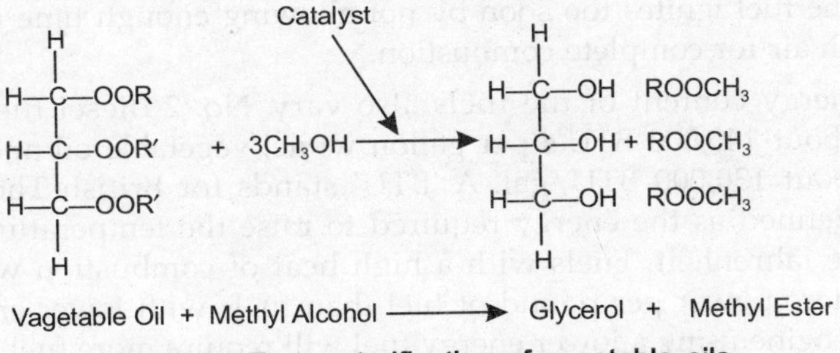

$$\begin{array}{c} H \\ | \\ H-C-OOR \\ | \\ H-C-OOR' \\ | \\ H-C-OOR' \\ | \\ H \end{array} + 3CH_3OH \xrightarrow{\text{Catalyst}} \begin{array}{c} H \\ | \\ H-C-OH \\ | \\ H-C-OH \\ | \\ H-C-OH \\ | \\ H \end{array} \begin{array}{c} ROOCH_3 \\ + ROOCH_3 \\ ROOCH_3 \end{array}$$

Vagetable Oil + Methyl Alcohol ⟶ Glycerol + Methyl Ester

Fig. 6.2 : Transesterification of vegetable oils

Some properties of various fuels are shown in table 6.1. They include diesel fuel, biodiesel, and vegetable oil. The main differences between diesel fuel, an ester fuel and vegetable oil are the viscosity, cetane number and heat of combustion. The viscosity of a fuel is important because it affects the atomization of the fuel being injected into the engine combustion chamber. A small fuel drop is desired so complete combustion occurs. A high viscosity fuel, such as raw vegetable oil, will produce a larger drop of fuel in an engine combustion chamber which may not burn as clean as a fuel that produces a smaller drop. Unburned oxidized fuel will build up in the engine around valves, injector tips and on piston sidewalls and rings. Previous NDSU tests using sunflower and other oils mixed with diesel fuel found significant buildup on piston sidewalls, stuck rings and in a few cases, broken rings. Biodiesel has a viscosity much closer to diesel fuel than vegetable oil. This helps produce a much smaller drop, which burns cleaner.

Table 6.1 : Fuel Properties

	Fuel Weight Lbs./gal.	Heat of Combustion BTU/gal.	Cetan Number	Viscosity Centistokes
No. 2 diesel	7.05	140,000	48	3.0
100% Biodiesel (B100) Methyl or ethyl ester	7.3	130,000	55	5.7
B20 mix (20/80)	7.1	138,000	50	3.3
Raw vegetable oil	7.5	130,000	35 to 45	40 to 50

Cetane rating varies considerably among the listed fuels (table 6.1) and is a measure of the self-ignition quality of the fuel. No. 2 diesel fuel usually has a cetane rating between 45 and 50 while vegetable oil is 35 to 45. Biodiesel is usually 50 to 60. The ignition quality affects engine performance, cold starting, warm up and engine combustion roughness. Cetane rating is related to the volatility of the fuel where more volatile fuels have higher ratings. A high cetane fuel also may lead to incomplete combustion and smoke if the fuel ignites too soon by not allowing enough time for the fuel to mix with air for complete combustion.

The energy content of the fuels also vary. No. 2 diesel fuel typically contains about 140,000 BTU's per gallon while, vegetable oil and biodiesel contain about 130,000 BTU/gal. A 'BTU' stands for British Thermal Unit which is defined as the energy required to raise the temperature of water one degree fahrenheit. Fuels with a high heat of combustion will usually produce more power per pound of fuel than fuels with lower energy. As a result, an engine using a lower energy fuel will require more fuel to produce the same power as diesel fuel. As a result of the lower energy content, biodiesel will require about 1.1 gallons of fuel to dp the same work as a gallon of diesel fuel.

Engine Studies

Several studies show biodiesel can run in a conventional diesel engine for an extended time. Researchers in several states including Missouri and Idaho, have run diesel engines in pickups, city buses, large trucks and tractors on various mixes of biodiesel/diesel fuel. These mixtures have ranged from 2/98% (B2), 20/80% (B20) up to 100% (B10p). The results of these studies look very promising.

Standard diesel engines will operate on 100 per cent biodiesel. In cold weather, biodiesel begins to cloud and thicken at about 30F. Biodiesel thickens at warmer temperatures than No. 2 diesel fuel, but additives are available that will lower the pour point. Pour point is the point at which flow of the fuel ceases; Mixing biodiesel with No. 1 diesel as is currently done with No. 2 will lower the pour point. Installing an in-tank or fuel line heater may also be needed to keep the fuel flowing in cold weather. A blend of biodiesel/diesel fuel has a lower pour point than 100 per cent biodiesel, but gelling may still occur unless care as mentioned earlier is taken.

New lower diesel engine emission requirements that dictate a reduction of sulphur in fuel is causing a reduction in the lubricating ability of fuel. This will shorten the operating life of the injection system and engine. Biodiesel blends, even at low rates (2%), indicate improved lubricating ability over diesel which should reduce wear and extend fuel system and engine life.

Studies show that some older engine fuel systems (engines built prior to 1993) may show fuel pump seal deterioration. They may have rubber or nitrile seals in the fuel pump and fuel system that could fail if 100 per cent biodiesel is used. It may be best to replace them with Viton or other non-rubber seals if 100 per cent biodiesel is used. A blend of 20 per cent biodiesel can be used in older engines with no changes, but it is recommended to watch for leaks. Also, biodiesel studies indicate some cleaning action of the fuel system, so a fuel filter may need replacement soon after switching to biodiesel.

Fig. 6.3 Various Mixtures of Biodiesel Have Been Used to Operate This 4 Cylinder Cummings Engine

Biodiesel and Air Pollution

Research with biodiesel show reductions in several contributors to air pollution. *Table 6.2* is a summary of engine tests completed at the University of Idaho.

These tests were, performed with a 100 per cent and a 20 per cent mix of ethyl and methyl ester of rapeseed oil. A U.S. Department of Energy publication indicates reductions in most emission components except for an increase in nitrous oxide. Biodiesel use could provide reductions in several air pollutants. This could provide significant improvements in cities where air quality is a concern.

Table 6.2 : Engine Emission Results from the University of Idaho

Emission	100% Ester Fuel (B100) in %	20/80 Mix (B20) in %
Hydrocarbons	–52.4	–19.0
Carbon Monoxide	–47.6	–26.1
Nitrous Oxides	–10.0	–3.7
Carbon Dioxide	+0.9	+.7
Particulates	+9.9	–2.8

Mixing and Storage of Biodiesel

Biodiesel mixes well with diesel fuel in any proportion and stays blended even in cold temperatures. A storage study completed over a 24-month period at the University of Idaho found that biodieseltends to store about as. well as diesel fuel. This study found that engine power decreased about 2 per cent and viscosity, density, peroxide and acid value inereasecl for biodiesel. Usually it is recommended not to store biodiesel longer than 6 months or at the most, a year: This recommendation is similar to diesel fuel storage periods.

Biodiesel Cost

The cost of biodiesel is higher than diesel fuel. Currently, there are seven producers of biodiesel in the United States. Pure biodiesel (100%) sells for about \$1.50 to \$2.00 per gallon before taxes. Fuel taxes will add approximately \$0.50 per gallon. A mix of 20 per cent biodiesel and 80 per cent diesel will cost about 15 to 20 more per gallon over the cost of 100 per cent diesel. Some suppliers are selling a 2 per cent biodiesel mix at the same price as diesel, but this price will probably not continue into the future. A more realistic price would be about 1 to 2 cents more per gallon than diesel. These prices would be more attractive to people. The U.S. Department of Energy is working with the biodiesel industry to reduce the cost of biodiesel. A subsidy for the industry similar to that for other alternate fuels may be needed to promote the fuel. Improvements in processing along with the use of waste cooking oil as a raw material may help reduce costs.

Currently, there are several service stations selling a mix of biodiesel and diesel in North Dakota.

Potential Fuel from Oil Crops

Currently, diesel fuel use in North Dakota is about 165 million gallons per year. About 85 million gallons are used on farms in crop production. In 2001, about 2.1 million acres of soybeans were produced in the state with an average yield of about 33 bushels per acre. Soybeans contain about 18 per cent oil so the average oil production per acre is about 49 gallons. If this oil were converted to an ester fuel, more than 100 million gallons of fuel could be produced. Soybean ester fuel could replace all the on-farm diesel fuel needs in the state. Other oil crops grown in the state could be used to produce additional fuel. Table 6.3 shows the production potential of biodiesel from the main oil crops grown in North Dakota.

Every gallon of vegetable oil will produce about 1 gallon of biodiesel. The total input/output energy ratio shows a very positive return. For every BTU of energy used to produce the crop and process the oil, about 3.3 BTU's is produced as fuel.

Table 6.3 : Potential fuel from North Dakota oil crops (2001)

Crop	Acres in State (millions)	Yield	Oil (%)	Gallons (per Acre)
Soybean	2.1	33 bu/acre	18	49
Sunflower	1.1	1400 lb/ac	44	84
Canola	1.2	1300 lb/ac	43	76

Fig. 6.4 Any Standard Diesel Engine will Operate Well on Biodiesel

Engine Warranties

Some people are concerned that using a new fuel in ah engine may cause damage. Several engine manufacturers guarantee their engines the same when using biodiesel as for diesel fuel as long as the amount of brodiesel does not exceed 20 per cent and the fuel must meet ASTM D6751 specifications.

- Peterson, C., & D. Reece. 1996, "Emissions Characteristics of Ethyl Truck". Transactions of the ASAE 39(2):805-816.
- Peterson, C.L., J.C. Thompson, J.S. Taberski, D.L. Reece, & G. Fleischman. 1999. "Long-Range On-road Test with Twenty Per Cent Rapeseed Biodiesel" Applied Engineering in Agriculture, ASAE-15(2):91-101.
- Marshall, W., Schumacher, L.G., Howeli, S. A. 1995. "Engine Exhaust Emissions Evaluation of a Cummins L10E When Fueled with a Biodiesel Blend". SAE Paper No. 952363. SAE, Warrendale, PA.
- Schumacher, L.G., S.C. Borgelt, & W.G. Hires. (1995) "Fueling a Diesel Engine with Methyl-Ester Soybean Oil". Applied Engineering in Agriculture. Vol. 11(1): 37-40.
- Thompson, J.C., C.L. Peterson, Reece, & S.M. Beck. 1998, "Two-Year Storage Study with Methyl and Ethyl Esters of Rapeseed Oil". Transactions of the ASAE 41(4):931-939.
- DOE. Feb. 2002. "Biodiesel-Clean, Green Diesel Fuel". DOE/GO-102001-1449, National Renewable.

7

Engine Lubricating Oil

Introduction

The major functions of lubricating oil is the reduction of friction and wear by the separation of surfaces, metallic or plastic, which are moving with respect to each other. Petroleum base lubricating oils are present in the residual fraction boiling above 370°C from the atmospheric distillation of selected crude oils of both Paraffinic and Naphthenic types. This residue is further distilled, under conditions of high vacuum, into series of fractions to provide light to heavy lubricating oil stocks. The number of fractions depends on the type of crude oil and the requirements of the refiner but 4 to 5 is a typical number. In the majority of cases to meet Specification requirements with respect to properties of base oils.

Petroleum based lubricating oils mainly consist of Paraffins, Naphthenes and Aromatics. The lubrication property of the particular lubricant depends on the distribution of these hydrocarbons. It Consists of C_{28} to C_{40} hydrocarbons. The most important characteristics governed by *IS 13696 are Specific* gravity, Flash point, Kinematic viscosity at 40°C and 100°C and Viscosity Index.

Apart from the above methods, the most significant parameter is *Total Base Number (TBN),* which gives an indication of additive treatment in oil. The basic characteristics of this are to neutralize the acidic constituents formed during use. This parameter is very important to predict a sample is adulterated or simulated.

Test Methods and Their Significance

Relative Density/Specific Gravity (P32 IS 1448 Methods of Test: ASTM D1298)

It is defined as a ratio of the mass of a given volume of substance at t°C to the mass of the equal volume of water at the same temperature and is determined at 15°C.

The Specific Gravity is determined by using:

- Hydrometer
- Specific Gravity Bottle
- Automatic density meter method

Specific gravity in many cases indicates the type or crude from which the product is made. Aromatics have the highest specific gravity where as paraffins the lowest. API gravity can be calculated from specific gravity (Section 2).

Significance

In case of used/reclaimed oils, lowering of specific gravity indicates:

- Presence of high boiling solvents or admixture of lower gravity oils
- If the Specific Gravity of the used/reclaimed oil is heavier than the original it indicates one or more of the following:
  * Oxidation of the oil charge
  * Presence of insolubles
  * Contamination with water
  * Addition of higher specific gravity oil.

The Specific Gravity of engine lubricating oil at 15°C normally varies from 0.85 to 0.90.

Viscosity:1 (P:25 IS 1448 methods of Test: IP 71: ASTM D 445 and 2170)

The Viscosity is the property of its resistance to flow. Different units of viscosity are in use, based on a number of seconds taken for a specific and measured quantity of oil to flow in a standard apparatus at a fixed temperature.

The universally accepted method is Kinematic Viscosity and is a measure of resistance to gravity flow of fluid, the pressure head being proportional to density. For the determination of Kinematic Viscosity, the time is measured in seconds for a fixed Volume of liquid flow under gravity, through a standard capillary of a calibrated viscometer at a closely controlled temperature. The Kinematic Viscosity is the product of time in seconds and calibration constant of the viscometer and is measured in centistokes at 40°C for Kerosene and Diesel.

- Canon Penske Viscometer — routine
- BS/IP U tube or any equivalent calibrated Viscometer

Method

The specific details of operation vary for the different types of viscometers. In all cases, the following procedure is followed:

Select a clean dry, calibrated viscometer having a range covering the estimated viscosity (that is, a wide capillary for a very viscous liquid and a narrower capillary for a more fluid liquid). The flow time should not be less than 200 seconds. Charge the viscometer in the manner dictated by the design of the instrument, this operation being in conformity with that employed when the instrument was calibrated. Should the sample contain, solid particles, filter during charging through a 75-micron IS Sieve. Constant temperature Viscometer bath can be utilized for measuring KV at a particular temperature. Allow the charged viscometer to remain in the bath long enough to reach the test temperature. Because this time will vary for the different instruments and for different temperatures, establish a safe temperature equilibrium time by trial (30 minutes should be sufficient). Use suction or pressure to adjust the head level of the test sample to a position in the capillary arm of the instrument about 5 mm ahead of the first timing mark. With the sample flowing freely, measure in seconds, to within 0.2 seconds and the time required for the meniscus to pass from the first timing mark to the second. If this flow time is less than the specified minimum select a viscometer with a capillary of smaller diameter and repeat the operation.

Calculation

Calculate this Kinematic Viscosity 'v' from the measured flow time 't' and the instrurnent constant 'C' by means of the following equation:

$$v = C \times t$$

Where

v = Kinematic Viscosity in centistokes

C = Calibration constant of the Viscometer in centistokes per second and

t = flow time in seconds

The Kinematic Viscosity can be measured in centistokes at two different temperatures 40°C and 100°C in order to find out the Index. Different grades of oil (SAE 5W, 10W, 20W and SAE 20, 30, 40, 50) are available based on their viscosity at 100°C. Low viscosity oil is required for high-speed bearings. High viscosity oil is required for heavily loaded and slow speed bearings.

Note:
- Viscosity is the most important single property of a lubricating oil
- In case of used oils if viscosity is lower than the original it indicates fuel dilution or admixture with low viscosity oils

Viscosity Index (P 56 IS 1448 Methods of Test: IP 226)

Viscosity Index (VI) is the rate of change of viscosity with respect to temperature. During the engine operation the moving parts get heated resulting the thinning of the oil layer between the mating surfaces resulting the poor lubrication. Since most of the oils have to be operated over a range of temperature.

Dean and Davis introduced a scheme by which a single number called Viscosity Index classified oil according to its viscosity temperature characteristics. They took two oil, one Paraffinic from Pennsylvanian crude and other Naphthenic oil from Gulf crude and determined viscosity at two different temperatures 100°F & 210°F (presently temperature followed are 40°C & 100°C). The Paraffinic oil which was assigned viscosity arbitrary number 100 and the Naphthenic oil which was assigned viscosity arbitrary number 0 were taken for calculating Viscosity Index by the following formula.

$$\text{Viscosity index (VI)} = \frac{L-U}{L-H} \times 100$$

Where

L = low VI oil (zero) but having the same viscosity at 100°C as of the unknown oil (oil in question)

H = high VI oil (100) having the same viscosity at 100°C as of the Unknown oil

U = Kinematic Viscosity of unknown oil at 40°C

The values of Land H can be obtained from table given in IS 1448 P: 56

It shows that L, H & U have the same viscosity at 100°C but different at 40°C

Note:
- A genuine oil will have higher Viscosity Index
- Decrease in VI indicates the possible adulteration with high boiling compound or admixture of low viscosity oils
- Blending lubricating oil shall have Viscosity Index 90 minimum
- Presence of diluents may result in the high viscosity index and in this case the oil should be checked for flash point. Lowering of the flash point is an indication of contamination/adulteration.

Flash Point (P 20 IS 1448 Methods of Test: ASTM D 56: D 92: D 93: D 1310 and 6450)

The flash point of a liquid is a lowest temperature at which application of flame causes the vapour above the sample to ignite. There are three types of apparatus used for the determination of Flash point namely Cleveland open cup, Pensky Marten closed cup (PMCC) and Abel. Abel is used for those liquids having flash point up to 70°C. Flash points indicate comparatively the degree of safety in storage, transportation and use of liquid Petroleum hydrocarbon products either in closed or Open containers.

The flash point of lubricating oil is carried out by Cleveland open cup/ Pensky Marten closed cup (Automatic) and Cleveland open cup (Automatic). About 75 ml of the sample is taken in a flash point cup and set all the parameters mentioned in the procedure manual are followed and their flash point is observed.

Carbon Residue (P8 IS 1448 Methods of Test: IP 13, 14)

It is an amount of carbonaceous material formed when a sample is evaporated and pyrolysed under specified conditions. The lighter will evaporate but the heavier more complex compounds will, decompose forming carbonaceous deposits. There are three methods for its determination.

- Conradson
- Ramsbottom

In the Conradson method sample is heated in a crucible under controlled conditions in absence of air and the residue left is weighed. Whereas, in Ramsbottom test the sample is placed in the tube with the capillary at the top and heated to 550°C in a bath of molten metal.

Neutralisation Value (P:1 IS 1448 Methods of Test: IP 177 ASTM D 974/97)

It is a measure of Acidity and Alkalinity of an oil. In order to improve the quality and life of an oil different types of additives are blended to it. The presence of acid and base number is an indication of additive treatment in a new oil. In new and used oils, the constituents considered to have acidic characteristics include organic and inorganic acids, esters, phenolic compounds, lactones, resins, salts of heavy metals and addition agents such as inhibitors and detergents. Similarly, constituents considered to have basic properties include organic and inorganic bases, amino compounds, salts of weak acids (soaps), basic salts of polyacidic bases, salts of heavy metals, and addition agents such as inhibitors and detergents.

Summary of Test Method

To determine the acid or base number, the sample is dissolved in a titrating solvent consists of toluene and isopropyl alcohol containing small amount of water and the resulting acid-phase solution is titrated at room temperature with standard non-aqueous alcoholic KOH or isopropyl alcoholic acid solution, respectively, to the end point indicated by the colour change of the added p-naphtholbenzein solution (orange in acid and green-brown in base).

Procedure for Acid Number

- Weigh a suitable quantity of the sample (about 2.0 gm) in a 250 ml flask.
- Add 100 ml of the titration solvent (500 ml toluene = 5 ml water to 495 ml of anhydrous isopropyl alcohol).

- Add 0.5 ml of the indicator (p-naphtholbenzein in a titration solvent – 10 gm/lit)
- If the mixture assumes yellow-orange coloration it is titrated against 0.1 M KOH.
- The end point is the colour change from orange to green or green-brown.
- Repeat for concordant values.
- Run blank determination by taking 100 ml of the titrating solvent and 0.5 ml of indicator solution.

Calculation

$$\text{Acid number; mg of KOH/g} = \frac{[(A-B)M \times 56.1]}{W}$$

Where,

A = KOH solution required for titration of the sample, ml

B = KOH solution required for titration for blank, ml

M = Molarity of KOH solution

W = Sample used in grams

Procedure for Base Number

- Weigh a suitable quantity of the sample (about 2.0 gm) in a 250 ml flask.
- Add 100 ml of the titration solvent (500 ml toluene = 5 ml water to 495 ml of anhydrous isopropyl alcohol)
- Add 0.5 ml of the indicator (p-naphtholbenzein in a titration solvent – 10 gm/lit)
- If the mixture assumes green or green-brown coloration it is titrated against 0.1 M HCl
- The end point is the colour change from green-brown to orange
- Repeat for concordant values
- Run blank determination by taking 100 ml of the titrating solvent and 0.5 ml of indicator solution. (same as in Acid Number)

Calculation

$$\text{Base number, mg of KOH/g} = \frac{[Em + FM)] \times 56.1}{W}$$

Where,

E = HCl solution required for titration of the sample, ml

m = molarity of HCl

M = Molarity of KOH solution

W = Sample used in grams

F = KOH required for titration of the acid number blank, ml

Total Base Number of New and Used Lubricating Oils (Mobil Lubricants)

Scope: A colour indicator titration test for TBN has been developed by MOBIL. This is applicable to oils containing Methyl and Amine type of additives. The sample is mixed with indicator solution and the solution titrated with perchloric acid to the end point, indicated by the colour change.

- PURPLE : When BASIC
- GREEN : When NEUTRAL
- AMBER : When ACIDIC

Reagents

1. Crystal Violet Indicator : 50 mgs of Crystal Violet Indicator is dissolved in glacial Acetic Acid and transferred to a one litre flask. Add 125 ml of Iso Octane. Make the volume to one litre with Glacial Aeetic Acid and shake. Keep the contents in a glass bottle.
2. Glacial Acetic Acid (AR grade)
3. Perchloric acid : Dilute 27.5 ml of Perchloric acid to one litre with Glacial Acetic Acid.
4. Weigh 400 mgs of Pot. Phthalate in a 100 ml flask and make up with glacial acetic acid

Procedure

Standardisation of Acid

- Titrate 25 ml of Pot. Phthalate solution with Perchloric acid using 15 ml of indicator solution to a green end point. Record the Volume of Acid used (v)
- Titrate a Blank (15 ml of indicator solution with 25 ml Glacial acetic acid) with Perchloric acid. Record the volume of Acid used (b).
- Calculate the Titre (T) of the acid as follows:

$$T = \frac{0.06869 \times W}{(v - b)} \quad W = \text{Wt. of Pot. Phthalate in mg.}$$

Total Base Number

- Weigh about 2 g of the oil in a 50 ml beaker and warm gently at 50°C
- Transfer to a tarred graduated (30 ml capacity) clean centrifuge tube upto 2 ml

- Reweigh the tube
- Add the indicator solution into the tube so that the total volume reach 10 ml
- Stopper the tube with a clean dry Teflon cork and shake it for 5 seconds
- Allow the contents of the tube to settle
- Add perchloric acid from the burette, till the colour of the tip becomes purple and allow to settle and note down the volume of acid used (V)
- Titrate a blank similarly
- Note down the volume of acid used (B)

$$\text{Total Base Number (TBN) mg of TBN KOH/mg} = \frac{T(V - B)}{S}$$

Where T = Titre of Acid asdetermined above

S = weight of the sample used

TBN can also be determined by Potentiometric method as per ASTM D 2896/98

Note:
- The finished genuine blended Engine Lubricating oils will have a required TBN as per Company Specifications.
- In general, the TBN of finished blended Engine Lubricating oil is 5 (minimum)
- Decrease in TBN (as per company specification) indicates the rpesence of possible adulterants preferably reclaimed/re-refined used engine oil
- Negligible TBN indicates the possible simulation with reclaimed/ re-refined engine oil
- TBN is an excellent parameter to find out the quality of an oil whether adulterated/simulated.

LUBRICATING GREASES

Introduction

Greases were well known from ancient time. Lime mixed in olive oil was in use to lubricate the axles of wooden carriage by Egyptians in 1400 B.C. The development of modern grease has followed the development of modern industrial age. Grease is nothing but dispersion of thickening agent in liquid lubricant making it Semi lucid product. In order to improve its quantities to meet the requirements of particular machine/machinery certain additives are incorporated which improves not only the performance but also the stability and life. In brief greases most fulfill the following tasks; in lubrication Technology.

- By slow separation of it, they must release a quantity of liquid lubricant sufficient to reduce friction and wear in the bearings over a wide range of temperature and long period of time.
- They must act as barrier against water and abrasive substances.

Classification of Greases

Greases are primarily classified by their thickness. The most common are metallic soaps. Other includes, poly-urea and inorganic thickeners, polymers, clay, lime etc. The grease manufactured/formulated must meet the respective specification laid down by Bureau of Indian Standard. Some of the important common and special types are covered as per the following specifications.

Graphite type IS 508
Automatiye IS 506
General purpose IS 507
Grease low temperature 7514
Antifriction bearing IS 712
Locomotive IS 720
Lithium base IS 7623
Calcium Complex IS 9136
Calcium base heat resistance IS 9917
Wheel bearing IS 10647
Calcium base P IS 11637
Lithium Base IS 12203
Non soap IS 12790
Silicon IS 14383 and many more

The most important properties in all the above greases are Acidity and Alkalinity, Drop Point, Evaporation. Loss, Corrosion, Oil Separation during storage, Cone penetration (Consistency), Viscosity of Mineral Oil, Heat stability, Sulphated ash; Oxidation stability etc.

Acidity and Alkalinity of Greases (P 53 IS 1448 Methods of Test)

This method describes the procedure for the determination of free acid, free alkali and insoluble carbonates, in Calcium, Sodium and lithium in greases of conventional type. A known quantity of sample is dissolved in n-hexane and to it alcohol is also added. Put few drops of indicator (Phenolphthalein). If the alcoholic layer after shaking becomes pink add known quantity of 0.5N HCl solution and titrate the excess acid back with 0.5 N alcoholic KOH solution and calculate the free alkalinity in term of Sodium Hydroxide. If the original alcoholic layer is not pink titrate the unheated solution with 0.5 M alcoholic KOH and calculate for acidity in term of Oleic acid.

Drop Point (ASTM D 2265: P 52 IS 1448 Methods of Test)

Dropping point is the temperature at which the first drop of the material falls from the cup.

Note: • Dropping Point is a temperature at which the grease passes from semi solid to a liquid state under the conditions of tests. Greases containing thickness other than conventional type may, without in state may separate oil. This temperature is useful to assist in identifying the grease and maintaining bench mark for quality control.

Evaporation Loss (ASTM D 972: P 61 & 68 IS 1448 Methods of Tests)

This method covers the determination of evaporation loss of lubricating greases and oils for applications where evaporation loss in a factor in the range of 99 to 149°C. The sample is placed in the evaporation cell kept in the bath at desired temperature. Heated air is passed over its surface for 22 hours. The evaporation loss is calculated from the loss in weight of the sample.

Note: • The evaporation toss method can be used to determine the loss of volatile material from greases but it does not co-relate with the service performance.

Corrosion (Copper Strip) ASTM D 4048: P 51 IS 1448 Methods of Tests

The method covers the detection of the corrosiveness to copper. The standard copper strip is immersed in a sample of grease and normally heated at 100°C for 24 hours. At the end of the period the strip is removed, washed and compared with ASTM Copper Strip corrosion Standard.

Note: • Test method measures the tendency of lubricating grease to corrode Copper under specific conditions. Predicting of possible chemical attack on lubricated parts such as bearing. Such corrosion for example may cause premature bearing failures.

Oxidation Stability (ASTM D 942: P 94 IS 1448 Methods of Tests)

It determines the resistance of lubricating greases to oxidation when stored in an oxygen atmosphere in a sealed system at an elevated temperatures under conditions of test. A sample of greases is taken in a Bomb and to it 110 PSI oxygen is charged. The Pressure is observed on the pressure gauge. The Bomb is immersed in the bath at 99°C. The degree of oxidation after a given period of time is determined by the corresponding decrease in oxygen pressure.

Note: • This method may be used for quality control to indicate batch to batch uniformity.

Oil Separation from Lubricating Greases During Storage (ASTM D 1742: P 85 IS 1448 Methods of Tests)

This method covers the determination of the tendency of lubricating greases to separate oil during storage in either normally filled of partially filled containers.

The sample of grease support on 75 mm is subjected to 0.25 PSI air pressure for 24 hours at 25°C. Any oil seepage that occurs draings into a beaker and weighed.

Note: • The results correlate directly with oil separation which occurs in 35 Ibs pails of greases during storage. It is not intended to predict oil separation tendencies of greases under dynamic service conditions.

Thermal Stability (P 89 IS 1448 Methods of Test)

This method describes the procedure for measuring the tendency of lubricating grease to separate oils at elevated temperature under static conditions. Suspend the cone containing known quantity of grease well exposed on its surface in a clean weighed beaker. Keep the beaker, at 100°C in an oven, tor 30 hours. After the test, weigh the beaker and report the per cent oil separated.

Cone Penetration (ASTM D 217: P 60 IS 1448 Methods of Tests)

The depth, in tenths of a millimeter that the standard cone penetrates the sample under the prescribed conditions of weight, time and temperature. The test procedures include for the measurement of penetration on unworked, worked, prolonged worked and block. Penetration upto 475 may be measured. Unworked penetrations does not generally represented the consistency of grease in use as effectively as do worked penetrations. The latter are usually preferred for inspecting greases.

Penetratian of blocked greases can be obtained on those products that are sufficiently hard to hold their shape. These greases have penetration below 85°C (working on the subjection of lubricating greases to the shearing of standard grease worker.

Worked Penetration

Penetration of a lubricating grease that has been subjected to 60 double strokes in a standard grease worker and penetrated without delay.

Prolonged Worked Penetration

Where the penetration has been subjected to more than 60 double strokes.

Block Penetration

Penetration of the grease, that is sufficiently hard to hold its shape, determined on the freshly prepared face of cube cut from a block of the grease. Penetration is determined.

FURNACE OIL/BLACK OIL

Introduction

The furnace oil or the black oil is the residual oil left after separating residual fuel distillate. It is brownish black in colour and consists hydrocarbons above C_{40} Based on Kinematic Viscosity different grades of furnace oil namely low viscous (LV), medium viscous (MV) and high viscous (HV) are available. It is normally used for heating furnaces. Forensic Sciences laboratory receives furnace oil related to Pilferage, Adulteration and Simulation cases.

The important characteristics governed by IS specifications (IS 1593) are Specific gravity, Flash point and Kinematic Viscosity.

Test Methods and Their Significance

Relative Density/Specific Gravity—Experimental (P 32 IS 1448 Methods of Test: ASTM D 1298)

Procedure is similar to that of Engine Lubricating Oil. The specific gravity of a typical standard Furnace oil falls within the range of *0.900 to 0.950.*

Viscosity: Experimental (P: 25 IS 1448 Methods of Test: IP 71: ASTM B 445 and 2170)

Test methods and Experimental Procedure is similar to that explained in Section-4 (Kerosene). The Kinematic Viscosity can be measured in centistokes at 50°C Different grades of oil (LV, MV1, MV2 & HV) are available based on their viscosity.

Significance

- Viscosity is the most important single property of a furnace oil
- Incase of used oils if viscosity is lower than the original it indicates fuel dilution or admixture with low viscosity oils.

Flash Point: Experimental (P 20 IS 1448 Methods of Test: ASTM D56: D 92: D 93: D 1310)

The flash point of lubricating oil is carried out by Fensky Marten closed cup (Automatic) and Cleveland open cup (Automatic) as the procedure given for lubricating oil.

Significance

- Genuinity of the sample can be found by Flash point

Carbon Residue (P8 IS 1448 Methods of Test: IP 13,14)

It is an amount of carbonaceous material formed when a sample is evaporated and paralyzed under specified conditions. The lighter will evaporate but the heavier more complex compounds will decompose forming carbonaceous deposits. There are two methods for its determination.

- Conradson
- Ramsbottom

In the Conradson method sample is heated in a crucible under controlled conditions in absence of air and the residue left is weighed. Whereas, in Ramsbottom test the sample is placed in the tube with the capillary at the top and heated to 550°C in a bath of molten metal.

Significance

- Carbon residue/High carbon content indicates the possible presence of bitumen + Kerosene (Simulation)

Water Content (IP 74: P 40 IS 1448 Methods of Test)

Petroleum products as marketed should be free from water. However products may pick up water during storage, handling or though condensation from atmosphere. The presence of water is undesirable in many cases.

Traces of water can be detected be means of crackle test. When a sample of oil is heated on a silent flame, crackling noise is heard, if any moisture is present in the oil. Water in percentage is estimated in special distillation apparatus known as Dean and Stark using toluene as asolvent.

Significance

Presence of water in lubricating oil is undesirable as it will tend to form emulsion and sludge in use.

like Naphtha (LAN & HAN), SBP Solvents etc.,

- Column : SP 2100 (packed)
- Carrier gas : Nitrogen (25 ml/min)
- Hydrogen : Flow (25 ml/min)
- Air : Flow (250 ml/min)
- Injector : 200°C
- Detector : Flame Ionisation Detector 220°C
- Programming mode : Initial temp 40°C hold 2 mts Ramp rate 5°C/min Ramp 1 : 60°C Ramp 2 : 90°C Ramp 3 : 150°C Ramp 4 : 180°C.

Experimental Conditions—Kerosene and Medium Boiling Hydrocarbon Solvents like Mineral Spirits, ATF, etc.

- Column : 5% SP 2100 on Chromosorb (packed)
- Carrier gas : Nitrogen (25 ml/min)
- Hydrogen : Flow (25 ml/min)
- Air : Flow (250 ml/min)
- Injector : 280°C
- Detector : Flame Ionisation Detector 300°C
- Programming mode : Initial temp 70°C hold 2 mts

  Ramp rate 5°C/min Ramp 1 : 100°C Ramp 2 : 150°C Ramp 3 : 200°C Ramp 4 : 250°C

Hydrocarbon Characterization of Petroleum Hydrocarbon Solvents by GC-DHA

Detailed Experimental Procedure and Hydrocarbon Profile is given in Section 2.

1. ASTM D 1298 /IP 160 “Density, Relative Density or API Gravity of Crude Petroleum and Liquid Petroleum Products by Hydrometer method.
2. ASTM D 4052/IP 365 Test Method for Density and Relative Density of Liquids Digital Density Meter.
3. ASTM D 1218 “Refractive Index and Refractive Dispersion of Hydrocarbon Liquids.
4. ASTM D 92/IP 36 “Flash and Fire Points by Cleveland Open Cup
5. ASTM D 93/IP 34 “Flash Point Fensky Marten Closed Tester”
6. ASTM D 1310 “Flash Point and Fire Points of Liquids by Tag open-cup Apparatus
7. ASTM D 86/IP 123 “Distillation of Petroleum Products”
8. ASTM D 5134 “Detailed Analysis of Petroleum Naphthas through n-nonane By Capillary Gas Chromatography.

Petroleum

Introduction

The petroleum industry began with the successful drilling of the first commercial oil well in 1859, and the opening of the first refinery two years later to process the crude into kerosene. The evolution of petroleum refining from simple distillation to today's sophisticated processes has created a need for health and safety management procedures and safe work practices. To those unfamiliar with the industry, petroleum refineries may appear to be complex and confusing places. Refining is the processing of one complex mixture of hydrocarbons into a number of other complex mixtures of hydrocarbons. The safe and orderly processing of crude oil into flammable gases and liquids at high temperatures and pressures using vessels, equipment, and piping subjected to stress and corrosion requires considerable knowledge, control, and expertise.

Safety and health professionals, working with process, chemical, instrumentation, and metallurgical engineers, assure that potential physical, mechanical, chemical, and health hazards are recognized and provisions are made for safe operating practices and appropriate protective measures. These measures may include hard hats, safety glasses and goggles, safety shoes, hearing protection, respiratory protection, and protective clothing such as fire resistant clothing where required. In addition, procedures should be established to assure compliance with applicable regulations and standards such as hazard communications, confined space entry, and process safety management.

This chapter of the technical manual covers the history of refinery processing, characteristics of crude oil, hydrocarbon types and chemistry, and major refinery products and by products. It presents information on technology as normally practiced in present operation. It describes the more common refinery processes and includes relevant safety and health information. Additional information covers refinery utilities and miscellaneous supporting activities related to hydrocarbon processing. Field personnel will learn what to expect in various facilities regarding typical materials and process methods, equipment, potential hazards, and exposures.

The information presented refers to tire prevention, industrial hygiene, and safe work practices, and is not intended to provide comprehensive guidelines for protective measures and/or compliance with regulatory requirements. As some of the terminology is industry—specific, a glossary is provided as an appendix. This chapter does not cover petrochemical processing.

Basic Refinery Process: Description and History

Petroleum refining has evolved continuously in response to changing consumer demand for better and different products. The original requirement was to produce kerosene as a cheaper and better source of light than whale oil. The development of the internal combustion engine led to the production of gasoline and diesel fuels. The evolution of the airplane created a need first for high-octane aviation gasoline and then for jet fuel, a sophisticated form of the original product, kerosene. Present-day refineries produce a variety of products including many required as feedstock for the petrochemical industry.

Distillation Processes: The first refinery, opened in 1861, produced kerosene by simple atmospheric distillation. Its by products included tar and naphtha. It was soon discovered that high-quality lubricating oils could be produced by distilling petroleum under vacuum. However, for the next 30 year kerosene was the product consumers wanted. Two significant events changed this situation: (1) invention of the electric light decreased the demand for kerosene; and (2) invention of the internal combustion engine created a demand for diesel fuel and gasoline (naphtha).

Thermal Cracking Processes: With the advent of mass production and World War I, the number of gasoline-powered vehicles increased dramatically and the demand for gasoline grew accordingly. However, distillation processes produced only a certain amount of gasoline from crude oil. In 1913, the thermal cracking process was developed, which subjected heavy fuels to both pressure and intense heat, physically breaking the large molecules into smaller ones to produce additional and distillate fuels. Visbreaking, another form of thermal cracking, was developed in the late 1930's to produce more desirable and valuable products.

Catalytic Processes: Higher-Compression gasoline engines required higher-octane gasoline with better antiknock characteristics. The introduction of catalytic cracking and polymerization processes in the mid-to late 1930's met the demand by providing improved gasoline yields and higher octane numbers.

Alkylation, another catalytic process developed in the early 1940's, produced more high-octane aviation gasoline and petrochemical feedstock for explosives and synthetic rubber. Subsequently, catalytic isomerization was develpod to convert hydrocarbons to produce increased quantities of alkylation feedstock. Improved catalysts and process methods such as hydrocracking and reforming were developed throughout the 1960's to increase gasoline yields and improve antiknock characteristics. These catalytic processes also produced hydrocarbon with a double bond (alkenes) and formed the basis of the modern petrochemical industry.

Treatment Process: Throughout the history of refining, various treatment methods have been used to remove non-hydrocarbons, impurities, and other constituents that adversely affect the properties of finished products or reduce the efficiency of the conversion processes. Treating can involve chemical reaction and/or physical separation. Typical examples of treating are chemical sweetening, acid treating, clay contacting, caustic washing, hydrotreating, drying solvent extraction, and solvent dewaxing. Sweetening compounds and acids desulphurize crude oil before processing and treat products during and after processing.

Following the Second World War, various reforming processes improved gasoline quality and yield and produced higher-quality products. Some of these involved the use of catalysts and/or hydrogen to change molecules and remove sulphur. A number of the more commonly used treating and reforming processes are described in this chapter of the manual. (*See Table 8.1 History of Refining on Next Page*).

Basics of Crude Oil

Crude oils are complex mixtures containing many different hydrocarbons compounds that vary in appearance and composition from one oil field to another. Crude oils range in consistency from water to tar—like solids, and in colour from clear to black. An 'average' crude oil contains about 84 per cent carbon, 14 per cent hydrogen, one per cent - three per cent sulphur, and less than one per cent each of nitrogen, oxygen, metals, and salts. Crude oils are generally classified as paraffinic, naphthenic, or aromatic based on the predominant proportion of similar hydrocarbon molecules. Mixed-base crudes have varying amounts of each type of hydrocarbon. Refinery crude base stocks usually consist of mixtures of two or more different crude oils.

Relatively simple crude oil assays are used to classify crude oils as paraffinic, naphthenic, aromatic, or mixed. One assays method (United States Bureau of Mines) is based on distillation, and another method (UOP 'K' factor) is based on gravity and boiling points. More Comprehensive crude

Table 8.1 : History of Refining

Year	Process name	Purpose	By-products, etc.
1862	Atmospheric distillation	Produce kerosene	Naphtha, tar, etc.
1870	Vacuum distillation	Lubricants(original) Cracking feedstocks (1930's)	Asphalt, residual Coker feedstocks
1913	Thermal cracking	Increase gasoline	Residual, bunker Fuel
1916	Sweetening	Reduce sulphur& odor	Sulphur
1930	Thermal reforming	Improve octane number	Residual
1932	Hydrogenation	Remove sulphur	Sulphur
1932	Coking	Produce gasoline basestocks	Coke
1933	Solvent extraction	Improve lubricant viscosity index	Aromatics
1935	Solvent dewaxing	Improve pour point	Waxes
1935	Cat. polymerization	Improve gasoline yield and octane	Petrochemical Feedstocks
1937	Catalytic cracking	Higher octane gasoline	Petrochemical Feedstocks
1939	Visbreaking	Reduce viscosity	Increased distillate, tar
1940	Alkylation	Increase gasoline octane and yield	High-octane aviation gasoline
1940	Isomerization	Produce alkylation feedstock	Naphtha
1942	Fluid catalytic Cracking	Increase gasoline yield and octane	Petrochemical Feedstocks
1950	Deasphalting	Increase cracking feedstock	Asphalt
1952	Catalytic reforming	Convert low-quality naphtha	Aromatics
1954	Hydrodesulphurization	Remove sulphur	Sulphur
1956	Inhibitor sweetening	Remove mercaptan	Disulfides
1957	Catalytic isomerization	Convert to molecules with high Octane number	Alkylation Feedstocks
1960	Hydrocracking	Improve quality and reduce sulphur	Alkylation
1974	Catalytic dewaxing	Improve pour point	Wax
1975	Residual Hydrocracking	Increase gasoline yield from residual	Heavy residuals

assays determine the value of the crude (*i.e.*, its yield and quality of useful products parameters. Crude oils are usually grouped according to yield structure.

Crude oils are also defined in terms of API (American Petroleum Institute) gravity. The higher the API gravity, the lighter the crude. For example, light crude oils have high API gravities and low specific gravities. Crude oils with low carbon, high hydrogen, and high API gravity are usually rich in paraffins and tend to yield greater proportions of gasoline and light petroleum products; those with high carbon, low hydrogen, and low API gravities are usually rich in aromatics.

Crude oils that Contain appreciable quantities of hydrogen sulphide or other reactive sulphur compounds are called 'sour' Those with less sulphur are called 'sweet.' Some exceptions to this rule are West Texas Crudes, Which are always considered 'sour' regardless of their H_2S Content, and Arabian high-sulphur crudes, which are not considered 'Sour' because their compounds are not highly reactive.

Basics of Hydrocarbon Chemistry

Crude oil is a mixture of hydrocarbon molecules, which are organic compounds of carbon and hydrogen atoms that may include from one to 60 carbon atoms. The properties of hydrocarbons depend on the number and arrangement if the carbon and hydrogen atoms in the molecules. The simplest hydrocarbon molecule is one carbon atom linked with four hydrogen atoms: methane. All other variations of petroleum hydrocarbons evolve from this molecule.

Hydrocarbons containing up to four carbon atoms are usually gases, those with 5 to 19 carbon atoms are usually liquids, and those with 20 or more are solids. The refining process uses chemicals, catalysts, heat and pressure to separate and combine the basic types of hydrocarbon molecules naturally found in crude oil into groups of similar molecules. The refining process also rearranges their structures and bonding patterns into different hydrocarbon molecules and compounds. Therefore it is the type of hydrocarbon (Paraffinic, naphthenic, or aromatic) rather than its specific chemical compounds that is significant in the refining process.

Three Principal Groups or Series of Hydrocarbons Compounds that Occur Naturally in Crude oil.

(a) ***Paraffins:*** The paraffinic series of hydrocarbon compounds found in crude oil have the general formula CnH_2n+2 and can be either straight chains (normal) or branched chains (isomers) of carbon atoms. The lighter, straight-chain paraffin molecules are found in gases and paraffin waxes. Examples of straight-chain molecules are methane, ethane, Propane, and butane (gases containing form one to four carbon atoms), and pentane and hexane (liquids with five to six carbon atoms). The branched-chain (isomer) paraffins are usually found in heavier fractions of crude oil and have higher octane numbers than normal paraffins. These compounds are saturated hydrocarbon, with all carbon bonds satisfied, that is, the hydrocarbon chain carries the full complement of hydrogen atoms.

(b) ***Aromatics*** are unsaturated ring-type (cyclic) compounds which react readily because they have carbon atoms that are deficient in hydrogen. All aromatics have at least one benzene ring (a single- ring compound characterized by three double bonds alternating with three single bonds between six carbon atoms) as part of their molecular structure. Naphthalenes are fused double-ring aromatic compounds. The most complex aromatics, polynuclears (three or more fused aromatic rings), are found in heavier fractions of crude oil.

(c) Naphthenes are saturated hydrocarbon groupings with the general formula CnH_2n, arranged in the from of closed rings (cyclic) and found in all fractions of crude oil except the very lightest. Single-ring naphthenes (monocycloparaffins) with five and six carbon atoms predominate, with two-ring naphthenes (dicycloparaffins) found in the heavier ends of naphtha.

(a) *Aikenes* are mono-olefms with the general fordmula CnH_2n and contain only one carbon-carbon double bond in the chain. The simplest alkene is ethylene, with two carbon atoms joined by a double bond and four hydrogen atoms. Olefms are usually formed by thermal and catalytic cracking and rarely occur naturally in unprocessed crude oil.

(b) *Dienes and Alknes.* Dienes, also known as diolefins, have two carbon-carbon double bonds. The alkynes, anther class of unsaturated hydrocarbons, have a carbon-carbon triple bond within the molecule. Both these series of hydrocarbons have the general formula $CnH_2n{-}2$. Diolefms such as 1,2- butadiene and 1,3-butadiene, and alkynes such as acetylene, occur in C_5 and lighter fractions from cracking. The olefins, diolefins and alkynes are said to be unsaturated because they contain less than the amount of hydrogen necessary to saturate all the valences of the carbon atoms. These compounds are more reactive than paraffins or naphthenes and readily combine with other elements such as hydrogen, chlorine and bromine.

Acetylene (C_2H_2)

H—C≡C—H

1,2-Butadiene (C_4H_6)

H_2C = C = C(H)—C(H)(H)—H = C_4H_6

1,3-Butadiene (C_4H_6)

H_2C = = = = C(H)—C(H) = = = = CH_2

Fig. 8.1 : Typical Diolefins and Lakynes

Non-hydrocarbons

(a) Sulphur Compounds: Sulphur may be present in crude oil as hydrogen sulphide (H_2), as compounds (*e.g.* mercaptans, sulphides, disulphides, thiophenes, etc.) or as elemental sulfur. Each crude oil has different amount and types of sulphur compounds, but as a rule the proportion, stability, and complexity of the compounds are greater in heavier crude-oil fraction. Hydrogen sulphide is a primary contributor to corrosion in refinery processing units. Other corrosive substances are elemental sulphur and mercaptans. Moreover, the corrosive sulphur compounds have an obnoxious odour.

Pyrophoric iron sulphide results from the corrosive action of sulphur compounds on the iron and steel used in refinery process equipment, piping, and tanks. The combustion of petroleum products containing sulphur compounds produces undesirables such as sulphuric acid and sulphur dioxide. Catalytic hydrotreating processes such as hydrodesulphurization remove sulphur compounds from refinery product streams. Sweetening processes either remove the obnoxious sulphur compounds or convert them to odourless disulphides, as in the case of mercaptans.

(b) Oxygen Compounds: Oxygen compounds such as phenols, ketones, and carboxylic acids occur in crude oils in varying amounts.

(c) Nitrogen Compounds: Nitrogen is found in lighter fractions of crude oil as basic compounds, and more often in heavier fraction of crude oil as non-basic compounds that may also include trace metals such as copper, vanadium, and/or nickel. Nitrogen oxides can from in process furnaces. The decomposition of nitrogen compounds in catalytic cracking and hydro-cracking processes forms ammonia and cyanides that can cause corrosion.

(d) Trace Metals: Metals, including nickel, iron and vanadium are often found in crude oils in small quantities and are removed during the refining process. Burning heavy fuel oils in refinery furnaces and boilers can leave deposits of vanadium oxide and nickel oxide and nickel oxide in furnace boxes, ducts, and tubes. It is also desirable to remove trace amounts of arsenic, vanadium, and nickel prior to processing as they can poison certain catalysts.

(e) Salts: Crude oils often contain inorganic salts such as sodium chloride, magnesium chloride, and calcium chloride in suspension or dissolved in entrained water (brine). These salts must be removed or neutralized before processing to prevent catalyst poisoning, equipment corrosion, and fouling. Salt corrosion is caused by the hydrolysis of some metal chlorides to hydrogen chloride (HCL) and the subsequent formation of hydrochloric acid when crude is heated. Hydrogen chloride may also combine with ammonia to form ammonium chloride (NH_4C_1), which causes fouling and corrosion.

(f) Carbon Dioxide: Carbon dioxide may result from the decomposition of bicarbonates present in or added to crude, or from steam used in the distillation process.

(g) Naphthenic Acids: Some crude oils contain naphthenic (organic) acids, which may become corrosive at temperatures above 450°F when the acid value of the crude is above a certain level.

Major Refinery Products

Gasoline: The most important refinery product is motor gasoline, a blend of hydrocarbons with boiling ranges are octane number from ambient temperatures to about 400°F. The important qualities for gasoline are octane number (antiknock), volatility (starting and vapor lock), and vapour pressure (environmental control). Additives are often used to enhance performance and provide protection against oxidation and rust formation.

Kerosene: Kerosene is a refined middle-distillate petroleum product that finds considerable use as a jet fuel and around the world in cooking and space heating. When used as jet fuel, some of the critical qualities are freeze point, flash point, and smoke point. Commercial jet fuel has a boiling range of about 375° – 525° F, and military jet fuel 130°–550°F. Kerosene, with less-critical specifications, is used for lighting, heating, solvents, and blending into diesel fuel.

Liquified Petroleum Gas (LPG): LPG, which consists principally of propane and butane, is produced for use as fuel and is an intermediate material in the manufacture of petrochemicals. The important specification for proper performance include vapour pressure and control of contaminants.

Distillate Fuels: Diesel fuels and domestic heating oils have boiling ranges of about Distillate Fuels. Diesel fuels and domestic heating oils have boiling ranges of about 400°–700°F. The desirable for distillate fuels include controlled flash and pour points, clean burning, no deposit formation in storage tanks, and a proper diesel fuel cetane rating for good starting and combustion.

Residual Fuels: Many marine vessels, power plants, commercial buildings and industrial facilities use residual fuels or combinations of residual and distillate fuels for heating and processing. The two most critical specifications of residual fuels are viscosity and low sulphur content for environmental control.

Coke and Asphalt: Coke is almost pure carbon with a variety of uses from electrodes to charcoal briquets. Asphalt, used for roads and roofing materials, must be inert to most chemicals and weather conditions.

Solvents: A variety of products, whose boiling points and hydrocarbon composition are closely controlled, are produced for use as solvents. These include benzene, toluene, and xylene.

Petrochemicals: Many products derived from crude oil refining, such as ethylene, propylene, butylenes, and isobutylene, are primarily intended for use as petrochemical feedstock in the production of plastics, synthetic fibres, synthetic rubbers, and other products.

Lubricants: Special refining processes produce lubricating oil base stocks. Additives such as demulsifiers, antioxidants, and viscosity improvers are blended into the base stocks to provide the characteristics required for more oils, industrial greases, lubricants, and cutting oils. The most critical quality for lubricating-oil base stock is a high viscosity index, which-provides for greater consistency under varying temperature.

Common Refinery Chemicals

Leaded Gasoline Additives: Tetraethyl lead (TEL) and tetramenthyl lead (TML) are additives formerly used to improve gasoline octane ratings but are no longer in common use except in aviation gasoline.

Oxygenates: Ethyl tertiary butyl ether (ETBE), methyl tertiary butyl ether (MTBE), tertiary amly methyl ether (TAME), and other oxygenates improve gasoline octane ratings and reduce carbon monoxide emissions.

Caustics: Caustics are added to desalting water to neutralize acids and reduce corrosion. They are also added to desalted crude in order to reduce the amount of corrosive chlorides in the tower overheads. They are used in some refinery treating processes to remove countaminants from hydrocarbon streams.

Sulphuric Acid and Hydrofluoric Acid: Sulphuric acid and hydrofluoric acid are used primarily as catalysts in alkylation processes. Sulphuric acid is also used in some treatment processes.

PETROLEUM REFINING OPERATIONS

Introduction

Petroleum refining begins with the distillation, or fractionation, of crude oils into separate hydrocarbon groups. The resultant products are directly related to the characteristics of the crude processed. Most distillation products are further converted into more usable products by changing the size and structure of the hydrocarbon molecules through cracking, reforming, and other conversion processes as discussed in this chapter. These converted products are then subjected to various treatment and separation processes such as extraction, hydrotreating, and sweetening to remove undesirable constituents and improve product quality. Integrated refineries incorporate fractionation, conversion, treatment, and blending operations and may also include petrochemical processing.

Refining Operations

Petroleum refining processes and operations can be separated into five basic areas:

Fractionation (distillation) is the separation of crude oil in atmospheric and vacuum'distillation towers into groups of hydrocarbon compounds of differing boiling-point ranges called 'fractions' or 'cuts.'

Conversion processes change the size and/or structure of hydrocarbon molecules.

These processes include:

Decomposition (dividing) by thermal and catalytic cracking;

Unification (combining) through alkylation and polymerization; and

Alteration (rearranging) with isomerization and catalytic reforming.

Treatment processes are intended to prepare hydrocarbon streams for additional processing and to prepare finished products. Treatment may include the removal or separation of aromatics and naphthenes as well as impurities and undesirable contaminants. Treatment may involve chemical or physical separation such as dissolving, absorption, or precipitation using a variety and combination of processes including desalting, drying, hydrodesulphurizing, solvent refining, sweetening, solvent extraction, and solvent dewaxing.

Formulating and Blending is the process of mixing and combining hydrocarbon fraction, additives and other components to produce finished products with specific performance properties.

Other Refining Operations include : light-ends recovery; sour-water stripping; solid waste and wastewater treatment; process-water treatment and cooling; storage and handling; product movement; hydrogen production; acid and tail-gas treatment; and sulphur recovery.

Auxiliary operations and facilities include : steam and power generation; process and fire water systems; flares and relief systems; furnaces and heaters; pumps and valves; supply of steam, air, nitrogen, and other plant gases; alarms and sensors; noise and pollution controls; sampling, testing and inspection; and laboratory, control room, maintenance, and administrative facilities.

DESCRIPTION OF PETROLEUM REFINING PROCESSES AND RELATED HEALTH AND SAFETY CONSIDERATIONS

Crude Oil Pretreatment (Desalting)

Description

(*a*) Crude oil often contains water, inorganic salts, suspended solids, and water-soluble trace metals. As a first step in the refining process, to reduce corrosion, plugging, and fouling of equipment and to prevent poisoning the catalysts in processing units, these contaminants must be removed by desalting (dehydration).

Table 8.2 : 2-3 Overview of Petroleum Refining Processes

Process name	Action	Method	Purpose	Feedstock	Product(s)
			Fractionation Processes		
Atmospheric Distillation	Separation	Thermal	Separate fractions	Desalted crude oil	Gas, gas oil, distillate, residual
Vacuum Distillation	Separation	Thermal	Separate w/o cracking	Atmospheric tower residual	Gas oil, lube Stock, residual
			Conversion Processed—Decomposition		
Catalytic	Alteration	Catalytic	Upgrade	Gas oil, coke	Gasoline
cracking			gasoline	distillate	petrochemical feedstock
Coking	Polymerize	Thermal	Convert vacuum residuals	Gas oil, coke distillate	Gasoline petrochemical feedstock
Hydro-cracking	Hydro-genate	Catalytic	Convert to lighter HC's	Gas oil, cracked oil, residual	Lighter, higher-quality products
*Hydrogen steam reforming	Decom-pose	Thermal/ Catalytic	Produce hydrogen	Desulfurized gas, O_2, steam	Hydrogen, CO, CO_2
*Steam cracking	Decom-pose	Thermal	Crack large molecules	Atm tower hvy fuel/ distillate	Cracked naphtha, coke, residual
Visbreaking	Decom-pose	Thermal	Reduce Viscosity	Atmospheric tower residual	Distillate, tar
			Conversion Processes—Unification		
Alkylation	Combining	Catalytic	Unite olefins and isoparaffins	Tower Isobutene/ cracker olefin	Iso-octane (alkylate)
Grease Compoun-ding	Combining	Thermal	Combine soaps and oils	Lube oil, fatty Acid, alky	Lubricating Grease
Polymeri-zing	Polymerize	Catalytic	Unite 2 or more olefins	Cracker olefins	High-octane
			Conversion Processes—Alteration or Rearrangement		
Catalytic reforming	Alteration/ dehydration	Catalytic	Upgrade low-Octane naphtha	Coker/hydro-cracker naphtha	High oct. Reformate/ aromatic
Isomeriza-tion	Rearrange	Catalytic	Convert straight chain to branch	Butane, Pentane, hexane	Isobutane/ Pentane/ hexane

...(Contd.)

Process name	Action	Method	Purpose	Feedstock	Product(s)
			Treatment Processes		
*Amine treating	Treatment	Absorption	Remove acidic contaminants	Sour gas, HCs w/CO_2 and H_2S	Acid free Gases and Liquid HCs
Desalting	Dehydration	Absorption	Remove contaminants	Crude oil	Desalted crude oil
Drying and Sweetening	Treatment	Abspt/ therm	Remove H_2O and sulphur compounds	Liq Hcs, LPG, Alky feedstk	Sweet and dry hydrocarbons
*Furfural extraction	Solvent extr.	Absorption	Upgrade mid Distillate and lubes	Cycle oils and Lube feed-Stocks	High quality diesel and lube oil
Hydrodesulphurization	Treatment	Catalytic	Remove sulphur Contaminants	High-sulphur Residual/ gas oil	Desulphurized Olefins
Hydrotreating	Hydrogenation	Catalytic	Remove impurities, Saturate HC's	Residuals, Cracked HC's	Cracker Feed, distillate, lube
*Phenol extraction	Solvent extr.	Abspt/ therm	Improve visc. Index, colour	Lube oil base Stocks	High quality Lube oils
Solvent deasphalting	Treatment	Absorption	Remove asphalt	Vac. tower residual, propane	Heavy lube Oil, asphalt
Solvent Dewaxing	Treatment	cool/filter	Remove from lube stocks	Vac. tower residual, propane	Heavy lube Oil, asphalt
Solvent extraction	Solvent exts.	Abspt./ precip.	Separate unsat. Oils	Gas oil, reformate, distillate	High-octane gasoline
Sweetening	Treatment	Catalytic	Remv H_2S, Convert mercaptan	Untreated distillate/ gasoline	High-quality distillate/ gasoline

Note: These processes are not depicted in the refinery process flow chart.

(*b*) The two most typical methods of crude-oil desalting, chemical and electrostatic separation, use hot water as the extraction agent. In chemical desalting, water and chemical surfactant (demulsifiers) are added to the crude, heated so that salts and other impurities dissolve into the water or attach to the water, and then help in a tank where they settle out. Electrical desalting is the application of high-voltage electrostatic charges to concentrate suspended water globules in the bottom of the setting tank. Surfactants are added only when the crude has a large amount of suspended solids. Both methods of desalting are continuous. A third and less-common process involves filtering heated crude using diatomaceous earth.

(*c*) The feedstock crude oil is heated to between 150° and 350° F to reduce viscosity and surface tension for easier mixing and separation of the water. The temperature is limited by the vapor pressure of the crude-oil feedstock. In both methods other chemicals may be added. Ammonia is often used to reduce corrosion. Caustic or acid may be added to adjust to pH of the water wash. Waste water and contaminants are discharged from the bottom of the setting tank to the waste water treatment facility discharged from the bottom of the setting tank to the wastewater treatment facility. The desalted crude is continuously from the top of the setting tanks and sent to the crude distillation (fractionating) tower.

Health and Safety Consideration

(*a*) **Fire prevention and Protection:** The potential for a fire due to a leak or release of crude from heaters in the crude desalting unit. Low boiling point components of crude may also be released if leak occurs.

(*b*) **Safety:** Inadequate desalting can cause fouling of heater tubes and heat exchangers throughout the refinery. Fouling restricts flow and heat transfer and leads to failures due to increased pressures and temperatures. Corrosion, which occurs due to the presence of hydrogen sulphide, hydrogen chloride, naphthenic (organic) acids, and other contaminants in the crude oil, also causes equipment failure. neutralized salts (ammonium chlorides and sulphides), when moistened by condensed water, can cause corrosion. Overpressuring the unit is another potential hazard that causes failures.

(*c*) **Health:** Because this is a closed process, there is little potential for exposure to crude oil unless a leak or release occurs. Where elevated operating temperatures are used when desalting sour crudes, hydrogen sulphide will be present. There is the possibility of exposure to ammonia, dry chemical demulsifiers, caustics, and /or acids during this operation. Safe work practices and/or the use of appropriate personal protective equipment may be needed for exposures to chemicals and other hazards such as heat, and during process sampling, inspection, maintenance, and turnaround activities.

Depending on the crude feedstock and the treatment chemicals used, the wastewater will contain varying amounts of chlorides, sulfides, bicarbonates, ammonia, hydrocarbons, phenol, and suspended solids. If diatomaceous earth is used in filtration, exposures should be minimized or controlled.Diatomaceous earth can contain silica in very fine particle size, making this a potential respiratory hazard.

Crude Oil Distillation (Fractionation)

Description

The first step in the refining process is the separation of crude oil into various fractions or straight—run cuts by distillation in atmospheric and vacuum towers. The main fractions or 'cuts' obtained have specific boiling-point ranges and can be classified in order of decreasing volatility into gases, light distillates, middle distillates, gasoils, and residum.

Atmospheric Distillation Tower

(*a*) At the refinery, the desalted crude feedstock is preheated using recovered process heat. The feedstock then flows to a direct-fired crude charge heater where it is fed into the vertical distillation column just above the bottom, at pressures slightly above atmospheric and at temperatures ranging from 650° to 700° F (heating crude oil above these temperatures may cause undesirable thermal cracking). All but the heaviest fractions flash into vapour. As the vapour rises in the tower, its temperature is reduced. Heavy fuel oil or asphalt residue is taken from the bottom. At successively higher points on the tower, the various major products including lubricating oil, heating oil, kerosene, gasoline, and uncondensed gases (which condense at lower temperatures) are drawn off.

(*b*) The fractionating tower, a steel cylinder about 120 feet high, contains horizontal steel trays for separating and collecting the liquids. At each tray, vapours from below enter perforations and bubble caps. They permit the vapours to bubble through the liquid on the tray, causing some condensation at the temperature of that tray. An overflow pipe drains the condensed liquids from each tray back to the below where the higher temperature causes re-evaporation. The evaporation, condensing, and scrubbing operation is repeated many times until the desired degree of product purity is reached. Then side streams from certain trays are taken off to obtain the desired fractions. Products ranging from uncondensed fixed gases at the top to heavy fuel oils at the bottom can be taken continuously from a fractionating tower. Steam is often used in towers to lower the vapour pressure and create a partial vacuum. The distillation process separates the major constituents of crude oil into so-called straight-run products. Sometimes crude oil is 'topped' by distilling off only the lighter fractions, leaving a heavy residue that is often distilled further under high vacuum.

Vacuum Distillation Tower: In order to further distill the residuum or topped crude from the atmospheric tower at higher temperatures, reduced pressure is required to prevent thermal cracking. The process takes place in one or more vacuum distillation towers. The principles of vacuum distillation resemble those of fractional distillation and except that larger-diameter columns are used to maintain comparable vapour velocities at the reduced

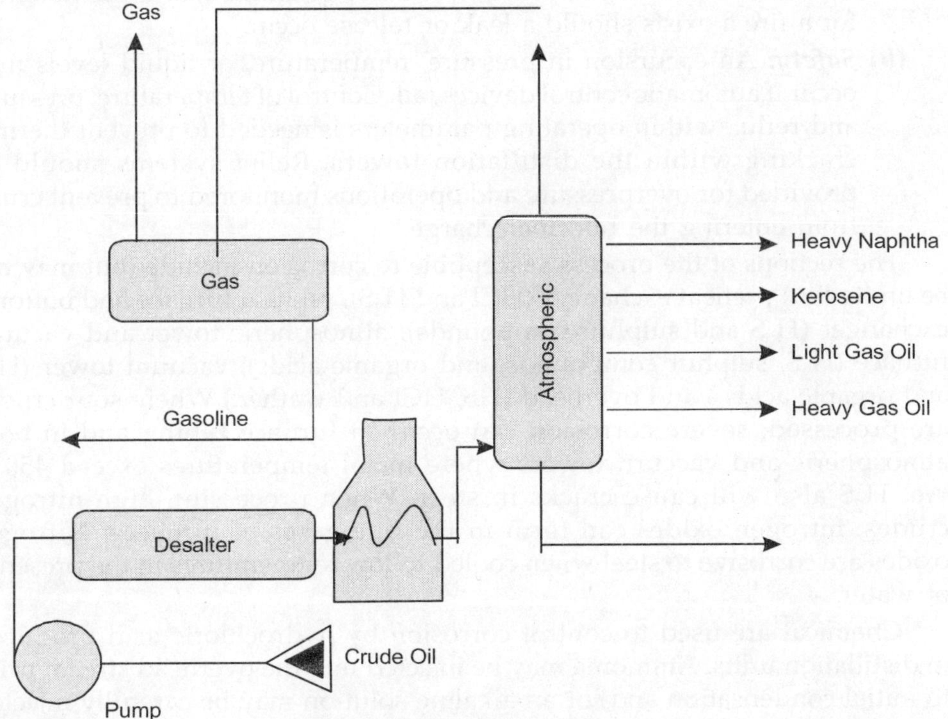

Fig. 8.2 : Atmospheric Distillation

pressures, the equipment is also similar. The internal designs of some vacuum towers are different from atmospheric towers in that random packing and demister pads are used instead of trays. A typical first-phase vacuum tower may produce gas oils, lubricating-oil stocks, and heavy residual for propane deasphalting. A second-tower operating at lower vacuum may distill surplus residuum from the atmospheric tower, which is not used for lube-stock processing, and surplus from the first vacuum tower not used for deasphalting.

Other Distillation (Columns): Within refineries there are numerous other, smaller distillation towers called columns, designed to separate specific and unique products. Columns all work on the same principles as the towers described above. For example, a depropanizer is a small column designed to separate propane and lighter gases from butane and heavier components. Another larger column is used to separate ethyl benzene and xylene. Small 'bubble' called strippers use steam to remove trace amounts of light products from heavier products streams.

Health and Safety Considerations

(a) ***Fire prevention and protections:*** Even though these are closed processes, heaters and exchangers in the atmospheric and vacuum

distillation units could provide a source of ignition, and the potential for a fire a exists should a leak or release occur.

(b) *Safety:* An excursion in pressure, temperature, or liquid levels may occur if automatic control devices fail. Control of temperature, pressure, and reflux within operating parameters is needed to prevent thermal cracking within the distillation towers. Relief systems should be provided for overpressure and operations monitored to prevent crude from entering the reformer charge.

The sections of the process susceptible to corrosion include (but may not be limited to) preheat exchanger (HCl and H_2S), preheat furnace and bottoms exchanger (H_2S and sulphur compounds), atmospheric tower and vacuum furnace (H_2S, sulphur compounds, and organic acids), vacuum tower (H_2S and organic acids) and overhead (HS, HCl and wather.) Where sour crudes are processed, severe corrosion can occur in furnace tubing and in both atmospheric and vaccurn towers where metal temperatures exceed 450°F. Wet H_2S also will cause cracks in steel. When processing high-nitrogen crudes, nitrogen oxides can form in the flue gases of furnaces. Nitrogen oxides are corrosive to steel when cooled to low temperatures in the presence of water.

Chemical are used to control corrosion by hydrochloric acid produced in distillation units. Ammonia may be injected into the overhead stream prior to initial condensation and/or an alkaline solution may be carefully injected into the hot crude-oil feed. If sufficient wash-water is not injected, deposits of ammonium chloride can from and cause serious corrosion. Crude feedstock may contain appreciable amounts of water in suspension which can separate during startup and, along with water remaining in the tower from steam purging, settle in the bottom of the tower. This water can be heated to the boiling point and create an instantaneous vapourization explosion upon contact with the oil in the unit.

(c) *Health:* Atmospheric and vacuum distillation are closed processes and exposures are expected to be minimal. When sour (high-sulphur) crudes are processed, there is potential for exposure to hydrogen sulphide in the preheat exchanger and furnace, tower flash zone and overhead system, vacuum furnace and tower, and bottoms exchanger. Hydrogen chloride may be present in the preheat exchanger, Hydrogen chloride may be preheat exchanger, tower top zones, and overheads. Wastewater may contain water-soluble sulphides in high concentrations and other water-soluble compounds such as ammonia, chlorides, phenol, mercaptans, etc., depending upon the crude feedstock and the treatment chemicals. Safe work practices and/or the use of appropriate personal protective equipment may be needed for exposures to chemicals and other hazards such as heat and noise, and during sampling, inspection, maintenance, and turnaround activities.

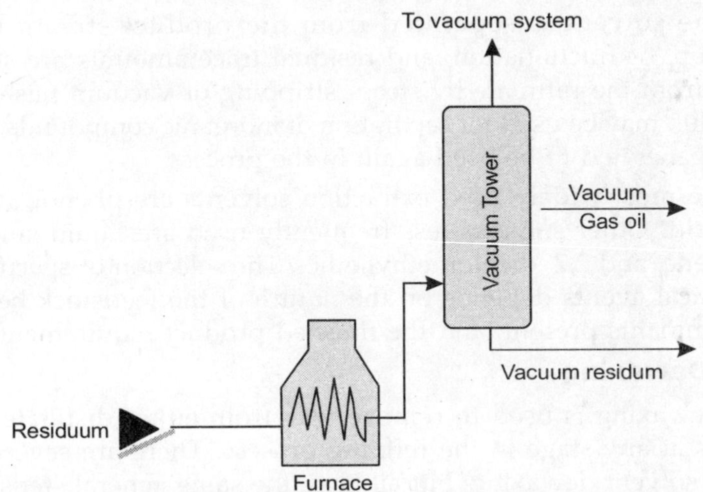

Fig. 8.3 : Vacuum Distillation

Solvent Extraction and Dewaxing

Description

Solvent treating is a widely used of refining lubricating oils as well as a host of other refinery stocks. Since distillation (fractionation) separates petroleum into groups only by their boiling-point ranges, impurities may remain. These include organic compounds containing sulphur, nitrogen, and oxygen; inorganic salts and dissolved metals; and soluble salts that were present in the crude feedstock. In addition, kerosene and soluble salts that were present in the crude feedstock. In addition kerosene and distillates may have trace amounts of aromatics and naphthenes, and lubricating oil base-stocks may contain wax. Solvent refining processes including solvent extraction and solvent dewaxing usually remove these undesirables at intermediate refining stages or just before sending the product to storage.

Solvent Extraction

(*a*) The purpose of solvent extraction is to prevent corrosion, protect catalyst in subsequent processes, and improve finished products by removing unsaturated, aromatic hydrocarbons from lubricant and grease stocks. The solvent extraction process separates aromatics, naphthenes, and impurities from the product stream by dissolving or precipitation. The feedstock is first dried and then treated using a continuous countercurrent solvent treatment operation. In one type of process, the feedstock is washed with a liquid the substances to be removed are more soluble than in the desired resultant product.In another process, selected solvents are added to causes impurities to precipitate out of the product. In the adsorption process, highly porous solid materials liquid molecules on their surfaces.

(*b*) The solvent is separated from the product stream by heating, evaporation, or fractionation, and residual trace amounts are subsequently removed from the raffmate by steam stripping or vacuum flashing. Electric precipitation may be used for separation of inorganic compounds. The solvent is then regenerated to be used again in the process.

(*c*) The most widely used extraction solvents are phenol, furfural, and cresylic acid. Other solvents less frequently used are liquid sulfur dioxide, nitrobenzene, and 2,2′ dichloroethyl ether. The selection of specific processes and chemical agents depends on the nature of the feedstock being treated, the contaminants present, and the finished product requirements.

Solvent Dewaxing

Solvent dewaxing is used to remove wax from either distillate or residual basestocks at any stage in the refining process. There are several processes in use for solvent dewaxing, but all have the same general steps, which are: (1) mixing the feedstock with a solvent; (2) precipitating the wax from the mixture by chilling; and (3) recovering the solvent from the wax and dewaxed oil for recycling by distillation and steam stripping. Usually two solvents are used: toluene, which dissolves the oil and maintains fluidity at low temperatures, and methyl ethyl ketone (MEK), which little wax at low temperatures and acts as a wax precipitating agent. Other solvents that are sometimes used include benzene, methyl isobutyl ketone, propane, petroleum naphtha, ethylene dichloride, methylene chloride, and sulphur dioxide. In addition, there is a catalytic process used as an alternate to solvent dewaxing.

Health and Safety Considerations

(a) Fire Prevention and Protection: Solvent treatment is essesntially a closed process and although operating pressures are relatively low, the potential exists for fire from a leak or spill contacting a source of ignition such as the drier or extraction heater. In solvent dewaxing, disruption of the vaccum will create a potential fire hazard by allowing air to enter the unit.

(b) Health: Because solvent extraction is a closed process, exposures are expected to be minimal under normal operating conditions. However, there is a potential for exposure to extraction solvents such as phenol, glycols, methyl ethyl ketone, amines, and other process chemicals. Safe work practices and/or the use of appropriate personal protective equipment may be needed for exposures to chemicals and other hazards such as noise and heat and during repair, inspection, maintenance and turnaround activities.

Thermal Cracking

Description

(*a*) Because the simple distillation of crude oil produces amounts and types of products that are not consistent with those required by the marketplace, subsequent refinery processes change the product mix by altering the molecular structure of the hydrocarbons. One of the ways of accomplishing this change is through 'cracking,' a process that breaks or cracks the heavier, higher boiling-point petroleum fractions into more valuable products such as gasoline, fuel oil, and gas oils. The two basic types of cracking are thermal cracking, using heat and pressure,and catalytic cracking.

(*b*) The first thermal cracking process was developed around 1913. Distillate fuels and heavy oils were heated under pressure in large drums until they cracked into smaller molecules with better antiknock characteristics. However, this method produced large amounts of solid, unwanted coke. This early process has evolved into the following applications of thermal cracking : visbreaking, steam cracking and coking.

Visbreaking Process: Visbreaking, a mild form of thermal cracking, significantly lowers the viscosity of heavy crude-oil residue without affecting the boiling point range. Residual from the atmospheric distillation tower is heated (800°–950°F) at atmospheric pressure and midly in a heater. It is then quenched with cool gas oil to control overcraking, and flashed in a distillation tower. Visbreaking is used to reduce the pour point of waxy residues the viscosity of residues used for blending with lighter fuel oils. Middle distillates may also be produced, depending on product demand. The thermally cracked residue tar, which accumulates in the bottom of the fractionation tower, is vacuum flashed in a stripper and the distillate recycled. Steam Cracking process. Steam cracking is a petrochemical process sometimes used in refineries to produce olefmic raw materials (*e.g.*, ethylene) from various feedstock for petrochemicals manufacture.

The feedstock range from ethane to vacuum gas oil, with heavier feeds giving higher yields of by products such as naphtha. The most common feeds are ethane, butane, and naphtha. Steam cracking out at temperatures of 1,500° –1,600°F and at pressures slightly above atmospheric. Naphtha produced from steam cracking contains benzene, which is extracted prior to hydrotreating. Residual from steam cracking is sometimes blended into heavy fuels. Coking Processes. Coking is a severe method of thermal cracking used to upgrade heavy residuals into lighter products or distillates. Coking produces straight-run gasoline (coker naphtha) and various middle-distillate fractions used as catalytic cracking feedstock. The process so completely reduces hydrogen that the residue is a from of carbon called 'coke' The two most common processes are delayed coking and continuous (contact or fluid) coking. Three typical of coke are obtained (sponge coke, honeycomb coke, and needle coke) depending upon the reaction mechanism, time temperature, and the crude feedstock.

(a) Delayed Coking: In delayed coking the heated charge (typically residuum from atmospheric distillation towers) is transferred to large coke drums which provide the long residence time needed to allow the cracking to proceed to completion. Initially the heavy feedstock is fed to a furnace which heats the residuum to high temperatures (900°–950°F) at low pressures (25-30 psi) and is designed and controlled to prevent coking in the heater tubes. The mixture is passed from the heater to one or more coker drums where the hot material is help approximately 24 hours (delayed) at pressures of 25-75 psi, until it cracks into lighter products. Vapours from the drums are returned to a fractionator where gas, naphtha, and gas oils are separated out. The heavier hydrocarbons produced produced in the fractionator are recycled through the furnace.

After the coke reaches a predetermined level in one drum, the flow is diverted to another drum to maintain continuous operation. The full drum is steamed to strip out uncracked hydrocarbons, cooled by water injection, and decoked by mechanical or hydraulic methods. The coke is mechanically removed by an auger rising from the bottom of the drum. Hydraulic decoking consists of fracturing the coke bed with high-pressure water ejected from a rotating cutter.

(b) Continuous Coking: Continuous (contact or fluid) coking is a moving-bed process that operates at temperatures higher than delayed coking. In continuous coking, thermal cracking occurs by using heat transferred from hot, recycled coke particles to feedstock in a radial mixer, called a reactor, at a pressure of 50 psi. Gases and vapours are taken from the reactor, quenched to stop any further redaction and fractionated. The reacted coke enters a surge drum and is lifted to a feeder and classifier where the larger coke particles are removed as product. The remaining coke is dropped into the recycling with feedstock. Coking occurs both in the reactor and in the surge drum. The process is automatic in that there is a continuous flow of coke and feedstock.

Health and Safety Considerations

(a) Fire Protection and Prevention: Because thermal cracking is a closed process, the primary potential for fire is from leaks or releases of liquids, gases, or vapours reaching an ignition source such as a heater. The potential for fire is present in coking operations due to vapor or product leaks. Should coking temperatures get out of control, an exothermic reaction could occur with in the coker.

(b) Safety: In thermal cracking when sour crudes are processed, corrosion can occur where metal temperatures are between 450° and 900°F. Above 900°F coke forms a protective layer on the metal. The furmace, soaking drums, lower part of the tower and high-temperature exchangers are usually subject to corrosion. Hydrogen sulfide corrosion in coking can also occur when temperatures are not properly controlled above 900°F.

Continuous thermal changes can lead to bulging and cracking of coke drum shells. In coking, temperature control must often be held within a 10°–20°F range, as high temperatures will produce coke that is too hard to cut out of the drum. Conversely, temperatures that are too low will result in a high asphaltic-content slurry. Water or steam injection may be used prevent buildup of coke in delayed coker furnace tubes, water must be completely drained from the coker, so as not to cause an explosion upon recharging with hot coke. Provisions for alternate means of egress from the working platform on top of coke drums are important in the event of an emergency.

(c) Health: The potential exists for exposure to hazardous gases such as hydrogen sulfide and carbon monoxide, and trace polynuclear aromatics (PNA') associated with coking operations. When coke is moved as a slurry, oxygen depletion may occur within confined spaces as storage siols, since wet carbon will adsorb oxygen. Wastewater may be highly alkaline and contain oil, sulphides, ammonia, and/or phenol. The potential exists in the exposure to burns when handling hot coke or the event-line leak, or from steam, hot water hot coke, or hot slurry that may be expelled when opening cokers. Safe work practices and/or the use of appropriate personal protective equipment may be needed for exposures to chemical and other hazards such as heat and noise, and during process sampling, inspection, maintenance, and turnaround activities.

Note: Coke produced from petroleum is a different product from that generated in the steel -industry coking process.

Catalytic Cracking

Description

(*a*) Catalytic craking breaks complex hydrocarbon into simler molecules in order to increase the quality, more desirable products and decrease the amount of residuals. This process rearranges the molecular structure of hydrocarbon compounds to convert heavy hydrocarbon feedstock in to lighter fractions such as kerosene, gasoline, LPG, heating oil, and petrochemical feedstock.

(*b*) Catalytic cracking similar to thermal cracking except that catalysts facilitate the conversion of the heavier molecules into lighter products. Use of a catalyst (a material that assists a chemical reaction but dose not take part in it) in the cracking reaction increases the yield of improved-quality products under much less severe operating conditions that in thermal cracking. Typical temperatures are from 850°–950°F at much lower pressures of 10-20 psi. The catalysts used in refinery cracking nits are typically solid materials (zeolite, aluminum hydrosilicate, treated bentonite clay, fuller's earth, bauxite, and silica-alumina) that come in the from of powders, beads,pellets or materials called extradite.

(*c*) There are three basic functions in the catalytic racking process:

Reaction: Feedstock reacts with catalyst and cracks into different Hydrocarbon;

Regeneration: Catalyst is reactivated by burning off coke; and

Fractionation: Cracked hydrocarbon stream is separated into various products.

(*d*) The three types of catalytic cracking processes are fluid catalytic cracking(FCC), moving-bed catalytic cracking, and Thermofor catalytic cracking (TCC). The catalytic cracking process is very flexible, and operating parameters can be adjusted to meet changing product demand. In addition to cracking, catalytic activities include dehydrogenation, hydrogenation and isomerization.

Fluid Catalytic Cracking

Description

(*a*) The most common process is FCC, in which the oil is cracked in the presence of a finely divided catalyst which is maintained in an aerated or fluidized state by the oil vapours. The fluid cracker consists of a catalyst section and a fractionating section that operate together as an integrated processing unit. The catalyst section contains the reactor and regenerator, which the standpipe and riser, forms the catalyst circulation unit. The fluid catalyst is continuously circulated between the reactor and the regenerator using air, oil vapours, and steam as the conveying media.

(*b*) A typical FCC process involves mixing a preheated hydrocarbon charge with hot, regenerated catalyst as it enters the riser leading to the reactor. The charge is combined with a recycle stream within the riser, vapourized, and raised to reactor temperature (900°–1,000°F) by the hot catalyst. As the mixture travels up the riser, the charge is cracked at 10-30 psi. In the more modern FCC units, all cracking takes place in the riser. The 'reactor' no longer functions as a reactor; it merely serves as a holding vessel for the cyclones. This cracking continues until the oil vapors are separated from the catalyst in the reactor cyclones. The resultant product stream (cracked product) is then charged to a fractionating column where it is separated into fractions, and some of the heavy oil is recycled to the riser.

(*c*) Spent catalyst is regenerated to get rid of coke that collects on the catalyst during the process. Spent catalyst flows through the catalyst stripper to the regenerator, where most of the coke deposits burn off at the bottom where preheated air and spent catalyst are mixed. Fresh catalyst is added and worn-out catalyst removed to optimize the cracking process. Moving Bed catalytic cracking. The moving-bed catalytic cracking process is similar to the FCC process. The catalyst is in the form of pellets that are moved continuously to the top of the unit by conveyor or pneumatic lift tubes to a storage hopper, then flow downward by gravity through the finally to a regenerator. The regenerator and hopper are isolated from the reactor by steam seals. The cracked product separated into recycle gas oil, clarified oil, distillate, naphtha,and wet gas.

Thermofor Catalytic Cracking: In a typical thermofor catalytic cracking unit, the preheated feedstock flows by gravity through the catalytic reactor bed. The vapours are separated from the catalyst and sent to fractionating tower. The spent catalyst is regenerated, cooled and recycled. The flue gas from regeneration is sent to a carbon-monoxide boiler for heat recovery.

Health and Safety Considerations

(a) Fire Prevention and Protection: Liquid hydrocarbons in the catalyst or entering the heated combustion air stream should be controlled to avoid exothermic reactions. Because of the presence of heaters in catalytic units, the possibility exists for fire due to a leak or vapor release. Fire protection including concrete of other insulation on the columns and supports, or fixed water spray or fog systems where insulation is not feasible and in areas where firewater hose streams cannot reach, should be considered.

In some processes, caution must be taken to prevent explosive concentrations of catalyst dust during recharge. When unloading any coked catalyst, the possibility exists for iron sulfide fires. Iron sulfide will ignite spontaneously when exposed to air and before must be wetted with water to prevent it from igniting vapours. Coked catalyst may be either cooled below 120°F before it is dumped from the reactor, or dumped into containers that have been purged and inerted with nitrogen and then cooled before further handling.

(b) Safety: Regular sampling and testing of the feedstock, product and recycle streams should be performed to assure that the cracking process is working as intended and that no contaminants have entered the process stream. Corrosives or deposits in the feedstock can foul gas compressors. Inspections of critical equipment including pumps, compressors, furnaces and heat exchangers should be conducted as needed. When processing sour crude, corrosion may be expected where temperatures are below 900°F. Corrosion takes place where both liquid and vapour phases exist, and at areas subject to local cooling such as nozzles and platform supports.

When processing high-nitrogen feedstock, exposure to ammonia and cyanide may occur, subjecting carbon steel equipment in the FCC overhead system to corrosion, cracking, or hydrogen blistering. These effects may be minimized by water wash or corrosion inhibitors. Water wash may also be used to protect overhead condensers in the main column subjected to fouling from ammonium hydrosulphide. Inspections should include checking for leaks due to erosion or other malfunction such as catalyst buildup on the expanders, coking in the overhead feeder lines from feedstock residues, and other unusual operating conditions.

(c) Health: Because the catalytic is a closed system, there is normally little opportunity for exposure to hazardous substances during normal operations. The possibility exists of exposure to extremely hot (700°F) hydrocarbon liquids or vaporus during process sampling or if a leak or release occurs. In addition, exposure to hydrogen sulfide and/or carbon monoxide gas may occur during a release of product or vapour.

Catalyst regeneration involves steam stripping and decoking, and produces fluid waste streams that may contain varying amounts of hydrocarbon, phenol, ammonia, hydrogen sulphide, mercaptan, and other materials depending upon the feedstock, crudes, and processes. Inadvertment formation of nickel carbonyl may occur in cracking processes using nickel catalysts, with resultant potential for hazardous exposures. Safe work practices and/or the use of appropriate personal protective equipment may be exposures to chemical and other hazards such as noise and heat; during process sampling inspection, maintenance and turnaround activities; and when handling spent catalyst, recharging catalyst, or if leaks or releases occur.

Hydrocracking

Description

(*a*) Hydrocarcking is a two-stage process combining catalytic cracking and hydrogenation, wherein heavier feedstock are cracked in the presence of hydrogen to produce more desirable products. The process employs high pressure, high temperature, a catalyst, and hydrogen. Hydrocracking is used for feedstock that are difficult to process by either catalytic or reforming, since these feedstock are characterized usually by a high polycyclic aromatic content and/or high concentrations of the two principal catalyst poisons, sulphur and nitrogen compounds.

(*b*) The hydrocracking process largely depends on the nature of the feedstock and the relative of the two competing reactions, hydrogenation and cracking. Heavy aromatic feedstock is converted into lighter products under a wide range of very high pressures (1,000-2,000 psi) and fairly high temperatures (750°-1,500°F), in the presence of hydrogen and special catalysts. When the feedstock has a high paraffmic content, the primary function of hydrogen is to prevent the formation of polycyclic aromatic compounds. Another important role of hydrogen in the hydrocracking process is to tar formation and prevent buildup of coke on the catalyst. Hydrogenation also serves to convert sulfur and nitrogen compounds present in the feedstock to hydrogen sulphide and ammonia.

(*c*) Hydrocracking producs relatively large amounts of isobutene for alkylation feedstock. Hydrocacking also performs isomerization for pour-point control and smoke-point control, both of which are important in high-quality jet fuel.

Hydrocracking Process

(*a*) In the first stage, preheated feedstock is mixed with recycled hydrogen and sent to the first-stage reactor, where catalysts convert sulfur and nitro-gen compounds to hydrogen sulphide and ammonia. Limited hydrocracking also occurs.

(*b*) After the hydrocarbon leaves the first stage, it is cooled and liquefied and run through a hydrocarbon. The hydrogen is recycled to the feedstock. The liquid is charged to a fractionator. Depending on the products desired (gasoline components jet fuel, and gas oil), the fractionator is run to cut out some portion of the first stage reactor out-turn. Kerosene-range material can be taken as a separate side-draw product or included in the fractionator bottoms with the gas oil.

(*c*) The fractionator bottoms are again mixed with a hydrogen stream and charged to the second stage. Since this material has already been subjected to some hydrogenation, cracking and reforming in the first stage, the operations of the second stage are more severe (higher temperatures and pressures). Like the outturn of the first stage, the second stage product is separated from the hydrogen and charged to the fractionator.

Health and Safety Considerations

(a) Fire Prevention and Protection: Because this unit operates at very high pressures and temperatures, control of both hydrocarbon leaks and hydrogen releases is important to prevent fires. In some processes, care is needed to ensure that explosive concentrations of catalytic dust do not recharging.

(b) Safety: Inspection and testing of safety relief devices are important due to the very high pressures in this unit. Proper control is needed to protect against plugging reactor beds. Unloading coked catalyst requires special precautions to prevent iron sulphide-induced fires. The coked should either be cooled to below 120°F before dumping, or be placed in nitrogen-inerted containers until cooled.

Because of the operating temperatures and presence of hydrogen, the hydrogen-sulphide content of the feedstock must be strictly controlled to a minimum to reduce the possibility of server corrosion. Corrosion by wet carbon dioxide in areas of condensation also must be considered. When processing high-nitrogen feedstock, the ammonia and hydrogen sulphide form ammonium and hydrogen sulphide form ammonium hydrosulphide, which causes serious corrosion at temperatures below the water dew point. Ammonium hydrosulphide is also present in sour water stripping.

*(c) **Health:*** Because this is a closed process, exposures are expected to be minimal under normal operating conditions. There is a potential for exposure to hydrocarbon gas and vapour emissions, hydrogen and hydrogen sulphide gas due to high-pressure leaks. Large quantities of carbon monoxide may be released during catalyst regeneration and changeover. Catalyst steam stripping and regeneration create waste streams containing sour water and ammonia. Safe work practices and/or the use of appropriate personal protective equipment may be needed for exposure to chemicals and other hazards such as noise and heat, during process sampling, inspection, maintenance, and turnaround activities, and when handling spent catalyst.

Catalytic Reforming

Description

(*a*) Catalytic reforming is an important process used to convert low-octane naphthas into high-octane gasoline components called reformate. Reforming represents the total effect of numerous such as cracking, polymerization, dehydrogenation and isomerization taking place simultaneously. Depending to the properties of the naphtha feedstock (as measured by the paraffin, olefm, naphthene, and aromatic content) and catalysts used reformates can be produced with very high concentrations of toluene, benzene, xylene, and other aromatics useful in gasoline blending and petrochemical processing. Hydrogen, a significant by product, is separated from the reformate for recycling and use in other processes.

(*b*) A catalytic reformer comprises a reactor section and a product-recovery section. More or less standard is a feed preparation section in which, by combination of hydrotreatment and distillation, the feedstock is prepared to specification. Most process use platinum as the active catalyst. Sometimes platinum is combined with a second catalyst (bimetallic catalyst) such as rhenium or another noble metal.

(*c*) There are many different commercial catalytic reforming processes including platforming, powerforming, ultraforming, and Thermofor catalytic reforming. In the platforming process, the first step is preparation of the naphtha feed to remove impurities from the naphtha and reduce catalyst degradation. The naphtha feedstock is then mixed with hydrogen, vapourized and passed through a series of alternating furnace and fixed-bed reactors containing a platinum catalyst. The effluent from the last reactor is cooled and sent to a separator to permit removal of the hydrogen-rich gas stream from the top of the separator for recycling. The liquid from the bottom of the separator is sent to a fractionator called a stabilizer (botanizer). It makes a bottom product called reformate; butanes and lighter go overhead and are sent to the saturated gas plant.

(*d*) Some catalytic reformers operate at low pressure (50-200 psi),and others operate at high pressures (up to 1,000 psi). Some catalytic reforming systems continuously regenerate the catalyst in other systems. One reactor at a time is taken off-stream for catalyst regeneration, and some facilities regenerate all of the reactors during turnarounds.

Health and Safety Considerations

(a) Fire Prevention and Protection: This is a closed system; however the potential for fire exists should a leak or release of reformate gas or hydrogen occur.

(b) Safety: Operating procedures should be developed to ensure control of hot spots during start-up. Safe catalyst handling is very important. Care must be taken not to break or crush the catalyst when loading the beds, as the small fines will plug up the reformer screens. Precautions against dust when regenerating or replacing catalyst should also be considered. Also water wash should be considered where stabilizer fouling has occurred due to the formation of ammonium chloride and iron salts. Ammonium chloride may from in pretreater exchangers and causes corrosion and fouling. Hydrogen chloride from the hydrogenation of chlorine compounds may form acid or ammonium chloride salt.

(c) Health: Because this is a closed prosess, exposures are expected to be minimal under normal operating conditions. There is potential for exposure to hydrogen sulfide and benzene should a leak or release occur.

Small emissions of carbon monoxide and hydrogen sulfide may occur during regeneration of catalyst. Safe work practices and/or appropriate personal protective equipment may be needed for exposures to chemical and other hazards such as noise and heat; during testing, inspecting, maintenance and turnaround activities; and when handling regenerated or spent catalyst.

Catalytic Hydrotreating

Description

Catalytic hydrotreating is a hydrogenation process used to removed about 90 per cent of contaminants such as nitrogen, sulfur, oxygen, and metals from liquid petroleum fractions. These contaminants, if not removed from the petroleum fractions as they travel through the refinery processing units, can have detrimental effects on the equipments, the catalysts and the quality of the finished product. Typically, hydrotreating is done prior to processes such as catalytic reforming so that the catalyst is not contaminated by untreated feedstock. Hydrotreating is also used prior to catalytic cracking to reduced sulphur and improve product yields and to upgrade middle-distillate petroleum fractions into finished kerosene, diesel fuel, and heating fuel oils. In addition, hydrotreating converts olefms and aromatics to saturated compounds.

Catalytic Hydrodesulphurization Process: Hydrotreating for sulphur removal is called hydroesulphurization. In a typical catalytic hydrodesulphuization unit, the feedstock is deaerated and mixed with hydrogen, preheated in a fired heater (600°-800°F) and then charged under pressure (up to 1,000 psi) through a fixed-bed catalytic reactor. in the reactor, the sulfur and nitrogen compounds in the feedstock are converted into H_2S and NH_3. The reaction products leave the reactor and after cooling to a low temperature enter a liquid/gas separator. The hydrogen-rich gas from the high-pressure separation is recycled to combine with the feedstock, and the low-pressure gas stream rich in H_2S is sent to a gas treating unit where H_2S is removed. The clean gas is then suitable as fuel for the refinery furnaces. The liquid stream is the product from hydrotreating and is normally sent to a stripping column for removal of H_2S and other undesirable components. In cases where steam is used for stripping, the product is sent to a vacuum drier for removal of water. Hydrodesulphurized products are blended or used as catalytic reforming feedstock.

Other Hydrotreating Processes

(*a*) Hydrotreating Processes differ depending upon the feedstock available and catalysts used. Hydrotreating can be used to improve the burining characteristics of distillates such as kerosene. Hydrotreatment of a kerosene fraction can convert aromatics into naphthenes, which are cleaner-burning compounds.

(*b*) Lube-oil hydrotreating uses catalytic treatment of the oil with hydrogen to improve product quality. The objectives in mild lube hydrotreating include saturation of olefins and improvements in colour, ordour and acid nature of the oil. Mild lube hydrotreating also may be used following solvent processing. Operating temperatures are usually below 600°F and operating pressures below 800 psi. Severer lube hydrotreating, at temperatures in the 600°-750°F range and hydrogen pressures up to 3,000 psi, is capable of saturating aromatic rings, along with sulphur and nitrogen removel, to impart specific properties not achieved at mild conditions.

(*c*) Hydrotreating also can be employed to improve the quality of pyrolysis gasoline (pygas), a by product from the manufacture of ethylene. Traditionally, the outlet for pygas has been motor gasoline blending, a suitable route in view of its high octane number. However, only small portions can be blended untreated owing to the unacceptable odour, colour, and gum-forming tendencies of this material. The quality of pygas, which is high in diolefm content, can be satisfactorily improved by hydrotreating, where by conversion of diolefms into mono-olefins provides an acceptable product for motor gas blending.

Health and Safety Considerations

(a) Fire Prevention and Protection: The potential exists for fire in the event of a leak or release of product or hydrogen gas.

(b) Safety: Many processes require hydrogen generation to provide for a continuous supply. Because of the operating temperatures and presence of hydrogen, the hydrogen sulphide content of the feedstock must be strictly controlled to a minimum to reduce corrosion. Hydrogen chloride may form and condense as hydrocholoric acid in the lower-temperature parts of the unit. Ammonium hydrosulphide may from in high-temperature, high-pressure units.Excessive contact time and/or temperature will create coking. Precautions need to be taken when unloading coked catalyst from the unit to prevent iron sulphide fires. The coked catalyst should be cooled to below 120°F before removal, or dumped into nitrogen-inerted bins where it can be cooled before further handling. Special antifoam additives may be used to prevent catalyst poisoning from silicone carryover in the coker feedstock.

(c) Health: Because this is a closed process, exposures are expected to be minimal under normal operating conditions. There is a potential for exposure to hydrogen sulphlde or hydrogen gas in the event of a release, or to ammonia should a sour-water leak or spill occur. Phenol also may be present in high boiling-point feedstock are processed. Safe work practices and/or appropriate personal protective equipment may be needed for exposures to chemicals and other hazards such as noise and heat; during process sampling, inspection, maintenance, and turnaround activities; and when handling amine or exposed to catalyst.

Isomerization

Description

(*a*) Isomerization converts n-butane, n-pentane and n-hexane into their respective isoparaffins of substantially higher octane number. The straight-chain paraffins are converted to their branched-chain counterparts whose component atoms are the same but are arranged ina different geometric structure. Isomerization is important for the conversion of n-butane into isobutene, to provide additional feedstock for alkylation units and the conversion of normal pentanes and hexanes into higher branched isomers for gasoline blending. Isomerization is similar to catalytic reforming in that the hydrocarbon molecules are rearranged but unlike catalytic reforming, isomerization just convert normal isoparaffins.

(*b*) There are two distinct isomerization processes, butane (C_4) and pentane/hexane (C_5/C_6). Butane isomrization produes feestock for alkylation. Aluminum chloride catalyst plus hydrogen chloride are universally used for the low-temperature processes. Platinum or another metal catalyst is used for the higher-temperature processes. In a typical low-temperature process, the feed to the isomerization plant is n-butane or mixed butanes mixed with hydrogen (to inhibit olefin formation) and passed to the reactor at 230°-340° psi. Hydrogen is flashed off in a high-pressure separator and the hydrogen chloride removed in a stripper column. The resultant butane mixture is sent to a fractionator (deisobutanier) to separate n-butane from the isobutene product.

(*c*) Pentane/hexane isomerization increases the octane number of the light gasoline components n-pentane and n-hexane, which are found in abundance in straight-run gasoline. In a typical C_5/C_6 isomerization process, dried and desulfurized feedstock is mixed with a small amount of organic and recycled hydrogen,and then heated to reactor temperature. It is then passed over supported-metal catalyst in the first reactor where benzene and olefins are hydrogenated. The feed next goes to the isomerization reactor where the paraffins are catalytically isomerized to isoparaffins. The reator effluent is then cooled and subsequently separated in the products separator into two streams: a liquid product (isomerate) and a recycle hydrogen gas stream. The isomerate is washed (caustic and water) acid stripped, and stabilized before going to storage.

Safety and Health Considerations

(a) Fire Protection and Prevention: Although this is a closed process, the potential for a fire exists should a release or leak contact a source of ignition such as the heater.

(b) Safety: If the feedstock is not completely dried and desulphurized, the potential exists for acid formation leading to catalyst poisoning and metal corrosion. Water or steam must not be allowed to enter areas where hydrogen chloride is present. Precautions are needed to prevent HCl from entering sewers and drains.

(c) Health: Because that is a closed process, exposures are expected to be minimal during normal operating conditions. There is a potential for exposure to hydrogen gas, hydrochloric acid,and hydrogen chloride and to dust when solid catalyst is used. Safe work practices and/or appropriate personal protective equipment may be needed for exposures to chemicals and other hazards such as heat and noise, and during process sampling, inspection, maintenance and turnaround activities.

Polymerization

Description

(*a*) Polymerization in the petroleum industry is the process of converting light olefin gases including ethylene, propylene, and butylenes into hydrocarbons of higher molecular weight and higher octane number that can be used as gasoline blending stocks. Polymerization combines two or more identical olefin molecules to form a single molecule with the same elements in the same proportions as the original molecules. Polymerization may be accomplished thermally or in the presence of a catalyst at lower temperatures.

(*b*) The olefin feedstock is pretreated to remove sulphur and other undersirable compounds. In the catalytic process the feedstock is either passed over a solid phosphoric acid catalyst or comes in contact with liquid phosphoric acid, where an exothermic polymeric reaction occurs. This reactions requires cooling water and the injection of cold feedstock into the reactor to control temperatures between 300° and 450°F at pressures from 200 psi to 1,200 psi. The reaction products leaving the reactor are sent to stabilization and/or fractionator system to separate saturated and unreacted gases from the polymer gasoline product.

Note: In the petroleum industry, polymerization is used to indicate the production of gasoline components, hence the term 'polymer' gasoline. Furthermore, it is not essential that only one type of monomer be involved. If unlike olefin molecules are combined, the process is referred to as 'copolymerization.' Polymerization in the true sense of the word is normally prevented, and all attempts are made to terminate the reaction at the dimer or trimer (three monomers joined together) stage. However, in the petrochemical section of a refinery, polymerization, which result in the production of, for instance, polyethylene, is allowed to proceed until materials of the required high molecular weight have been produced.

Safety and Health Considerations

(a) Fire Prevention and Protection: Polymerization is a closed process where the potential for a fire exists due to leaks or releases reaching a source of ignition.

(b) Safety: The potential for an uncontrolled exothermic reaction exists should loss of cooling water occur. Servere corrosion leading to equipment failure will occur should water make contact with the phosphoric acid, such as during water washing at shutdowns. Corrosion may also occur in piping manifolds, reboilers, exchangers, and other locations where acid may settle out.

(c) Health: Because this is a closed system, exposures are expected to be minimal under normal operating conditions. There is a potential for exposure to caustic wash (sodium hydroxide) to phosphoric acid used in the process or washed out during turnarounds, and to catalyst dust. Safe work practices and/or appropriate personal protective equipment may be needed for exposures to chemicals and other hazards such as noise and heat and during process sampling, inspection, maintenance and turnaround activities.

Alkylation

Description

Alkylation combines low-molecular-weight olefms (primarily a mixture of propylene and butylene) with isobutene in the presence of a catalyst, either sulphuric acid or hydrofluoric acid. The product is called alkylate and is composed of a mixture of high-octane, branched-chain paraffmic hydrocarbons. Alkylate is a premium blending stock because it has exceptional antiknock properties and is clean burning. The octane number of the alkylate depends mainly upon the king of olefms used and upon operating conditions,

Sulphuric Acid Alkylation Process

(*a*) In cascade type sulphuric acid (H_2SO_4) alkylation units, the feedstock (propylene, butylene, amylene and fresh isobutene) enters the reactor and contacts the concentrated sulfuric acid catalyst (in concentrations of 85 per cent to 95 per cent for good operation and to minimize corrosion). The reactor is divided into zones, with olefins fed through distributors to each zone, and the sulphuric acid and isobutanes flowing over baffles from zone to zone.

(*b*) The reactor effluent is separated into hydrocarbon and acid phases in a settler, and the acid is returned to the reactor. The hydrocarbon phase is hot-water washed with caustic for pH control before being successively depropanized, deisobutanized and debutanized. The alkylate obtained from the deisobutanizer can then go directly to motor-fuel blending or be rerun to produce aviation-grade blending stock. The isobutene is recycled to the feed.

Hydrofluoric Acid Alylation Process: Philips and UOP are the two common types of hydrofluoric acid alkylation processes in use. In the Phillips process, olefin and isobutene feedstock are fed to a combination reactor/ settler system. Upon leaving the reaction zone, the reactor effluent flows to a settler (separating vessel) where the acid separates from the hydrocarbons.The acid layer at the bottom of the separating vessel is recycled. The top layer of hydrocarbon (hydrocarbon phase), consisting of propane, normal butane, alkylate, and excess (recycle) isobutene, is charged to the main fractionator, the bottom product of which is motor alkylate. The main fractionator overhead consisting mainly of propane, isobutene and HF, goes to a depropanizer. Propane with trace amount of HF goes to an HF stripper for HF removal and is then catalytically defluorinated, treated and sent to storage. Isobutene is withdrawn from the main fractionator and recycled to the reactor/settler, and alkylate from the bottom of the main fractionator is sent to product blending.

The UOP process uses two reactors with separate settlers. Half of the dried feedstock is charged to the first reactor, along with recycle and make up isobutene. The reactor effluent then goes to its settler where the acid is recycled and the hydrocarbon charged to the second reactor. The other half of the feedstock also goes to the second reactor, with the settler acid being recycled and the hydrocarbons charged to the main fractionator. Subsequent processing is similar to the Phillips process. Overhead from the main fractionator goes to a depropanizer. Isobutene is recycled to the reaction zone and alkylate zone and alkylate is sent to product blending.

Health and Safety Considerations

(a) Fire Protection and Prevention: Alkylation units are closed processes; however, the potential exists for fire should a leak or release occur that allows product or vapour to reach a source of ignition.

(b) Safety: Sulphuric acid and hydrofluoric acid are potentially hazardous chemicals. Loss of coolant water, which is needed to maintain process temperatures, could result in an upset. Precautions are necessary that equipment and materials that have been in contact with acid are handled carefully and are thoroughly cleaned before they leave the process area or refinery. Immersion wash vats are often provided for neutralization of equipment that has come into contact with hydrofluoric acid. Hydrofluoric acid units should be thoroughly drained and chemically cleaned prior to turnarounds and entry to remove all traces of iron fluoride and hydro-fluoric acid. Following shutdown, where water has been used the unit should be thoroughly dried before hydrofluoric acid is introduced.

Leaks, spills, or releases involving hydrofluoric acid or hydrocarbons containing hydrofluoric acid can be extremely hazardous. Care during delivery and unloading of acid is essential. Process unit containment by curbs, drainage and is essential. Process unit containment by curbs, drainage and isolation so that effluent can be neutralized before release to the sewer system is considered. Vents can be routed to soda-ash scrubbers to neutralize fluoride gas or hydrofluoric acid vapours before release. Pressure on the cooling water and steam side of exchangers should be kept below the minimum pressure on the acid service side to prevent water contamination.

Some corrosion and fouling in sulphuric acid units may occur from the breakdown of sulphuric acid esters or where caustic is added for neutralization. These esters can be removed be fresh acid treating and hot-water washing. To prevent corrosion from hydrophluoric acid, the hydrofluoric acid, the acid concentration inside the process unit should be maintained above 65 per cent and moisture below 4 per cent.

(c) Health: Because this is a closed process, exposures are expected to be minimal during normal operations. There is a potential for exposure should leaks, spills or release occur. sulphuric acid and (particularly) hydrofluoric acid are potentially hazardous chemicals. Special precautionary emergency preparedness measures and protection appropriate to the potential hazard and areas possibly affected need to be provided. Safe work practices and appropriate skin and respiratory personal protective equipment are needed for potential exposures to hydrofluoric and sulphuric acids during normal operations such as reading gauges inspecting, and process sampling, as well as during emergency response, maintenance and turnaround activities. Procedures should be in place to ensure that protective equipment and clothing worn in hydrofluoric acid activities are decontaminated and

inspected before reissue. Appropriate personal protection for exposure to heat and noise also may be required.

Sweetening and Treating Processes

Description

(*a*) Treating is a means by which contaminants such as organic compounds containing sulfur, nitrogen, and oxygen; dissolved metals and inorganic salts; and soluble salts dissolved in emulsified water are removed from petroleum fractions or streams. Petroleum refiners have a choice of several different treating processes, but the primary of the majority of them is the elimination of unwanted sulphur compounds. A variety of intermediate and finished products, including middle distillates, gasoline, kerosene, jet fuel, and sour gases are dried and sweetened. Sweetening, a major refinery treatment of gasoline, treats sulphur compounds (hydrogen sulphide, thiophene and mercaptan) to improve colour, ordour, and oxidation stability. Sweetening also reduces concentration of carbon dioxide.

(*b*) Treating can be accomplished at an intermediate stage in the refining process, or just before sending the finished product to storage. Choices of a treating method depend on the nature of the petroleum fractions, amount and type of impurities in the fractions to be treated, the extant to which the removes the impurities, and end-product specifications. Treating materials include acids, solvents, alkalis, oxidizing, and adsorption agents.

Acid, Caustic, or Clay Treating: Sulphuric acid is the most commonly used acid treating process. Sulphuric acid treating result in partial or complete removal of unsaturated hydrocarbons, sulphur, nitrogen, and oxygen compounds, and resinous and asphaltic compounds. It is used to improve the odour, colour, stability, carbon residue and other properties of the oil. Clay/lime treatment of acid-refined oil removes traces of asphaltic materials and other compounds improving product colour, odour, and stability. Caustic treating with sodium (or potassium) hydroxide is used to improve odour and colour by removing organic acids (naphthenic acids, phenols) and sulphur compounds (mercaptans, H_2S) by a caustic wash. By combining caustic soda solution with various solubility promoters (*e.g.*, methyl alcohol and cresols), up to 99 par cent of all meracaptans as well as oxygen and nitrogen compounds can be dissolved from petroleum fractions.

Drying and Sweetening: Feedstock from various refinery units are sent to gas treating plants where butanes and butanes are removed for use as alkylation feedstock, heavier components are sent to gasoline blending, propane is recovered for LPG, and propylene is removed for use in petrochemicals. Some mercaptans are removed by water-soluble chemicals that react with the mercaptans. Caustic liquid (sodium hydroxide) amine compounds (diethanolamine) or fixed-ded catalyst sweetening also may be used. Drying is accomplished by the use of water absorption or adsorption agents to remove water from the products. Some processes simultaneously dry and sweeten by adsorption on molecular sieves.

Sulphur Recovery: Sulphur recovery converts hydrogen sulphide in sour gases and hydrocarbon streams to elemental sulphur. The most widely used recovery system is the Claus process, which uses both thermal and catalytic-conversion reactions. A typical process produces elemental sulphur by burning hydrogen sulphide under controlled conditions. Knockout pots are used to remove water and hydrocarbons from gas streams. The gases are than exposed to a catalyst to recover additional sulphur. Sulphur vapour from burning and conversion is condensed and recovered.

Hydrogen Sulphide Scrubbing: Hydrogen sulphide scrubbing is a common treating process in which the hydrocarbon feedstock is first scrubbed to prevent catalyst poisoning. Depending on the feedstock and the nature of contaminants, desulphurization methods vary from ambient temperature-activated charcoal absorption to high-temperature catalytic hydrogenation followed by zinc oxide treating.

Health and Safety Considerations

(a) Fire Protection and Prevention: The potential exists for fire from a leak or release of feedstock or product. Sweetening processes use air or oxygen. If excess oxygen enters these processes, it is possible for a fire to occur in the settler due to the generation of static electricity, which acts as the ignition source.

(b) Health: Because these are closed processes, exposures are expected to be minimal under normal operating conditions. There is a potential for exposure to hydrogen sulphide, caustic (sodium hydroxide), spent caustic, spent catalyst (Merox), catalyst dust and sweetening agents (sodium carbonate and sodium bicarbonate). Safe work practices and/or appropriate personal protective equipment may be needed for exposures to chemical and other hazards such as noise and heat and during process sampling, inspection, maintenance and turnaround activities.

Unsaturated Gas Plants

Description

Unsaturated (unsat) gas plants recover light hydrocarbons (C_3 and C_4 olefins) from wet gas streams from the FCC, TCC and delayed coker overhead accumulators or fractionation receivers. In a typical unsat gas plant the gases are compressed and treated with amine to remove hydrogen sulphide either before or after they are sent to a fractionating absorber where they are mixed into a concurrent flow of debutanized gasoline. The light fractions are separated by heat in a reboiler, the offgas is sent to a sponge absorber, and the bottoms are sent to a debutanizer. A portion of the debutanized hydrocarbon is recycled, with the balance sent to the splitter for separation. The overhead gasges go to a depropanizer for use as alkylation unit feedstock.

Health and Safety Considerations

(a) Fire Prevention and Protection: The potential of a fire exists should spills releases, or vapours reach a source of ignition.

(b) Safety: In unsat gas plants handling FCC feedstock, the potential exists for corrosion from moist hydrogen sulfide and cyanides. When feedstock are from the delayed coker or the TCC, corrosion from hydrogen sulphide and deposits in the high pressure sections of gas compressors from ammonium compounds is possible.

(c) Health: Because these are closed processes, exposures are expected to be minimal under normal operating conditions. There is a potential for exposures to amine compounds such as monoethanolamine (MEA), diethanolamine (DEA) and methyldiethanolamine (MDEA) and hydrocarbons. Safe work practices and/or appropriate personal protective equipment may be needed for exposures to chemicals and other hazards such as noise and heat and during process sampling, inspection, maintenance, and turnaround activities.

Amine Plants

Description

Amine plants remove acid contaminants from sour gas and hydrocarbon streams. In amine plants, gas and liquid hydrocarbon streams containing carbon dioxide and/or hydrogen sulfide are charged to a gas absorption tower or liquid contractor where the acid contaminants are absorbed by counterilowing amine solutions (*i.e.,* MEA, DEA, MDEA.) The stripped gas or liqiuid is removed overhead and the amine is sent to a regenerator. In the regenerator, the acidic components are stripped by heat and reboiling action and disposed of and the amine is recycled.

Health and Safety Considerations

(a) Fire Protection and Prevention: The potential for fire exists where a spill or leak could reach a source of ignition.

(b) Safety: To minimize corrosion, proper operating practices should be established and regenerator bottom and reboiler temperatures controlled. Oxygen should be kept out of the system to prevent amine oxidation.

(c) Health: Because this is a closed process, exposures are expected to be minimal during normal operations. There is potential for exposure to amine compounds (*i.e.,* monoethanolamine, diethanolamine, methydiethano-

lamine), hydrogen sulphide and carbon dioxide. Safe work practices and/or appropriate personal protective equipment may be needed for exposures to chemicals and other hazards such as noise and heat and during process sampling, inspection, maintenance and turnaround activities.

Saturate Gas Plants

Description

Saturate (sat) gas plants separate refinery gas components including butanes for alkylation, pentanes for gasoline blending, LPG' for fuel, and ethane for petrochemicals. Because sat gas processes depend on the feedstock and product demand, each refinery uses different systems, usually absorption-fractionation or straight fractionation. In absorption-fractionation, gases and liquids from various refinery units are fed to an absorber-deethanizer where C_2 and lighter fractions are separated from heavier fractions by lean oil absorption and removed for use as fuel gas or petrochemical feed. The heavier fractions are stripped and sent to a debutanizer and the lean oil is recycled back to the absorber-deethanizer. C_3/C_4 is separated from pentanes in the debutanizer, scrubbed to remove hydrogen sulphide and fed to a splitter where propane and butane are separated. In fractionation sat gas plants, the absorption stage is eliminated.

Health and Safety Considerations

*(a) **Fire Protection and Prevention:*** The potential for fire if a leak or release reaches a source of ignition such as the unit reboiler.

*(b) **Safety:*** Corrosion could occur from the presence of hydrogen sulphide, carbon dioxide, and other compounds as a result of prior treating. Streams containing ammonia should be dried before processing. Antifouling additives may be used in absorption oil to protect heat exchanger. Corrosion inhibitors may be used to control corrosion in overhead systems.

*(c) **Health:*** Because this is a closed process, exposures are expected to be minimal during normal operations. There is potential for exposure to hydrogen sulphide, carbon dioxide and other products such as diethanolamine or sodium hydroxide carried over from prior treating. Safe work practices and/or appropriate personal protective equipment may be needed for exposures to chemicals and other hazards such as noise and heat and during process sampling, inspection, maintenance and turnaround activities.

Asphalt Production

Description

(*a*) Asphalt is a portion of the residual fraction that remains after primary distillation operations. It is further processed to impart characteristics required by its final use. In vacuum distillation, generally used to produce road-tar asphalt, the residual is heated to about 750°F and charged to a column where vacuum is applied to prevent cracking.

(*b*) Asphalt for roofing materials os produced by air blowing. Residual is heated in a pipe still almost to its flash point and charged to a blowing tower where hot air is injected for a predetermined time. The dehydrogenization of the asphalt forms hydrogen sulphide, and the oxidation creates sulphur dioxide. Steam, used to blanket the top of the tower to entrain the various contaminants, is then passed through a scrubber to condense the hydrocarbons.

(*c*) A third process used to produced asphalt is solvent deasphalting. In this extraction process, which uses propane (or hexane) as a solvent, heavy oil fractions are separated to produce heavy lubricating oil, catalytic feedstock, and asphalt. Feedstock and liquid propane are pumped to an extraction tower at precisely controlled mixtures, temperatures (150°-250°F), and pressures of 350-600 psi. Separation occurs in a rotating disc contactor, based on differences in solubility. The products are then evaporated and steam stripped to the propane, which is recycled. Deasphalting also removes some sulphur and nitrogen compounds, metals, carbon resdues and paraffins from the feedstock.

Health and Safety Considerations

(a) Fire Protection and Prevention: The potential for fire exists if a product leak or release contracts a source of ignition such as the process heater. Condensed steam from the various asphalt and deasphalting processes will contain trace amounts of hydrocarbons. Any disruption of the vacuum can result in the entry of atmospheric air and subsequent fire. In addition, raising the temperature of the vaccum tower bottom to improve efficiency can generate methane by thermal cracking. This can create vapours in asphalt storage tanks that are not detectable by flash testing but are high enough to be flammable.

(b) Safety: Deasphalting requires exact temperature and pressure control. In addition, moisture, excess solvent, or a drop in operating temperature may cause foaming which affects the product temperature control and may create an upset.

(c) Health: Because these are closed processes, exposures are expected to be minimal during normal operations. Should a spill or release occur, there is a potential for exposure to residuals and asphalt. Air blowing can some polynuclear aromatics. Condensed steam from the air-blowing asphalt process may also contain contaminants. The potential for exposure to hydrogen sulphur dioxide exists in the production of asphalt. Safe work practices and/or appropriate personal protective equipment may be needed for exposures to chemicals and other hazards such as noise and heat, and during process sampling, inspection, maintenance, and turnaround activities.

Hydrogen Production

Description

(*a*) High-purity hydrogen (95-99%) is required for hydrodesulphurization, hydrogenation, hydrocracking and petrochemical processes. Hydrogen, produced as a by product of refinery processes (principally hydrogen recovery from catalytic reformer product gases), often is not enough to meet the total refinery requirements, necessitating the manufacturing of additional hydrogen or obtaining supply from external sources.

(*b*) In steam-methane reforming, desulfurized gases are mixed with superheated steam (1,100°-1,600°F) and reformed in tubes containing a nickel base catalyst. The reformed gas, which consists of steam, hydrogen, carbon monoxide and carbon dioxide, is cooled and passed through converters containing an iron catalyst where the carbon monoxide reacts with steam to from carbon dioxide and more hydrogen. The carbon dioxide is removed by amine washing. Any remaining carbon monoxide in the product stream is converted to methane.

(*c*) Steam-naphtha reforming is a continuous process for the production of hydrogen from liquid hydrocarbons and is, in fact similar to steam-methane reforming. A variety of naphthas in the gasoline boiling range may be employed, including fuel containing up to 35 per cent aromatics. Following pre-treatment to remove sulphur compounds, the feedstock is mixed with steam and taken to the reforming furnace (1,250°-1,500°F) where hydrogen is produced.

Health and Safety Considerations

(a) Fire Protection and Prevention: The possibility of fire exists should a leak or release occur and reach an ignition source.

(b) Safety: The potential exists for burns from hot gases and superheated steam should a release occur. Inspections and should be considered where the possibility exists for valve failure due to contaminants in the hydrogen. Carryover from caustic scrubbers should be controlled to prevent corrosion in pre-heaters. Chlorides from the feedstock or steam system should be prevented from entering reformer tubes and contaminating the catalyst.

(c) Health: Because these are closed processes, exposures are expected to be minimal during normal operating conditions. There is a potential for exposure to excess hydrogen, carbon monoxide, and/or carbon dioxide. Condensate can be contaminated by process materials such as caustics and amine compounds, with resultant exposures. Depending on the specific process used, safe work practices and/or appropriate personal protective equipment may be needed for exposures to chemicals and other hazards such as noise and heat, and during process sampling, inspection, maintenance and turnaround activities.

Blending

Description

Blending is the physical mixture of a different liquid hydrocarbons to produce a finished product with certain characteristics. Products can be blended in-line through a manifold system, or batch blended in tanks and vessels. In-line blending of gasoline, distillates, jet fuel, and kerosene is accomplished by injecting proportionate amounts of each component into the main stream where turbulence promotes thorough mixing. Additives including octane enhancers, metal deactivators, anti-oxidants, anti-knock agents, gum and rust inhibitors, detergents, etc. are added during and/or after blending to provide specific properties not inherent in hydrocarbons.

Health and Safety Considerations

(a) Fire Prevention and Protection: Ignition sources in the area need to be controlled in the event of a leak of release.

(b) Safety: If feedwater runs low and boilers are dry, the tubes will overheat and fail. Conversely, excess water will be carried over into the steam distribution system and damage the turbines. Feedwater must be free of contaminants that could affect operation. Boilers should have continuous or intermittent blowdown systems to remove water from steam drums and limit buildup of scale on turbine blades and superheater tubes. Care must be taken not to overheat the superheater during startup and shut-down. Alternate fuel sources.

(c) Health: Safe work practices and/or appropriate personal protective equipment may be needed for exposures to chemicals and other hazards such as noise and heat; when handling additives; and during inspection, maintenance, and turnaround activities.

Lubricant, Wax and Grease Manufacturing Processes

Description

Lubricating oils and waxes are refined from the residual fractions of atmospheric and vacuum distillation. The primary objective of the various lubricating oil refinery processes is to remove asphalts, sulphonated aromatics, and paraffinic and isoparaffmic waxes from residual fractions. Reduced crude from the vacuum unit is deasphalted and combined with straight-run lubricating oil feedstock, pre-heated, and solvent-extracted (usually with phenol or furfural) to produce raffinate.

Wax Manufacturing Process: Raffmate from the extraction unit contains a considerable amount of wax that must be removed by solvent extraction and crystallization. The raffmate is mixed with a solvent (propane) and pre-cooled in heat exchangers. The crystallization temperature is attained by the evaporation of propane in the chiller and filter tanks. The wax is continuously removed by filters and cold solvent-washed to recover retained oil. The solvent is recovered from the oil by flashing and steam stripping.The wax is then heated with hot solvent, chilled, filtered and given a final wash to remove all oil.

Lubricating Oil Provess: The dewaxed raffimate is blended with other distillate fractions and further treated for viscosity index, colour, stability, carbon residue, sulphur, additive response, and oxidation stability in extremely selective extraction processes using solvents (furfural, phenol, etc.). In a typical phenol unit, the raffimate is mixed with phenol in the treating section at temperatures below 400°F. Phenol is then separated from the treated oil and recycled. The treated lube-oil base stocks are then mixed and/or compounded with additives to meet the required physical and chemical characteristics of motor oils, industrial lubricants, and metal working oils.

Grease Compounding: Grease is made by blending metallic soaps (salts of long chained fatty acids) and additives into a lubricating oil medium at temperatures of 400°-600°F. Grease may be either batch-produced or continuously compounded. The characteristics of the grease depend to a great extent on the metallic element (calcium, sodium, aluminum, lithium, etc.) in the soap and the additives used.

Health and Safety Considerations

(a) Fire Protection and Prevention: The potential for fire exists if a product or vapour leak or release in the lube blending and wax processing areas reaches a source of ignition. Storage of finished products, both bulk and packaged, should be in accordance with recognized practices.

While the potential for fire is reduced in lube oil blending, care must be taken when making metal-working oils and compounding greases due to the use of higher blending and compounding temperatures and lower flash point products.

(b) Safety: Control of treater temperature is important as phenol can cause corrosion above 400°F. Batch and in-line blending operations require strict controls to maintain desired product quality. Spills should be cleaned and leaks repaired to avoid slips and falls. Additives in drums and bags need to be handled properly to avoid strain. Wax can clog sewer or oil drainage systems and interfere with wastewater treatment.

(c) Health: When blending, sampling and compounding, personal protection from steam, dusts, mists vapours, metallic salts, and other additives is appropriate. Skin contact with any formulated grease or lubricant should be avoided. Safe work practices and/or appropriate personal protection may be needed for exposures to chemicals and other hazards such as noise and heat; during inspection, maintenance, and turnaround activities;

and while sampling and handling hydrocarbons and chemicals during the production of lubricating oil and wax.

OTHER REFINERY OPERATIONS

Heat Exchangers, Coolers and Process Heaters

Heating Operations: Process heaters and heat exchangers preheat feedstock in distillation towers and in refinery processes to reaction temperatures. Heat exchangers use either steam or hot hydrocarbon transferred from some other section of the process for heat input. The heaters are usually designed for specific process operations, and most are of cylindrical vertical or box-type designs. The major portion of heat provided to process units comes from fired heaters are fuelled by refinery or natural gas, distillate and residual oils. Fired heaters are found on crude and reformer pre-heaters, coker heaters, and large-column reboilers.

Cooling Operations: Heat also may be removed from some processes by air and water exchangers, fin fans, gas liquid coolers, and overhead condensers, or by transferring heat to other systems. The basic mechanical vapour-compression refrigeration system, which may serve one or more process units, includes an evaporator, compressor, condenser, controls, and piping common coolants are water, alcohol/water mixtures, or various glycol solutions.

Health and Safety Considerations

(a) Fire Protection and Prevention: A means of providing adequate draft or steam purging is required to reduce the chance of explosions when lighting fires in heater furnaces. Specific start-up and emergency procedures are required for each type of unit. If fire impinges on fin fans, failure could occur due to overheating. If flammable product escapes from heat exchanger due to a leak, fire could occur.

(b) Safety: Care must be taken to ensure that all pressure is removed from heater tubes before removing header or fitting plugs. Consideration should be given to providing for pressure relief in heat-exchanger piping systems in the event they are blocked off while full of liquid. If controls fail, variations of temperature and pressure could occur on either side of the heat exchanger. If heat exchanger tubes fail and process pressure is greater than heater pressure, product could enter the heater with downstream consequences. If the process pressure is less than heater pressure, the heater stream could enter into the process fluid. If loss of circulation occurs in liquid or gas coolers, increased product temperature could affect downstream operations and require pressure relief.

(c) Health: Because these are closed systems, exposures under normal operating conditions are expected to be mnimal. Depending on the fuel,

process operation, and unit design, there is a potential for exposure to hydrogen sulphide to hydrogen sulphide, carbon monoxide hydrocarbons, steam boiler feed-water-treatment chemicals. Skin contact should be avoided with boiler blowdown, which may contain phenolic compounds. Safe work practices and/or appropriate personal protective equipment against hazards may be needed may be needed during process maintenance, inspection, and turnaround activities and for protection from radiant heat superheated steam, hot hydrocarbon and noise exposures.

Steam Generation

Heater and Boiler Operations: Steam is generated in main generation plants, and/or at various units using heat flue gas or other sources. Heaters (furnaces) include burners and a combustion air system, the boiler enclosure in which heat transfer takes place, draft or pressure system to remove flue gas from the furnace, soot blowers, and compressed-air systems that seal openings to prevent the escape of flue gas. Boilers consist of a number of tubes that carry the water-steam mixture through the furnace for maximum heat transfer. These tubes run between steam-distribution drums at the top of the boiler and water-collecting drums at the bottom of the boiler. Steam flows from the steam drum to the superheater before entering the steam distribution system.

Heater Fuel

(*a*) Heaters may use any one or combinations of fuels including refinery gas, natural gas, fuel oil, and powdered coal. Refinery off-gas is collected from process units and combined with natural gas and LPG in a fuel-gas balance drum. The balance drum provides constant system pressure, fairly stable Btu-content fuel, and automatic separation of suspended liquids in gas vapours, and in prevents carryover of large slugs of condensate into the distribution system. Fuel oil is typically a mix of refinery crude oil with straight-run and cracked residues and other products. The fuel-oil system delivers fuel to process-unit heaters and steam generators at required temperatures and pressures. The fuel oil is heated to pumping temperature, sucked through a coarse suction strainer, pumped to a temperature-control heater, and then pumped through a fine-mesh strainer before being burned.

(*b*) In one example of process-unit heat generation, carbon monoxide boilers recover heat in catalytic units as carbon monoxide in flue gas is burned to complete combustion. In other processes, waste-heat recovery units use heat from the flue gas to make steam.

Steam Distribution: The distribution system consists of valves, fittings piping, and connections suitable for the pressure of the steam transported. Steam leaves the boilers at the highest pressure required by the process units or electrical generation. The steam pressure is then reduced in turbines that drive process pumps and compressors. Most steam used in the refinery is condensed to water in various types of heat exchangers. The condensate is reused as boiler feedwater or discharged to wastewater treatment. When refinery steam is also used to drive steam turbine generators to produce electricity, the steam must be produced at much higher pressure than required for process steam. Steam typically is generated by heaters (furnaces) and boilers combined in one unit.

Feedwater

(*a*) Feedwater supply is an important part of steam generation. There must always be as many pounds of water entering the system as there are pounds of steam leaving it. Water used in steam generation must ne free of contaminants including minerals and dissolved impurities that can damage the system or affect its operation. Suspended materials such as silt, sewage, and oil, which from scale and sludge, must be coagulated or filtered out of the water. Dissolved gases, particularly carbon dioxide and oxygen, cause boiler corrosion and are removed by deaeration and treatment. Dissolved minerals including metallic salts, calcium carbonates, etc., that cause scale, corrosion, and turbine blade deposites are treated with lime or soda ash to precipitate them from the water. Recirculated cooling water must also be treated for hydrocarbon and other contaminants.

(*b*) Depending on the characteristics of raw boiler feedwater, some or all of the following six stages of treatment wilt be applicable:

- Clarification;
- Sedimentation;
- Filtration;
- Ion exchange;
- Deaeration; and
- Internal treatment.

Health and Safety Considerations

(a) Fire Protection and Prevention: The most potentially hazardous operation in steam generation is heart startup. A flammable mixture of gas and air can build up as a result of loss of flame at one or more burners during light-off. Each type of unit requires specific startup and emergency procedures including purging before light off and in the event of misfire or loss of burner flame.

(b) Safety: If feedwater runs low and boilers are dry, the tubes will overheat and fail. Conversely, excess water will be carried over into the steam distribution system and damage the turbines. Feedwater must be free of contaminants that could affect operations. Boilers should have continuous or intermittent blowdown system to remove water from steam drums and limit buildup of scale on turbine blades and superheater tubes. Care must be taken not to overneat the superheater during startup and shut-down. Alternate fuel sources should be provided in the event of loss of gas due to refinery unit shutdown or emergency. Knockout pots provided at process units remove liquids from fuel gas before burning.

(c) Health: Safe work practices and/or appropriate personal protective equipment may be needed for potential exposures to feedwater chemicals, steam, hot water, radiant heat, and noise, and during process sampling, inspection, maintenance, and turnaround activities.

Pressure-Relief and Flare Systems

Pressure-Relief Systems: Pressure-relief control vapours and liquids that are released by pressure-relieving devices and blow-downs. Pressure relief is an automatic, planned release when operating pressure reaches a pre-determined level. Slowdown normally refers to the intentional release of material, such as blowdowns from process unit startups, furnace blowdowns, shutdowns, and emergencies. Vapour depressuring is the rapid removal of vapours from pressure vessels in case of fire. This may be accomplished by the use of a rupture disc, usually set at a higher pressure than the relief valve.

Safety Relief Valve Operations: Safety relief valves, used for air, steam, and gas as well as for vapour and liquid the valve to open in proportion to the increase in pressure over the normal operating pressure. Safety valves designed primarily to release high volumes of steam usually pop open to full capacity. The overpressure needed to open liquid-relief valves where large-volume discharge is not required increases as the valve lifts due to increased spring resistance. Pilot-operated safety relief valves, with up to six times the capacity of normal relief valves are used where tighter sealing and larger volume discharges are required. Non-volatile liquids are usually pumped to oil-water separation and recovery systems, and volatile liquids are sent to units operating at a lower pressure.

Flare Systems: A typical closed pressure release and flare system includes relief valves and lines from process units for collection of discharges, knockout drums to separate vapours and liquids, seals, and/or purge gas for flashback protection, and a flare and igniter system which combusts vapours when discharging directly to the atmosphere is not permitted. Steam may be injected into the flare tip to reduce visible smoke.

Pressure Relief Health and Safety Considerations

(a) Fire Protection and Prevention: Vapours and gases must not discharge where sources of ignition could be present.

(b) Safety: Liquids should not be discharged directly to a vapour disposal system. Flare knockout drums and flares to be large enough to handle

emergency blowdowns. Drums should be provided with relief in the event of over pressure. Pressure relief valves must be provided where the potential exists for overpressure in refinery processes due to the following causes: Loss of cooling water, which may greatly reduce pressure in condensers and increases the pressure in the process unit. Loss of reflux volume, which may cause a pressure drop in condensers and a pressure rise in distillation towers because the quantity of reflux affects the volume of vapours leaving the distillation tower.

Rapid vapourization and pressure increase from injection of a lower boiling-point liquid including water into a process vessel operating at higher temperatures. Expansion of vapour and resultant over-pressure due to overheated process steam, malfunctioning heaters, or fire. Failure of automatic controls outlets, heat exchanger failure, etc. Internal explosion, chemical reaction, thermal expansion, or accumulated gases. Maintenance is important because valves are required to function properly. The most common operating problems are listed below.

Failure to open at set pressure, because of plugging of the valve inlet or outlet, or because corrosion prevents proper operation of the disc holder and guides. Failure to reseat after popping open due to fouling, corrosion, or deposits on the seat or moving parts, or because solids in the gas stream have cut the valve disc. Chattering and premature opening, because operating pressure is too close to the set point.

(c) Health: Safe work practices and/or appropriate personal protective equipment may be needed to protect against hazards during inspection, maintenance, and turnaround activities.

Wastewater Treatment

Description

Wastewater treatment is used for process, runoff, and sewerage water prior to discharge or recycling. Wastewater typically contains hydrocarbons, dissolved materials, suspended solids, phenols, ammonia, sulphides, and other compounds. Wastewater includes condensed steam, stripping water, spent caustic solutions, cooling tower and boiler blowdown, wash, alkaline and acid waste neutralizations water, and other process-associated water.

Pre-treatment Operatrions: Pre-treatment is the separation of hydrocarbons and solids from wastewater. API separators, interceptor plates, and settling ponds remove suspended hydrocarbons, oily sludge, and solids by gravity separation, skimming, and filtration. Some oil-in-water emulsions must be heated to assist in separating the oil and water. Gravity separation depends on the specific gravity differences between water and immiscible oil globules oil globules and allows free oil to be skimmed off the surface of the wastewater. Acidic wastewater is neutralized using ammonia, lime, or soda ash. Alkaline wastewater is treated is treated with sulfuric acid hydrochloric acid, carbon dioxide-rich flue gas, or sulphur.

Secondary Treatment Operations: After pretreatment, suspended solids are removed by sedimentation or air flotation. Wastewater with low levels of solids may be screened or filtered. Flocculation agents are sometimes added to help separation. Secondary treatment processes biologically degrade and oxidize soluble organic matter by the use of activated sludge, unaerated or aerated lagoons, trickling filter methods, or anaerobic treatments. Materials with high adsorption characteristics are used in fixed-bed filters or added to the wastewater to from as slurry which is removed by sedimentation or filtration. Additional treatment methods are used to remove oils and chemicals from wastewater containing sulphides and/or ammonia, and solvent extraction is used to remove phenols.

Tertiary Treatment Operations: Tertiary treatments remove specific pollutants to meet regulatory discharge requirements. These treatments include chlorination, ozonation, ion exchange, reverse osmosis, actived carbon adsorption, etc. Compressed oxygen is diffused into wastewater streams to oxidize certain chemicals or to satisfy regulatory oxygen-content requirements. Wastewater that is to be recycle may require cooling to remove heat and/or oxidation by spraying or air stripping to remove any remaining phenols, nitrates, and ammonia.

Health and Safety Considerations

(a) Fire Protection and Prevention: The potential for fire exists if vapours from wastewater containing hydrocarbons hydrocarbons reach a source of ignition during treatment.

(b) Health: Safe work practices and/or appropriate persona protective equipment may be needed for exposures to chemicals and waste products during process sampling, inspection, maintenance, and turnaround activities as well as to noise, gases, and heat.

Cooling Towers

Description

Cooling towers remove heat from process water by evaporation and latent heat transfer between hot water and air. The two types of towers are crossflow and counterflow. Crossflow towers introduce the airflow at right angles to the water flow throughout the structure. In counterflow cooling towers, hot process water is pumped to the upper most plenum and allowed to fall through the tower. Numerous slats or spray nozzles located throughout the length of the tower disperse the water and help in cooling. Air enters at the tower bottom and flows upward against the water. When the fans or blowers are at the air inlet, the air is considered to be forced draft. Induced draft is when the fans are at the air outlet.

Cooling Water: Recirculated cooling water must be treated to remove impurities and dissolved hydrocarbons. Becauses the water is saturated with oxygen from being cooled with air, the chances for corrosion are increased. One means of corrosion prevention is the addition of a material to the cooling water that forms a protective film on pipes and other metal surfaces.

Health and Safety Considerations

(a) Fire Protection and Prevention: When cooling water is contaminated by hydrocarbons, flammable vapors can be evaporated into the discharge air. If a source of ignition is present, or if lightning occurs, a fire may start. A potential fire hazard also exists where there are relatively dry areas in induced-draft cooling towers of combustible construction.

(b) Safety: Loss of power to cooling tower fans or water pumps could have serious consequences in the refinery. Impurities in cooling water can corrde and foul pipes and heat exchangers, scale from dissolved salts can deposit on pipes, and wooden cooling towers can be damaged by micro organisms.

(c) Health: Cooling-tower water can be process materials and by-products including sulphur dioxide, hydrogen sulphide, and carbon dioxide, with resultant exposures. Safe work practices and/or appropriate personal protective equipment may be needed during process sampling, inspections, maintenance, and turnaround activities; and for exposure to hazards such as those related to noise, water-treatment chemicals, and hydrogen sulphide when wastewater is treated in conjunction with cooling towers.

Electrical Power

Description

Refineries may receive electricity from outside sources or produced their own power with generators driven by steam turbines or gas engines. Electrical substations receive power from the utility or power plant for distribution throughout the facility. They are usually located in non-classified areas, away from sources of vapor or cooling-tower water spray. Transformers, circuit breakers, and feed-circuit switches are usually located in substations feed power to distribution stations with in the process unit areas. Distribution stations can be located in classified areas, providing that classification requirements are met. Distribution stations usually have a liquid-filled transformer and an oil-filled or air-break disconnect device.

Health and Safety Considerations

(a) Fire Protection and Prevention: Generators that are not properly classified and are located too close to process units may be a source of ignition should a spill or release occur.

(b) Safety: Normal electrical safety precautions including dry footing, high-voltage warning signs, and guarding must be taken to protect against electrocution. Lockout/tagout and other appropriate safe work practices must be established to prevent energization while work is being performed on high-voltage electrical equipment.

(c) Health: Safe work practices and/or the use of appropriate personal protective equipment may be needed for exposures to noise, for exposure to hazards during inspection and maintenance activities, and when working around transformers and switches that may contain a dielectric fluid which requires special handling precautions.

Gas and Air Compressors

Description

Both reciprocating and centrifugal are used throughout the refinery for gas and compressed air. Air compressor systems include compressors, coolers, air receivers, air dryers, controls, and distribution piping. Blowers are used to provide air to certain processes. Plant air is provided for the operation of air-powered tools, catalyst regenerations, process heaters, steam-air decoking, sour-water oxidation, gasoline sweetening, asphalt blowing, and other uses. Instrument air is provided for use in pneumatic instruments and controls, air motors and purge connections.

Health and Safety Considerations

(a) Fire Protection and Prevention: Air compressors should be located so that the suction does not take in flammable vapours or corrosive gases. There is a potential for fire should a leak occur in gas compressors.

(b) Safety: Knockout drums are needed to prevent liquid surges from entering gas compressors. If gases are contaminated with solids materials, strainers are needed. Failure of automatic compressor controls will affect processes. If maximum pressure could potentially be greater than compressor or process-equipment design pressure, pressure relief should be provided. Guarding is needed for exposed moving parts on compressors. Compressor buildings should be properly electrically classified, and provisions should be made for proper ventilation.

Where plant air is used to back up instrument air, interconnections must be upstream of the instrument air drying system to prevent contamination of instruments with moisture. Alternate sources of instrument air supply, such as use of nitrogen, may be needed in the event of power outages or compressor failure.

(c) Health: Safe work practices and/or appropriate personal protective equipment may be needed for exposure such as during inspection and maintenance activities. The use of appropriate safeguards must be considered

so that plant and instrument air is not used for breathing or pressuring potable water systems.

Marine, Tank Car, and Tank Truck Loading and Unloading

Description

Facilities for loading liquid hydrocarbons into tank cars, tank trucks, and marine vessels and barges are usually part of the refinery operations. Product characteristics, distribution needs, shipping requirements, and operating criteria are important when designing loading facilities. Tank trucks and rail tank cars are either top or bottom-loaded, and vapour-recovery systems may be provided where required. Loading and unloading liquefied petroleum gas (LPG) require special considerations in addition to those for liquid hydrocarbons.

Health and Safety Considerations

(a) Fire Protection and Prevention: The potential for fire exists where flammable vapours from spills or releases can reach a source of ignition. Where switch-loading is permitted, safe practices need to be established and followed. Bonding is used to equalize the electrical charge between the loading rack and the tank truck or tank car. Grounding is used at truck and rail loading facilities to prevent flow of stray currents. Insulating flanges are used on marine dock piping connections to prevent static electricity buildup and discharge. Flame arrestors should be installed in loading rack and marine vapour-recovery lines to prevent flashback.

(b) Safety: Automatic or manual shutoff systems at supply headers are needed for top and bottom loading in the event of leaks or overfills. Fall protection such as railings are needed for top-loading racks where employees are exposed to falls. Drainage and recovery systems may be provided for storm drainage and to handle spills and leaks. Precautions must be taken at LPG loading facilities not to overload or over pressurize tank cars and trucks.

(c) Health: The nature of the health hazards at loading and unloading facilities depends upon the products being loaded and the product previously transported in the tank cars, tank trucks, or marine vessels. Safe work practices and/or appropriate personal protective equipment may be needed to protect against hazardous exposures when loading or unloading, cleaning up spills or leaks, or when gauging, inspecting, sampling, or performing maintenance activities on loading facilities or vapour-recovery systems.

Turbines

Description

Turbines are usually gas or steam-powered and are typically used to drive pumps, compressors, blowers, and other refinery process equipment. Steam enters turbines at high temperatures and pressures, expands across and drives rotating blades while directed by fixed blades.

Health and Safety Considerations

(a) Safety: Steam turbines used for exhaust operating under vacuum should have safety relief valves on the discharge side, both for protection and to maintain steam in the event of vacuum failure. Where maximum operating pressure could be greater than design pressure, steam turbines should be provided with relief devices.Consideration should be given to providing governors and over speed control devices on turbines.

(b) Health: Safe work practices and/or appropriate personal protective equipment may be needed for noise, steam and heat exposures, and during inspection and maintenance activities.

Pumps, Piping and Valves

Description

(*a*) Centrifugal and positive-displacement (*i.e.*, reciprocating) pumps are used to move hydrocarbons, process water, fire water,and wastewater through piping within the refinery. pumps are driven by electric motors, steam turbines, or internal combustion engines. The pump type, capacity, and construction materials depends on the service for which it is used.

(*b*) Process and utility piping distribute hydrocarbons, steam, water and other products throughout the facility. Their size and construction depend on the type of service, pressure, temperature, and nature of the products. Vent, drain, and sample connections are provided on piping, as well as provisions for blanking.

(*c*) Different types of valves are used depending on their operating purpose. These include gate valves, bypass valves, globe and ball valves, plug valves, block and check valves. Valves can be manually or automatically operated.

Health and Safety Considerations

(a) Fire Protection and Prevention: The potential for fire exists should hydrocarbon pumps, valves, or lines leaks that could allow vapors to reach sources of ignition. Remote sensors, control valves, fire valves, and isolation valves should be used to limit the release of hydrocarbons of hydrocarbons at pump suction lines in the event of leakage and/or fire.

(b) Safety: Depending on the product and service, backflow prevention from the discharge line may be needed. The failure of automatic pump controls could cause a deviation in process pressure and temperature. Pumps operated with reduced or no flow can overheat and rupture. Pressure relief in the discharge piping should be provided where pumps can be over pressured. Provisions may be made for pipeline expansion, movement, and temperature changes to avoid rupture. Valves and instruments that require servicing or other work should be accessible at grade level or from an operating platform. Operating vent and drain connections should be provided with double-block valves, a block valve and plug, or bling flange for protection against releases.

(c) Health: Safe work practices and/or appropriate personal protective equipment may be needed for exposure to hazards such as those related to liquids and vapours when opening or draining pumps, valves, and/or lines and during product sampling, inspection, and maintenance activities.

Tank Storage

Description

Atmospheric storage tanks and pressure storage tanks are used throughout the refinery for storage for storage of crudes, intermediate hydrocarbons (during the process), and finished products. Tanks are also provided for fire water, process and treatment water, acids, additives,and other chemicals. The type, construction, capacity and location of tanks depends on their use and materials stored.

Health and Safety Considerations

(a) Fire Protection and Prevention: The potential for fire exists should hydrocarbon storage tanks be overfilled or develop leaks that allow vapours to escape and reach sources of ignition. Remote sensors, control valves, isolation valves, and fire valves may be provided at tanks for pump-out or closure in the event of a fire in the tank or in the tank dike or storage area.

(b) Safety: Tanks may be provided with automatic overflow control and alarm systems, or manual gauging and checking procedures may be established to control overfills.

(c) Health: Safe work practices and/or appropriate personal protective equipment may be needed for exposure to hazards to related to product sampling, manual gauging, inspection, and maintenance activities including confined space entry where applicable.

9

Ethanol

Introduction

India imports nearly 70 per cent of its annual crude petroleum requirement, which is approximately 110 million tons. The prices are in the range of US$ 50-70 per barrel, and the expenditure on crude purchase is in the range of Rs. 1600 billion per year, impacting in a big way, the country's foreign exchange reserves.

The petroleum industry now looks very committed to the use of ethanol as fuel as it is expected to benefit sugarcane farmers as well as the oil industry in the long run. Ethanol (FUEL ETHANOL) can also be produced from wheat, corn, beet sweet sorghum etc. Ethanol is one of the best tools to fight vehicular pollution contains 35 per cent oxygen that helps complete combustion of fuel and thus reduces harmful tailpipe emissions. It also reduces particulate emissions that pose health hazard.

Ethanol (ethyl alcohol, grain alcohol, ETOH) is a clear, colourless liquid with a characteristic, agreeable odour. In dilute aqueous solution, it has a somewhat sweet flavour, but in more concentrated solutions it has a burning taste. Ethanol, CH_3CH_2OH, is an alcohol, a group of chemical compounds whose molecules contain, a hydroxyl group, –OH, bonded to a carbon atom. The word alcohol derives from Arabic al-kuhul, which denotes a fine powder of antimony produced by distilling antimony and used as an eye makeup. Alcohol originally referred to any fine powder, but mediaeval alchemists later applied the term to the refined products of distillation, and this led to the current usage.

Ethanol melts at –114.1°C, boils at 78.5°C, and has a density of 0.789 g/mL at 20°C. Its low freezing point has made it useful as the fluid in thermometers for temperatures below–40°C, the freezing point of mercury, and for other low-temperature purposes, such as for anti-freeze in automobile radiators.

Ethanol has been made since ancient times by the fermentation of sugars. ethanol and more than half of industrial ethanol is still made by this process. Simple sugars are the raw material. Zymase, an enzyme from yeast, changes the simple sugar: into ethanol and carbon dioxide. The fermentation reaction, represented by the simple equation $C_6H_{12}O_6$ $2CH_3CH_2OH + 2\ CO_2$ is actually very complex, and impure cultures of yeast produce varying amounts of other substances, including glycerine and various organic acids. In the production of beverages, such as whiskey and brandy, the impurities supply the flavour. Starches from potatoes, corn, wheat, and other plants can also be used in the production of ethanol by fermentation. However, the starches must first be broken down into simple sugars. An enzyme released by germinating barley, diastase, converts starches into sugars. Thus, the germination of barley, called malting, is the first step in brewing beer from starchy plants, such as corn and wheat.

Ethanol as a Fuel

Ethanol is used as an automotive fuel by itself and can be mixed with gasoline to form what has been called 'gasohol' Fuel Ethanol—the most common blends contain 10 per cent ethanol and 85 per cent ethanol mixed with gasoline. Because the ethanol molecule contains oxygen, it allows the engine to more completely combust the fuel, resulting in fewer emissions. Since ethanol is produced from plants that harness the power of the sun, ethanol is also considered a renewable fuel. Therefore, ethanol has many advantages as an automotive fuel.

Most industrial ethanol is denatured to prevent its use as a beverage. Denatured ethanol contains small amounts, one or two per cent each, of several different unpleasant or poisonous substances. The removal of all these substances would involve a series of treatments more expensive than the federal excise tax on alcoholic beverages. These denaturants render ethanol unfit for some industrial uses. In such industries undenatured ethanol is used under close federal supervision.

India is initiating the use of ethanol as an automotive fuel. A move has been made by distilleries in India to use surplus alcohol as a blending agent or an oxygenate in gasoline. Based on experiments by the Indian Institute of Petroleum, a 10 per cent ethanol blend with gasoline and a 15 per cent ethanol blend with diesel are being considered for use in vehicles.in at least one state.

To address global warming concerns, the amount of carbon dioxide produced while burning fossil fuels must be reduced. Ethanol-blended gasoline and ethanol-blended diesel are being considered as viable alternatives to further lower emission levels.

Alcohol Specifications India
Indian Standard 321 of 1964
Requirements for Absolute (Anhydrous) Alcohol

S. No.	Particulars	Special Grade	Grade 1	Grade 2	Test-method*
1.	Ethanol content, per cent by volume at 15.6°C:	99.50	99.50	99.50	C**
2.	Miscibillty with water:	Miscible	Miscible	Miscible	D
3.	Alkalinity:	Nil	Nil	Nil	E
4.	Acidity, as acetic acid, per cent by weight, maximum:	0.006 (60 ppm)	0.006 (60 ppm)	0.006 (60 ppm)	E
5.	Residue on evaporation, per cent by weight, maximum:	0.005 (50 ppm)	0.005 (50 ppm)	0.005 (50 ppm)	F
6.	Aldehydes, as acetaldehyde, g/100 ml, maximum:	0.10 (1000 ppm)	0:006 (60 ppm) ppm)	0.10 (1000	G
7.	Esters, as ethyl acetate, g/100 ml, maximum:	0.02 (200 ppm)	—	—	H
8.	Copper, as Cu, g/100 ml, maximum:	—	0,0004 (4 ppm)	—	J
9.	Lead, as Pb, g/100 ml, maximum	—	0.0001 (1 ppm)	—	K
10.	Methyl alcohol:	— test.	To satisfy	—	L
11.	Fusel oil:	— test.	To satisfy	—	M
12.	Ketones, isoproply alcohol and tertiary butyl alcohol	—	To satisfy test.	—	A***
13.	Total sulphur and sulphur compounds, as S, per cent by weight, maximum	0.001 (10 ppm)	—	—	P
14.	Sulphur dioxide, as SO_2, per cent by weight, maximum	0.0005 (0.5 ppm)	—	—	Q

* For test methods, reference should be made to the appendix of the Indian Standard 323 of 1959 for rectified spirit (with the exception of item marked ***, as noted below).

** Test method C should be used; with the modification that Table II in Appendix B of this standard should be used in place of Table IV of Indian Standard 323 of 1959.

*** Reference should be made to test method A in the Appendix of this standard.

Ethanol World-wide

Other countries are either producing and using ethanol in large quantities or are providing incentives to expand ethanol production and use. Brazil and Sweden are using large quantities of ethanol as a fuel. Some Canadian provinces promote ethanol use as a fuel by offering subsidies of up to 45 cents per gallon of ethanol.

India is initiating the use of ethanol as an automotive fuel. A move has been made by distilleries in India to use surplus alcohol as a blending agent or an oxygenate in gasoline. Based on experiments by the Indian Institute of Petroleum, a 10 per cent ethanol blend with gasoline and a 15 per cent ethanol blend with diesel are being considered for use in vehicles in at least one state.

In France, ethanol is produced from grapes that are of insufficient quality for wine production. Prompted by the increase in oil prices in the 1970s, Brazil introduced a programme to produce ethanol for use in automobiles in order to reduce oil imports. Brazilian ethanol is made mainly from sugar cane. Pure ethanol (100% ethanol) is used in approximately 40 per cent of the cars in Brazil. The remaining vehicles use blends of 24 per cent ethanol with 76 per cent gasoline. Brazil consumes nearly 4 billion gallons of ethanol annually. In addition to consumption, Brazil also exports ethanol to other countries.

Sweden has used ethanol in chemical production for many years. As a result, Sweden's crude oil consumption has been cut in half since 1980. During the same time period, the use of gasoline and diesel for transportation has also increased. Emissions have been reduced by placing catalytic converters in vehicle exhaust systems which decrease carbon monoxide, hydrocarbon, and nitrogen oxide emissions. To address global warming concerns, the amount of carbon dioxide produced while burning fossil fuels must be reduced. Ethanol-blended gasoline and ethanol-blended diesel are being considered as viable alternatives to further lower emission levels.

The Gazette of India: Extraordinary [Part I—Sec. I] Ministry of Petroleum and Natural Gas Resolution New Delhi, 3rd September, 2002 No. P-45018/28/2000-C.C.

With a view to give boost to agriculture sector and reduce environmental pollution, Government of India have been examining for quite some time supply of ethanol-doped-petrol in the country. In order to ascertain financial and operational aspects of blending five per cent ethanol with petrol as allowed in the specifications of Bureau of Indian Standards for petrol. Government had launched three pilot projects; two in Maharashtra and one in Uttar Pradesh during April and June 2001 and these pilot projects have been supplying five per cent ethanol-doped-petrol only to the retail outlets under their respective supply areas since than. Apart from the aforesaid field through pilot projects, R & D studies also were undertaken simultaneously. Both pilot projects and R & D studies have been successful and established blending of ethanol up to five per cent with petrol and usage of ethanol-doped-petrol in vehicles.

Discussions were held with concerned agencies including the Governments of major sugar producing States. While the Society for Indian

Automobile Manufacturers (SIAM) has confirmed the acceptance for use of five per cent ethanol-doped-petrol in vehicles. State Governments of major sugar producjng States and the representatives of sugar/distillery industries have confirmed availability/capacity to produce ethanol. Government have set up an Expert Group headed by the Executive Director of the Centre for High Technology for examining various options of blending ethanol with petrol including use of ETBE in refineries. Considering the logistical and financial advantages, this Group has recommended blending of ethanol with petrol at supply locations (terminals/depots) of oil companies. In view of the above, Government have now resolved that with effect from 1-1-2003, five per cent ethanol-doped-petrol will be supplied in the following nine States and Four contiguous Union Territories:

States: 1. Andhra Pradesh; 2. Goa; 3. Gujrat; 4. Haryana; 5. Karnataka; 6. Maharashtra; 7. Punjab; 8. Tamilnadu; 9. Uttar Pradesh.

Union Territories: 1. Damman and Diu; 2. Dadra and Nagar Haveli; 3. Chandigarh; 4. Pondicherry.

Process-of-manufacture

Absolute alcohol is an important product required by industry. As per IS Specification it is nearly 100 per cent pure/water free alcohol, Alcohol as manufactured is rectified spirit, which is 94.68 per cent alcohol, and rest is water. It is not possible to remove remaining water from rectified spirit by straight distillation as ethyl alcohol forms a constant boiling mixture with water at this concentration and is known as azeotrope. Therefore, special, process for removal of water is required for manufacture of absolute alcohol. In order to extract water from alcohol it is necessary to use some dehydrate, which is capable of separating, water from alcohol. Simple dehydrate is unslacked lime, Industrial alcohol is taken in a reactor and quick lime is added to that and the mixture is left over night for complete reaction. It is then distilled in fractionating column to get absolute alcohol. Water is retained by quick lime. This process is used for small-scale production of absolute alcohol by batch process.

The process used for dehydration of alcohol using *molecular sieves* is as follows:

Molecular-sieve-dehydration

The salient features of the process are given herewith:

I. Dehydration-with-Molecular-Sieve-Process

The rectified spirit from the rectifier is superheated with steam in feed super-heater. Super-heated rectified spirit from feed super-heater is passed to one of the pair of molecular sieve beds for several minutes. On a timed basis, the flows of superheated rectified spirit vapour is switched to the alternate bed of the pair. A portion of the anhydrous ethanol vapour leaving the fresh adsorption bed is used to regenerate the loaded bed. A moderate vacuum is applied by vacuum pump operating after condensation of the regenerated ethanol water mixture. This condensate is transferred from recycle drum to the Rectified Column in the hydrous distillation plant via Recycle pump. The net make of anhydrous Absolute alcohol draw is condensed in product condenser and passed to product storage. The life of molecular sieve may be around five to seven years. However, the operating cost is considerably less than *azeotropic distillation*.

Molecular Sieve Ethanol Dehydration Technology for Fuel Ethanol

Most of the ethanol dehydration plants for production of absolute alcohol are based on Azeotropic distillation. It is a mature and reliable technology capable of producing a very dry product. However, its high capital cost, energy consumption, reliance on toxic chemicals like benzene and sensitivity to feedstock impurities, has virtually eliminated the use of azeotropic distillation in modern ethanol plants. Benzene has been used as entrainer of' choice of ethanol dehydration but it is now known to be a powerful carcinogen.

Advantages of Molecular Sieve technology for ethanol dehydration are as follows:

1. The basic process is very simple, making it easy to automate which reduces Labour and training requirements;
2. The process is inert. Since no chemicals are used, there are no material handling or liability problems, which might endanger workers;
3. Molecular sieves can easily process ethanol-containing contaminants, which would cause immediate upset in an azeotropic distillation system;

   In addition to ethanol, a properly designed sieve can dehydrate a wide variety of other chemicals, thereby providing added flexibility in future operating options;
4. The molecular sieve desiccant material has a very long potential service life, with failure occurring only due to fouling of the media or by mechanical destruction. A properly designed system should exhibit a desiccant service life in excess of 5 years;
5. It can be configured to function as a stand-alone system or to be integrated with the distillation system. This lets the customer make the trade-off between maximum operating flexibility versus maximum energy efficiency;
6. If fully integrated with the distillation system, steam consumption rate only slightly above the absolute theoretical minimum for the separation can be achieved; and

7. A properly designed molecular sieve can reliably dehydrate 160-proof ethanol to 190 + proof, making strict control of rectifier overhead product-quality-unnecessary.

Process-description

From Feed Tank, rectified spirit is pumped to the Stripper/Rectifier Column. A partial steam of vapours from the Column are condensed in Condenser and sent back to the column as reflux. Rest of the vapours are passed through a super-heater and taken to the Molecular Sieve units for dehydration. The vapour passes through a bed of molecular sieve beads and water in the incoming vapour stream is adsorbed on the molecular sieve material and anhydrous ethanol vapour exists from the Mol. Sieve Unit. Hot anhydrous ethanol vapour from the Mol. Sieve Units is condensed in the Mol. Sieve Condenser. The anhydrous ethanol product is then further cooled down in the product cooler, to bring it close to the ambient temperature. The two Mol, Sieve units operate sequentially and are cycled so that one is under regeneration while the other is under operation, adsorbing water from the vapour stream. The regeneration is accomplished by applying vacuum to the bed undergoing regeneration. The adsorbed from the molecular sieves material desorbs and evaporates into the ethanol vapour stream. This mixture of ethanol and water is condensed and cooled against cooling tower water in the Mol. Sieves Regenerant Condenser. Any uncondensed vapour and entrained liquid leaving the Mol. Sieve Regenerant Condenser enters the Mol. Sieve Regenerant Drum, where it is contacted with cooled regenerant liquid.

The cooled regenerant liquid is weak in ethanpl concentration, as it contains all the water desorbed from the Molecular Sieve Beds. This low strength liquid is recycled back to the Stripper Column for recovering the ethanol. The water leaves from the bottom of the column and contains only traces of alcohol.

Advantages of the System (Molecular Sieves)

- Minimal Labour
- Stable operation
- Near theoretical recovery
- Steam consumption minimized by multi-stage preheating to permit substantial heat recovery and reuse.
- An advanced control system, developed through years of experience, to provide sustained, stable, automatic operation.

Demand Supply for Ethanol

The Center's 'Gasohol Programme'of blending 5 per cent ethanol in petrol has given an assured scope for ethanol industry in the country. The Centre's Kisan-friendly imitative has definitely been a boost to the venture. Following statistics could show how there is definite market potential for such industry.

Petrol Consumption

10000000	kilo Litres
500000	kilo Litres — 5% alcohol required
500000000	Ltrs.

Demand All Over Country	5000	Lac litres
Existing Production	1840	Lac litres
Total demand	2460	Lac litres
Demand in Maharashtra	700	Lac litres

Source: *The information is taken from document published by Government of India, Ministry of Petroleum and Natural Gas.*

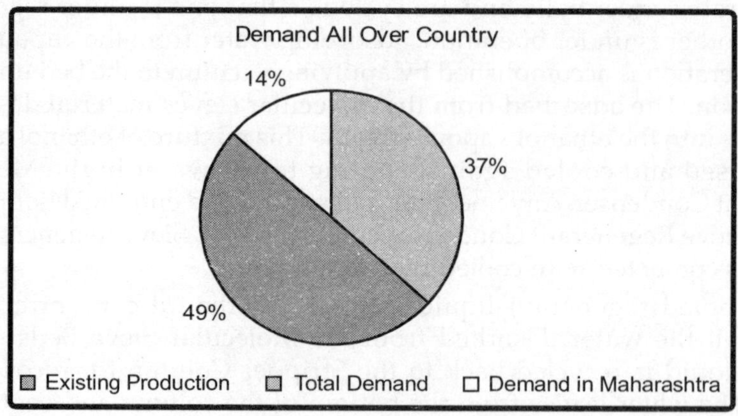

In parts of 4 states of Andhra Pradesh, Maharashtra, Punjab, Uttar Pradesh and Goa five per cent of ethanol blended petrol has already been started and till 30th June 2003, it will be fully covered. Gujarat, Haryana, Karnataka, Tamilnadu and the Union Territories of Chandigarh, Dadra and Nagar Haveli, Daman and Diu and Pondicherry are also covered till the end of July 2003.

The entire country will be covered in 2nd Phase and ethanol content to be increased to 10 per cent in 3rd Phase.

Most important R & D Studies are successful of blending ethanol with Diesel, which itself is a very significant point in developing ethanol.

All this significance shows a definite assured market for the industry leading the project to most viable and safe for financial assistance.

Anhydrous Ethanol Potential for Gasoline Blending

The statistics published by the Ministry of Petroleum the potential is as follows:

For five per cent Blend in Gasoline

Requirement on all India Basis — 500 million litres. per annum

Requirement in 8 States — 300 million litres. per annum

Requirement in UP and Maharashtra — 40 and 70 million litres. per annum respectively.

This statistics show a direct potential.

Source: *The information is taken from document published by Government of India, Ministry of Petroleum and Natural Gas.*

Due to government promoting ethanol to mix in petrol there is drastic demand for ethanol, which could overcome the existing unutilized capacity and thus creating an excess demand.

Now, Government of India has approved 10 per cent of Ethanol in petrol for which same has been incorporated in IS 2796 : 2008 specification. If it is introduced, India will promote the industry of sugar and in turn we can control some percentage of environmental problems.

A Sugar Industry Perspective and Ethanol Production

India is the largest producer of sugar in the world. In terms of sugarcane production, India and Brazil are almost equally placed. In Brazil, out of the total cane available for crushing, 45 per cent goes for sugar production and 55 per cent for the production of ethanol directly from sugarcane juice. This gives the sugar industry in Brazil an additional flexibility to adjust its sugar production keeping in view the sugar price in the international market as nearly 40 per cent of the sugar output is exported.

The annual projected growth rate in the area under sugarcane at 1.5 per cent per annum has doubled during the last five years. This is because it is considered to be an assured cash crop with good returns to the farmers *vis-a-vis* other competing crops.

India is currently passing through a glut situation with closing stocks at the end of the year of over 100 lakh tons since 1999-2000. Correspondingly, molasses production has also increased. The table below gives the production of molasses, alcohol utilization by the alcohol-based chemical industry, potable sector and the surplus at the end of each year. It is therefore evident that along with sugarcane production, phenomenal growth is also taking place in the production of molasses, the basic raw material for the production of ethanol from sugarcane. Of course, there are also other agro routes available to produce ethanol.

According to MPNG, five per cent ethanol blends on an all-India basis would require 500 million litres. The current availability of molasses and alcohol would be adequate to meet this requirement after fully meeting the requirement of the chemical industry and potable sectors.

Availability

In the absence of a well knit policy in the past for purchasing and blending ethanoi, not many distilleries have been producing ethanol. Only three distilleries attached to sugar mills had war years' experience, and were able to gear themselves up to supply ethanol immediately. Now, about 11 factories in Uttar Pradesh will be adding facilities to produce about 75 million litres of anhydrous alcohol by end-September; seven units in Tamil Nadu (production capacity of 62.5 million liters of anhydrous alcohol); eight in Karnataka (anhydrous alcohol production capacity of 66.5 million litres); and four units in Andhra Pradesh (capacity of over 40 million litres). Similar steps have also betaken up by the cooperative sector units in Maharashtra, Punjab and UP. By the end of the year it is estimated that about 300 million litres capacity would have been created for the production of anhydrous alcohol.

As capacities are built up, the oil sector should also be able to generate that much demand for ethanol to guard against any idling capacity. The Petroleum Ministry may therefore like to look into this matter and ensure that the oil sector speeds up the creation of requisite facilities for blending ethanol with petrol. So far generation of demand for ethanol has been very low and it takes considerable time for IOC's units to finalize purchase of ethanol against offers made by distilleries in response to their tenders.

In the Indian Sugar Mill Association, this matter was recently examined and it was concluded that instead of taking up the scheme on a state-wise basis, it would be appropriate to take it up in metropolitan and other cities where environmental pollution is a major concern. The blending should be taken up to 10 per cent and introduced selectively to make a better impact on the environment, as no changes in the engine or carburetor are required, and other countries are already carrying this out successfully.

Cost

There is considerable scope for further reduction in the cost of production of both sugarcane and sugar in India with liberalization of controls on the sugar industry. Consolidation of land holdings and corporate farming on the raw material side and expansion of capacity on the unit size are important developments and would lead to substantial improvements in productivity, thereby rendering India a cost-effective producer of sugar in the world.

The area under sugarcane is presently less than two per cent of total cultivable area in the country and about three per cent of the irrigated area. There is considerable scope for increasing the area under sugarcane considering the fact that it is more profitable compared to other crops. The Planning Commission has visualized a conservative increase in area under sugarcane by six lakh hectares during the 10th Plan period, but considering past trends, the area under cane is likely to exceed five million hectares.

During the 10th Plan period, the annual incremental growth in consumption has been estimated at nine lakh tons per annum. For the first time the Indian Government has fixed a target of 15 lakh tons per annum for export for this period. However, the production target was fixed at 21.3 million tons keeping in view the large carry forward stocks at the beginning of the period and to correct the demand-supply distortions presently caused. These targets are achievable looking at the performance of the industry in the past with a production of 18.5 million tons achieved in 2000-01.

Conclusion

In conclusion, the sugar industry will not be lacking in meeting the requirement of ethanol. In a market economy, there, would be a considerable shift from the gur and khandsari sectors which are inefficient producers with poor quality. In the current scenario of glut in sugar production, it may be advisable to divert such additional cane for the production of alcohol after meeting the sweetener requirement. The additional availability of alcohol on the assumption that the entire cane is utilized for the production of sweeteners will be about 200 million litres over and above that indicated in the table. Alternatively, if additional cane available is utilized for the production of alcohol to bring in a balance in the demand and supply of sugar, the alcohol production at the end of the 10th Plan would be around 1,485 million litres.

Such a flexibility has become very relevant in the current scenario of economy liberalization and more particularly as a means to correct the aberrations in sugar production.

Alcohol Production

(in million litres)

Alcohol Year	Molasses Prod.	Production of Alcohol	Industrial Use	Potable Use	Other Uses	Surplus Availability
1998-99	7.00	1411.8	534.4	584.0	55.2	238.2
1999-00	8.02	1654.0	518.9	622.7	57.6	455.8
2000-01	8.33	1685.9	529.3	635.1	58.8	462.7
2001-02	8,77	1775.2	539.8	647.8	59.9	527.7
2002-03	9.23	1869.7	550.5	660.7	61.0	597.5
2003-04	9.73	1969.2	578.0	693.7	70.0	627.5
2004-05	10.24	2074.5	606.9	728.3	73.5	665.8
2005-06	10.79	2187.0	619.0	746.5	77.2	742.3
2006-07	11.36	2300.4	631.4	765.2	81.0	822.8

The task force on the sugar industry for the Tenth Five Year Plan has suggested the evolution of a national policy on alternative fuels, which would include the use of ethanol-blended gasoline.

Until such a policy is evolved, sugar factories and distifleries should be encouraged to produce ethanol from the surplus alcohol available with them, a report of the task force says. For this, it suggests providing loans from the Sugar Development Fund at six per cent per annum for up to 60 per cent of the project cost.

The ministry of petroleum and natural gas and the oil companies, in consultation with the department of food and public distribution, the All-India Distilleries Association and the apex bodies of the sugar industry/can set a reasonable price for ethanol produced by distilleries for the purpose of blending with gasoline.

There is a need to compare ethanol prices with other oxygenates-cum-octane boosters such as MTBE, and not with gasoline, the report states. As an oxygenate, ethanol contains oxygen, which naturally reduces its calorific value but improves the combustion efficiency and significantly reduces air pollution.

Considering the environment-friendly characteristics of ethanol-blended gasoline as an automobile fuel, the pricing of ethanol needs to be viewed not only in terms of a financial cost-benefit analysis, but also in terms of an economic cost-benefit analysis, the report adds.

In Brazil 20-24 per cent of ethanol is blended in gasoline. In the US, 10 per cent of ethanol, produced mainly from maize, is blended with gasoline.

There has been a steady increase in the production of alcohol in India, with the estimated production rising from 887.2 million litres in 1992-93 to nearly 1,654 million litres in 1999-2000. Surplus alcohol leads to depressed prices for both alcohol and molasses.

According to the task force, the projected alcohol production in the country will increase from 1869.7 million litres in 2002-03 to 2,300.4 million litres in 2006-07. Thus the surplus alcohol available in the country is expected to go up from 527.7 million litres in 2002-03 to 822.8 million litres in 2006-07.

Utilization of molasses for the production of ethanol in India will not only provide value-addition to the byproduct, it can also ensure better price stability and price realization of molasses for the sugar mills. This will improve the viability of the sugar mills, which will in turn benefit cane growers.

With gasoline demand expected to increase from 7.9 million tones in 2001-02 to 11.6 million tones in 2006-07, the requirement of ethanol at five per cent blending is expected to rise from 465 million litres to 682 million litres.

Petroleum is one of the most precious natural energy resources. With India growing at a fast pace, the demand for oil is set to rise. India and China will account for 45 per cent of the increase in global primary energy demand by 2030.

India has become a significant consumer of energy resources. Its oil consumption has risen to 3.3 million barrels per day in 2009, from 643,000 barrels of oil per day in 1980, making it the world's fourth biggest consumer of oil.

India is also the fourth largest producer of ethanol in the world. Ethanol production in India has an advantage as its production could potentially leave sugar prices unaffected. By blending petrol with 10 per cent biofuel, 80 million litres of petrol could be saved annually in India, says a report by the Institute of Defence Studies and Analyses.

In India, ethanol made its foray into the transport sector as a fuel additive in 2001. The government launched three EBP pilot projects/the first in Uttar Pradesh, followed by two others in Maharashtra.

In order to enhance the country's energy security, the Government of India mandated blending of five per cent ethanol with petrol in 9 States and 4 Union Territories in the year 2003 and subsequently mandated five per cent blending of ethanol with petrol in 20 States and 8 Union Territories in November 2006 on an all-India basis except a few North East states and Jammu and Kashmir.

The programme was a significant step in utilising alternative, renewable and environment-friendly sources of energy like ethanol to supplement fossil fuels.

The sugar industry agreed to all the terms of the oil marketing companies (OMCs), which include agreeing to a fixed price for three years and has also demonstrated adequate availability of ethanol to increase the blending proportion to 10 per cent.

Despite the group of ministers (GoM) headed by the finance minister endorsing a price of Rs. 27 per litre in April 2010, the programme continues to hang fire.

Why Ethanol Blended Petrol

The EBP programme is primarily based on indigenously produced ethanol from sugarcane molasses, which, besides augmenting fuel availability in the country, would also provide better returns for sugarcane farmers.

Further, ethanol is environment-friendly as it enhances combustion of petrol, resulting in lower emission of pollutants.

With reduced dependence on crude oil consumers can pay less for petrol and enjoy the benefits of a clean and healthy environment.

Ethanol is an organic solvent, similar in properties to the hundreds of other components of petroleum-derived gasoline. Yet, there is a big difference: ethanol burns cleaner itself, and also it burns more completely the petrol it is blended into.

Ethanol can be made from natural resources, organic liquids or coal beside grains, cassava etc. but the sources that are most common, cheaper and also renewable are natural raw materials such as sugarcane juice or molasses.

This is because the raw material will be remade in exactly the same way during the following crop cycle. This is a result of the action of photosynthesis upon the carbon dioxide.

In India, ethanol is mainly derived by sugarcane molasses, which is a by-product in the conversion of sugarcane to sugar. Therefore, ethanol does not compromise on the food security front.

The government's EBP programme would lead to better returns for sugar cane farmers and therefore better sugarcane and sugar production.

In India, ethanol production does not take away land from food crops. Ethanol production = Higher cane price = Rural prosperity.

Ethanol and Your Car

Engine performance and total emissions are both improved by the addition of ethanol to petrol.

Another performance benefit from ethanol is its high octane addition to fuel. Of all the commercially viable octane boosters possible, nothing delivers more punch than ethanol. The populace still feels the ill effects of the tonnes of poisonous lead that are spewed into urban environments because of the poor decision to accept lead over ethanol as the octane additive of choice.

Other benefits due to ethanol in cars are technical in nature, but may be summarised as follows:

1. Cleans engine overtime, especially harmful combustion chamber deposits;
2. Improved front end volatility for better cold start and improved operation (driveability and distillation curve effects);
3. Dissolves any fuel line and fuel tank water, which are sources of corrosion, and eliminates them out through the exhaust;
4. The higher octane of the ethanol blend allows the new cars with higher compression ratio to run smoothly without any change in engines;

Blending ethanol up to 10 per cent has technical benefits without impacting on engine performance and fuel efficiency in cars.

Exhaust *versus* Evaporative Emissions

Adding ethanol to regular unleaded petrol at 10 per cent is an easy way to make unleaded premium, and it extends supplies by 10 per cent.

Without any modification of the base petrol, however, the vapour pressure of the fuel will increase slightly, leading to more evaporative, or fugitive emissions. These are primarily vapours that escape the carbon canister on the automobile, or are forced into the air as the level in a fuel tank rises. They do not include fuel spills, because normally the entire volume of a gasoline spill will evaporate in any case.

The question is whether this greater evaporative mass gives rise to greater pollution potential than the large benefit of exhaust emissions reduction.

In the view of some fuel scientists the nature of the chemical make-up of this new vapour space is less harmful that the unblended, but lower pressure, base gasoline has. Ethanol itself, for example, which is now part of the vapour, has a lower ozone-forming potential than olefins and aromatics.

Adding ethanol to regular unleaded extends supplies to the extent of blending and lowers risks of ozone formation.

Ethanol and Health

After years of ethanol use in once-polluted major cities in the United States, Europe and Brazil, the air is demonstrably cleaner and within federal guidelines for a healthy lifestyle.

Not only are toxic species reduced, such as carbon monoxide and aromatics, but also the potential to produce ground level ozone is lower because the elements necessary for its production have been greatly lessened, in particular, high octane benzene, known to cause leukaemia, can be nearly eliminated because ethanol can provide the octane it once did.

The benefit to citizens of urban airsheds is enormous. Cleaner air means healthier people, especially those that suffer from respiratory diseases. Mortality rates will improve, health care visits will decrease in number and severity, healthcare costs and insurance rates will benefit, and productivity will improve as absenteeism and performance is improved.

Advantages of Ethanol Fuel

Ethanol Fuel is a type of Alternative fuel to put back the traditional fuels as a step taken to protect the environment and we are going to discuss *ethanol fuel advantages,* there are many advantages to adopt Ethanol as a fuel.

Ethanol Fuel as Organic Fuel

The origin of *Ethanol fuel* is organic and therefore known as bio-fuel, It is produced directly and Indirectly from crop. It is obtained directly from corn, sugarcane and grains and indirectly from paper waste. By the process of fermentation these things are converted into Ethanol.

Ethanol Fuel as a Source of Renewable Energy

A very important point regarding Ethanol is that it is a renewable source of energy. In present scenario renewable source of energies are in demand so is the case with Ethanol As the demand is increasing so is the Ethanol production.

Ethanol Fuel Ease of Access

Ethanol is a bio-fuel and is/present in large/quantities therefore easily accessible, Ethanol Fuel is a renewable source of energy and has the capacity to be available in future. As corn is the staple food so it is cultivated in many countries as a source for fuel. You need not to bother about its consumption.

Ethanol Fuel Advantage of Independency

A big harvest of corn or other *bio mass* is a great source of fuel to replace the fossil fuel. This gives independency of personal fuel needs. There remains no need to import fuels from other countries. In this way a large amount is saved for the better consumption.

Ethanol Fuel Advantage of Employability

When the production of Ethanol is increased it has also provided the opportunity of employment. Employability is directly proportional to the cultivation of *Ethanol source.*

Ethanol Fuel is Cost-effective

As every country has the capacity to produce, bio-fuel therefore it is not expensive. As compared to the fossil fuels, ethanol fuel is quite economic. Fossil fuel which is imported from other countries to meet the demands, plays havoc upon the economy. It is better to harvest a big crop of ethanol which would not only be cost-effective individually but also save the revenue.

Ethanol Fuel Reduces GHG Gases

The biggest *advantage of Ethanol Fuel*, is that it does not increase the pollution level. Burning Ethanol Fuel in vehicle produces less toxic effects in the environment. Ethanot. is prepared as a fuel by adding Ethanol and gasoline in the proportion of 85/15. This less amount of gasoline does the work of igniter and then; Ethanol performs the rest of function. This proportion reduces the amount of GHG gases in environment as it burns cleaner as compared to gasoline.

Ethanol Fuel is Environment Friendly

Damaging Ozone layer has been becoming a global issue as it is destroying the environment for the healthy survival of living beings on earth. Now the world is standing at the orifice of destruction. Advantage of Using *Ethanol* fueling system acts as a souvenir to the earth a little bit we must shake hand with.

Ethanol Fuel Promotes Agriculture

For the production of *Ethanol Fuel* there is needed to increase the agriculture revenue. Such step taken by the government will really work as a booster for the agriculture to set a base for self sufficient fueling reservoirs.

Ethanol Fuel is Hydrogen Producer

Ethanol Fuel itself works as a fuel. Researchers are busy carrying out to make it a better fuel removing all its side effects to make it an efficient energy source. Still there are some disadvantages come in front while using Ethanol as a fuel. Although it burn cleaner yet it starts corrosion very soon in the engine. To use it in a better and productive way scientists are thinking to convert it in hydrogen form which is an alternative source of fuel. It is considered to be more effective way of using Ethanol in the form of hydrogen fuel.

Ethanol Challenges in a Current Scenario and Technical Tips

Today ethanol one of the renewable fuel, has been considered a blend component for gasoline in an automobile industry without effecting the performance of engine. As per Government regulatory, the use of ethanol as a gasoline blend component has been incorporated in IS Specification. First time in India, ethanol blend petrol is being marketed by oil companies and stored at their supply point. Due to scarcity of ethanol, it is not fully used properly for which Government's interference is required to take care of environmental problems.

With the growth the production and demand of ethanol in near future come increased challenges. Suppliers and markets joining the biofuel marketplace for the first time are facing these associated complexities, but they can benefit from the experience gathered by others.

What are the Key Issues Related to E10 Ethanol Use?

Ethanol is often blended into gasoline at low levels ranging from 3 per cent to 10 per cent. An ethanol level of 10 per cent is used in many/markets and widely known as E10. Ethanol differs from gasoline in some key properties and all low ethanol blends present unique and significant challenges. These challenges are as various as they are complex, and producers and blenders must overcome these obstacles in order to be successful in the market.

E10 Performance Issues Fuel Properties

Ethanol differs from gasoline in some specific properties that can have a large affect on the final fuel blend. Ethanol has a high octane value and has often been used to enhance the final octane of gasoline blends. Since gasoline is a blend of different hydrocarbon with individual boiling points, the mixture creates a fuel with a distillation curve. Ethanol has a single boiling point causing a change in the distillation curve of the final blend. By itself, ethanol has a very low vapour pressure. However, when blended with gasoline, the resultant fuel blend can have a vapour pressure that is higher than the gasoline or ethanol alone.

Deposits

Intake valve deposits are an issue that must be addressed in any gasoline. Blending low levels of ethanol into gasoline tends to increase intake valve deposits. For that reason, all E10 ethanol blends must be properly treated with the right fuel additives to minimize intake valve deposits and the effect those deposits have on engine performance.

Additive Compatibility

Gasoline additives need to be designed and tested for use in low level ethanol blended gasoline. Additives that are not properly formulated could cause potential compatibility problems.

Ethanol	**Gasoline**
Specific Gravity = 0.794	Specific Gravity = 0.72 – 0.78
Boiling Temperature = 77.8°C	Boiling Range = 27 – 225°C
Flash Point = 12.8°C	Flash Point = –42°C
Energy Content = 23,550 kJ/kg	Energy Content = 44,540 kJ/kg
RVP = 15.8 kPa	RVP = 55 – 103 kPa
Blending Octane	Octane
RON = 108 – 120	RON : Various

Corrosion

The effects of corrosion can be amplified with the use of ethanol blended fuels. In some markets, the ethanol itself is treated with corrosion inhibitors to protect the final fuel blend. However, in other markets this may not be the case, and corrosion becomes a greater concern for the fuel blender and marketer.

Fuel Economy

Ethanol has a lower energy content than gasoline. The use of ethanol blended fuels can result in a slight loss in overall fuel economy. Certain fuel additive packages are designed to overcome this issues and improve fuel economy.

E10 Blending and Handling Issues

Blending and handling ethanol fuel blends can bring numerous challenges to the fuel marketer as well. Phase Separation One of the most challenging and potentially catastrophic issues related to ethanol fuel blends involves the stability of the mixture. Ethanol and gasoline are normally blended through an in-line blender at a fuel terminal and the two components result in a homogenous solution. The problem occurs when water is introduced to the mix. Even a relatively small amount of water accidentally entering into the fuel can cause the gasoline and ethanol to separate into two layers, gasoline on top and ethanol/water on the bottom, rendering the fuel useless. For this reason, cleanliness and good housekeeping practices are considered to be key means to ensuring successful ethanol blends. This is particularly true when a system is first changing over from gasoline to ethanol blended gasoline. At this time, the operator needs to be concerned about both phase separation and the ability of ethanol blends to remove varnish from older tanks.

Equipment Compatibility

Equipment compatibility can be an issue with ethanol blends. Everything from the storage tanks, hoses, filters, and pumps to the water finding pastes need to be considered as they all can be affected by ethanol blends.

Tech Tips

As E10 fuel has been introduced into various regions all over the world, reports, good and bad, have been widely circulated in the general public. Alternative fuel blends to decrease our dependence on foreign oil/will be. with us until internal, combustion engines are replaced with alternate power sources. Following are questions and answers that may help you when addressing customer issues and questions.

Q. **What is E10 fuel?**

A. E10 fuel is a blend of ethanol (10%) and gasoline (90%).

Q. **What is ethanol?**

A. Ethanol is highly refined alcohol that is made from grain (typically corn) or the cellulose from other plants.

Q. **Why is ethanol added to gasoline?**

A. Energy Policy. Act requires the increased use of renewable motor fuels. In most areas, ethanol is the most readily available renewable fuel that can be added to conventional gasoline without major changes.

Q. **When is ethanol added to gasoline?**

A. Ethanol is added to gasoline by local or regional distributors.

Q. **What are the negative properties of ethanol?**

A. Ethanol has several properties that contribute to fuel system issues.

- Ethanol is a strong cleaner (solvent).
- Ethanol is hygroscopic (*e.g.*, it has a strong attraction to moisture).
- E10 fuel's usable life span may be less than the normal length of off- season storage.

Q. **Wouldn't the cleaning properties of ethanol be good for a fuel system?**

A. No, fuel systems that have been used for non-oxygenated gasoline will have varnish deposits and surface corrosion (rust and aluminum oxides). This includes the tanks and pipes used for fuel storage and transportation. Ethanol will clean varnish as well as surface corrosion from any surface it contacts. Ethanol may dissolve plastic resins used to make some fiberglass-tanks. The amount, of material cleaned from alt of these systems can quickly exceed the filtration capacity of fuel system filters resulting in restricted fuel flow. Ultimately engine performance is reduced and potentially damage to the engine can occur.

Q. **What issues are caused by ethanol's attraction to water?**

A. Ethanol molecules have a stronger bond to water molecules than to gasoline molecules. In the absence of water, ethanol and gasoline molecules will bond. When water is added to E10 fuel, the bond between the ethanol arid gasoline will weaken. When the percentage of water in E10 fuel reaches approximately 0.5 per cent, the bond between the ethanol and gasoline molecules will breakdown and the ethanol molecules will attach to the water molecules. This is called phase separation.

Q. **What happens when phase separation occurs?**

A. Several things happen.

- The ethanol and water molecules settle to the bottom of the fuel tank forming a distinct layer of water and ethanol on the bottom and gasoline without ethanol on the top.
- Fuel for the engine is drawn from the bottom of the tank. An engine will not run properly, if at all, on ethanol and water. The thanol and water mixture is very corrosive to some metals and can damage internal engine components.
- The remaining gasoline, without ethanol, will have an octane level below the original E10 fuel's octane level, approximately 2 ~ 3 points lower. This octane level may be below the requirements of the engine.

Q. **Can phase separation be reversed?**

A. No, there are no additives or processes that will recombine phase separated ethanol and gasoline.

Q. **Can I use the gasoline remaining after removal of the phase separated water and alcohol?**

A. No, as mentioned above, the remaining gasoline will have a lower octane level that may not be compatible with our engine.

Q. **How long can E10 fuel be stored?**

A. There are many different opinions concerning how long it is ok to store any fuel (E10 fuel or gasoline), 2 weeks, 90 days, 1 year, or longer, before losing the properties that are required for proper and safe operation of your engine. There are too many variables (*e.g.*, the age of fuel when purchased, temperature, humidity, use of stabilizers and the type of storage containers) to accurately predict how long.

BIOETHANOL

Introduction

With fossil fuel stocks in rapid decline and scientist around the world arguing the case for global warming, caused by increased CO_2 emissions, the race is on to find both a greener and cheaper alternative to petrol.

Normal ethanol can be easily derived from petrol, however because bioethanol fuel is derived from plants it is viewed as a green fuel. The energy from the sun is used by the plants to make sugar, which in turn is converted into bioethanol. In addition during the growing process the plant is also absorbing high levels of carbon dioxide from the atmosphere, making the whole process greener than the refinement of conventional fossil fuels.

The bioethanol is produced firstly by the action of enzymes and micro-organisms on the crops to release the starch and sugars, and then by a process of distilling and dehydration to produce a product that can be used as fuel in the internal combustion car engine. The added benefit of bioethanol is that ft has a higher octane rating than standard fuel, 104 as against 97, and so using bioethanol will offer increased performance.

Sadly you cannot put bioethanol into a standard petrol combustion engine without first making some modifications. The engine management system needs to be upgraded, so that the engine can determine which fuel it is running on, and secondly the engine internal components need to be toughened up, because ethanol can react with certain materials to form corrosive acids.

Whilst Bioethanol certainly has green credentials it is not viable as a fuel for the masses in its current state, due to the huge land resources required. However there are now second generation biofuels derived from waste, stocks and third generation biofuels derived from algae. Algae biofuels produce 30 times more energy per acre than biofuel crops, and so could ultimately be part of the future of green energy production.

One of the ways in which these modern environmentally friendly cars can be energy efficient and help improve fuel economy is by using the latest, high technology car *bulbs* which draw very low levels of power and so take less energy from the engine.

What is Bioethanol?

The principle fuel used as a petrol substitute for road transport vehicles is bioethanol. Bioethanol fuel is mainly produced by the sugar fermentation process, although it can also be manufactured by the chemical process of reacting ethylene with steam.

The main sources of sugar required to produce ethanol come from fuel or energy crops. These crops are grown specifically for energy use and include corn, maize and wheat crops, waste straw, willow and popular trees, sawdust, reed canary grass, cord grasses, Jerusalem artichoke, myscanthus and sorghum plants. There is also ongoing research and development into the use of municipal solid wastes to produce ethanol fuel.

Ethanol or ethyl alcohol (C_2H_5OH) is a clear colourless liquid, it is biodegradable, low in toxicity and causes little environmental pollution if spilt. Ethanol burns to produce carbon dioxide and water. Ethanol is a high octane fuel and has replaced lead as an octane enhancer in petrol. By blending ethanol with gasoline we can also oxygenate the fuel mixture so it burns more completely and reduces polluting emissions. Ethanol fuel blends are widely sold in the United States. The most common blend is 10 per cent ethanol and 90 per cent petrol (E10). Vehicle engines require no modifications to run on E10 and vehicle warranties are unaffected also. Only flexible fuel vehicles can run on up to 85 per cent ethanol and 15 per cent petrol blends (E85).

What are the Benefits of Bioethanol?

Bioethanol has a number of advantages over conventional fuels. It comes from a renewable resource *i.e.*, crops and not from a finite resource and the crops it derives from can grow well in the UK (like cereals, sugar beet and maize). Another benefit over fossil fuels is the greenhouse gas emissions. The road transport network accounts for 22 per cent (www.foodfen.org.uk) of all greenhouse gas emissions and through the use of bioethanol, some of these emissions will be reduced as the fuel crops absorb the CO_2 they emit through growing. Also, blending bioethanol with petrol will help extend the life of the UK's diminishing oil supplies and ensure, greater fuel security, avoiding heavy reliance on oil producing nations. By encouraging bioethanol's use, the rural economy would also receive a boost from growing; the necessary crops. Bioethanol is also biodegradable and far less toxic that fossil fuels. In addition, by using bioethanol in older engines can help reduce the amount of carbon monoxide produced by the vehicle thus improving air quality. Another advantage of bioethanol is the ease with which it can be easily integrated into the existing road transport fuel system. In quantities up to 5 per cent, bioethanol can be blended with conventional fuel without the need of engine modifications. Bioethanol is produced using familiar methods, such as fermentation, and it can be distributed using the same petrol forecourts and transportation systems as before.

Bioethanol Production

Ethanol can be produced from biomass by the hydrolysis and sugar fermentation processes. Biomass wastes contain a complex mixture of carbohydrate polymers from the plant cell walls known as cellulose, hemi cellulose and lignin. In order to produce sugars from the biomass, the biomass is pre-treated with acids or enzymes in order to reduce the size of the feedstock and to open up the plant structure. The cellulose and the hemi cellulose portions are broken down (hydrolysed) by enzymes or dilute acids into sucrose sugar that is then fermented into ethanol. The lignin which is also present in the biomass is normally used as a fuel for the ethanol production plants boilers. There are three principle methods of extracting sugars from biomass. These are concentrated acid hydrolysis, dilute acid hydrolysis and enzymatic hydrolysis.

Concentrated Acid Hydrolysis Process

The Arkanol process works by adding 70-77 per cent sulphuric acid to the biomass that has been dired to a 10 per cent moisture content. The acid is added in the ratio of 1.25 acid to 1 biomass and the temperature is controlled to 50°C. Water is then added to dilute the acid to 20-30 per cent and the mixture is again heated to 100°C for 1 hour. The gel produced from this mixture is then pressed to release an acid sugar mixture and a chromatographic column is used to separate the acid and sugar mixture.

Dilute Acid Hydrolysis

The dilute acid hydrolysis process is one of the oldest, simplest and most efficient methods of producing ethanol from biomass. Dilute acid is used to hydrolyse the biomass to sucrose. The first stage uses 0.7 per cent sulphuric acid at 190°C to hydrolyse the hemi cellulose present in the biomass. The second stage is optimised to yield the more resistant cellulose fraction. This is achieved by using 0.4 per cent sulphuric acid at 215°C. The liquid hydrolates are then neutralised and recovered from the process.

Enzymatic Hydrolysis

Instead of using acid to hydrolyse the biomass into sucrose, we can use enzymes to break down the biomass in a similar way. However, this process is very expensive and is still in its early stages of development.

Wet Milling Processes

Corn can be processed into ethanol by either the dry milting or the wet milling process. In the wet milling process, the corn kernel is steeped in warm water, this helps to break down the proteins and release the starch present in the corn and helps to soften the kernel for the milling process. The corn is then milled to produce germ, fibre and starch products. The germ is extracted to produce corn oil and the starch fraction undergoes centrifugation and saccharifcation to produce gluten wet cake. The ethanol is then extracted by the distillation process. The wet milling process is normally used in factories producing several hundred million gallons of ethanol every year.

Dry Milling Process

The dry milling process involves cleaning and breaking down the corn kernel into fine particles using a hammer mill process. This creates a powder with a course flour type consistency. The powder contains the corn germ, starch and fibre. In order to produce a sugar solution the mixture is then hydrolysed or broken down into sucrose sugars using enzymes or a dilute acid. The mixture is then cooled and yeast is added in order to ferment the mixture into ethanol. The dry milling process is normally used in factories producing; less than 50 million gallons of ethanol every year.

Sugar Fermentation Process

The hydrolysis process breaks down the cellulostic part of the biomass or corn into sugar solutions that can then be fermented into ethanol. Yeast is added to the solution, which is then heated. The yeast contains an enzyme called invertase, which acts as a catalyst and helps to convert the sucrose sugars into glucose and fructose (both $C_6H_{12}O_6$).

The chemical reaction is shown below:

$$\underset{\text{Sucrose}}{C_{12}H_{22}O_{11}} + \underset{\text{Water}}{H_2O} \xrightarrow[\text{Catalyst}]{\text{Invertase}} \underset{\text{Fructose}}{C_6H_{12}O_6} + \underset{\text{Glucose}}{C_6H_{12}O_6}$$

The fructose and glucose sugars then react with another enzyme called zymase, which is also contained in the yeast to produce ethanol and carbon dioxide.

The chemical reaction is shown below:

$$\underset{\text{Fructose/Glucose}}{C_6H_{12}O_6} + \xrightarrow[\text{Catalyst}]{\text{Zymase}} \underset{\text{Ethanol}}{2C_2H_5OH} + 2CO_2$$

The fermentation process takes around three days to complete and is carried out at a temperature of between 250°C and 300°C.

Fractional Distillation Process

The ethanol, which is produced from the fermentation process, still contains a significant quantity of water, which must be removed. This is achieved by using the fractional distillation process. The distillation process works by boiling the water and ethanol mixture. Since ethanol has a lower boiling point (78.3°C) compared to that of water (100°C), the ethanol turns into the vapour state before the water and can be condensed and separated.

11

Bioethanol from Lignocellulose

Bioethanol

Ethanol or ethyl alcohol (CH_3CH_2OH) is an important organic chemical because of its unique properties, and therefore can be used widely for various purposes. Under ordinary conditions, ethanol is a volatile, flammable, clear, colourless liquid, miscible in both water and non-polar solvents.

The production of ethanol has two routes: synthetic and biological. The synthetic ethanol production is commonly carried out by a catalytic hydration of ethylene in vapour phase and often as a by product of certain industrial operations (Logsdon, 2006). The ethanol produced from this process is mostly used as a solvent (60%) and chemical intermediate (40%). Fermentative ethanol production accounts for 93 per cent* of the total ethanol production in the world. The ethanol is produced from fermentation of sugars extracted mostly from crops. *Saccharomyces cerevisiae* is the most popular microorganism used for ethanol production due to its high ethanol yield and high tolerance to rather high ethanol concentration. The ethanol produced is mostly used as fuels (92%); industrial solvents and chemicals (4%), and beverages (4%) (Logsdon, 2006).

Crops are the main feedstock used for ethanol production now-a-days. Brazil is the largest ethanol producer with a capacity of 15.5 Giga-L (in 2004) and uses sugarcane as feedstock, while the USA in second place (12.9 Giga-L) uses corn as feedstock (Rosillo-Calle and Walter, 2006). However,

*Data were retrieved from http:/www.distill.com/berg/

these crops are also food for human and animals, thus the expansion of production capacity, especially as ethanol becomes a worldwide alternative fuel, is limited by supply of the feedstock. In contrast, cheap abundant lignocetlulosic materials in the form of agricultural and forestry wastes as well as municipal and industrial wastes are available as alternative feedstock for ethanol production. Therefore, the use of lignocellulosic materials for ethanol production is very promising.

In this chapter, ethanol as fuel and lignocellulosic material as feedstock for ethanol production are in focus. The first part discusses the advantages of ethanol as fuel in regard to combustion as well as to its environmental impact, while the second part discusses the structure of lignocellulosic materials, followed by the hydrolysis process which breaks down of lignocellulosic to obtain fermentable sugars. Furthermore, inhibition caused by inhibitors released during acid hydrolysis is also discussed.

Ethanol as Fuel

The use of ethanol as fuel goes back to the origin of the use of vehicles itself. For example, Henry Ford's Model T, built in 1908, ran on ethanol. It was continued until the availability of cheap petrol effectively killed off ethanol as a major transport fuel in the early part of the 20th century. The energy crisis of the 1970s renewed interest in ethanol production for fuels and chemicals. Although the interest waned in the following decade due to oil price abatement, the environmental issue of reducing greenhouse gas, rising vehicle fuel demand, and the security of energy supply sustain the development of ethanol production from renewable resources.

Ethanol is used in vehicles either as a sole, fuel or blended with gasoline. As an oxygenated compound, ethanol provides additional oxygen in combustion, and hence obtains better combustion efficiency. The physico-chemical properties of some oxygenated high-octane additives are shown in Table 11.1. Since the completeness of combustion is increased by the present of oxygenated fuels, the emission of carbon monoxide is reduced by 32.5 per cent while the emission of hydrocarbons is decreased by 14.5 per cent (Rasskazchikova *et al.*, 2004). In addition, the emission of nitrogen oxides is reduced by using ethanol as additive.

Methyl-tertiary-butyl-ether (MTBE) has properties similar to those of gasoline, but a higher octane number, and therefore is very suitable for high-octane additive. However, MTBE is reportedly responsible for groundwater pollution as a result of *e.g.*, leaking underground, tanks. Low levels of MTBE can make drinking-water supplies undrinkable due to its offensive taste and odour*. MTBE has higher water solubility compare with other gasoline constituents, thus is rather difficult to purge from ground water (Rong, 2001). Moreover, biodegradatidn of MTBB needs a lot of oxygen which is almost

*Summarized from http://www.epa.gov/mtbe/faq.ht .ı

Table 11.1 : The Physicochemical Properties of some Oxygenated High-octane Additives to Gasoline*

Properties	Gasoline	Oxygenates		
		Methanol	Ethanol	MTBE
Density at 15.56°C, kg/m^3	719-779	794	792	742
Heat, kJ/kg				
Combustion (lower)	41,800-44,200	19,934	26,749	35,123
Evaporation	~349	1104	839	326
Flash point, °C	–42.8.	6.5	12	–28
Octane number				
Research (RON)	90-100	107	108	116
Motor (MON)	81-90	92	92	101
Reid vapour pressure, kPa	55-103	32	16	54

impossible to carry out naturally in ground water. The use of methanol as oxygenated is limited, or in many countries prohibited, due to its high toxicity, volatility and hygroscopic behaviour. Ethanol has become more competitive as an oxygenated fuel especially because ethanol is produced from renewable resources by fermentation, resulting in less dependency on fossil fuel. Moreover, ethanol is less hygroscopic, contains a reasonable heat of combustion, has lower evaporation heat and, most importantly, is not toxic like methanol. In addition, acetaldehyde as a product of partial oxidation of ethanol in the exhaust gas of vehicles is much less toxic than formaldehyde which is formed when using methanol.

As a high-octane additive, ethanol has drawbacks: emitting acetaldehyde of 2-4 times as much as does gasoline; highly corrosive, which is a function of water content; a negative effect on rubber and plastic; and the blend with gasoline tends to separate in the presence of traces of water (Rasskazchikova *et al.*, 2004). Fortunately, these drawbacks have been overcome. An additional 5 per cent of water in a blend of ethanol and gasoline can reduce the emission of acetaldehyde. Furthermore, stabilizers like higher alcohols, fusel oil, aromatic amines, ethers or ketones are useful to prevent separation. For example, 2.5-3 per cent of isobutanol stabilized the gasoline-ethanol blend in the presence of 5 per cent water at low temperature of –20°C. Some corrosion inhibitor such as hydroxyethylated alkylphenols and alkyl imidazolines can attain essential anticorrosion resistance. Additionally, polymer industries have developed special materials that are resistant to penetration of alcohols (Rasskazchikova *et al.*, 2004).

---

*Adopted from *'Properties of Fuels'* which available at http:www.eere.energy.gov/

Environmental Impact

The main environmental advantages of fuel ethanol are its sustainability in using a renewable resource as a feedstock, thus promoting independence of fossil fuel, and maintaining the level of greenhouse gas (CO_2). Carbon dioxide in the atmosphere is assimilated through photosynthesis and metabolized to be a building block of plants. The energy of sunlight is used to make carbohydrates stored in crops and in the whole plant body. While crops are useful as energy sources for human and animals, some crops like starch or oil-containing crops can be converted to fuels or chemicals. Combustion of these fuels produces CO_2 gas which would be assimilated again by plants. In total, almost no net CO_2 is produced by using fuels generated from biomass (Fig. 11.1)

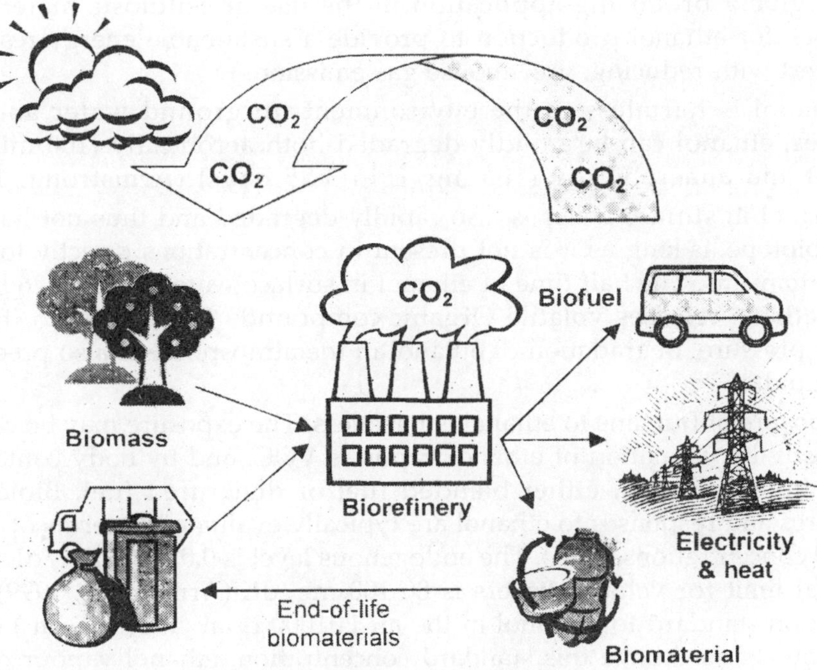

Fig. 11.1. The schematic diagram of carbon-cycle in the use of ethanol for fuels and chemicals

How effectively ethanol reduces greenhouse gas emission has been widely discussed. The issues are mainly related to the net energy content in ethanol, and depend on the assumption of ethanol production routes. A number of life-cycle assessments have been studied, and show that a change from fossil fuel to biofuels could reduce CO_2 emission by factor of 1/2 to 1/5, depending on how significant the use of renewable fuels is at all stages in the process (Bernesson *et al.*, 2006; Hu *et al.*, 2004; Kadam, 2002; Kirn and

Dale, 2005; Rosillo-Calle and Walter, 2006; von Blottnitz and Curran, 2006). Even though a couple of reports claim that ethanol production from corn gives negative net energy content, *i.e.*, that the amount of energy required to produce ethanol exceeds the energy contained in ethanol itself, more reports claim that ethanol has positive net energy, content (Farrell *et al.*, 2006; Kim and Dale, 2005). The net energy content of ethanol is reported as 2.5-8 MJ/L which is related to 60-100 g CO_2 emitted/MJ-ethanol energy (gasoline has almost zero net energy and about 95 g CO_2 emission/MJ-gasoline energy). In addition, Farrell *et al.*, (2006) developed the "Energy and Resources Group (ERG) Biofuel Analysis. Meta Model" (EBAMM) to predict net energy and GHG emission of ethanol produced from cellulosic material, and reported that those values are 23 MJ/L and 10 g CO_2 emission/MJ-ethanol energy respectively. Although it is still, a theoretical calculation,, the results give a promising application in the use of cellulosic material as feedstock for ethanol production to provide a sustainabie energy resource in concert with reducing, greenhouse gas emission.

Ethanol is harmless to the environment. In ground water and soil mixtures, ethanol can be rapidly degraded both aerobically (100 ml/L in 7 days) and anaerobically (100 mg/L in 3-25 days) (Armstrong, 1999).

Ethanol in surface water is also rapidly degraded and thus not harmful to the biotope as long as it is not present in concentrations directly toxic to microorganisms. The half-time of ethanol in surface water is 6.5 to 26 hours. While ethane releases volatile Organic compounds (VOC) due to its low vapour pressure, degradation of ethanol in the atmosphere is also predicted to be rapid.

Exposure of humans to ethanal is harmless. The exposure may be carried out mostly by inhalation of ethanol vapor as VOC, and by body contact or, rarely, ingestion from either blended fuel or denatured fuel. Biological exposures and responses to ethanol are typically evaluated in terms of blood ethanol concentrations (BEC). The endogenous level is 0.02-0.15 mg/dL while the legal limit for vehicle drivers is 80-100 mg/dL (Armstrong, 1999), The occupation standard for ethanol in the air is 1000 ppm (1900 mg/m^3) on an eight-hour basis. Above this standard concentration, ethanol vapour causes eye and upper respiratory tract irritation, fatigue, headache and sleepiness. In practice, this level is far above actual conditions; for instance, the average ambient level in air in the city of Porto Alegre, Brazil, where 17 per cent of the vehicles run entirely on ethanol, is 12 ppb (0.023 mg/m^3) (Armstrong, 1999).

In addition, Massad *et al.*, (1985) studied the potential health effects of gasoline and ethanol engine exhaust fumes. He concluded that the acute toxicity of the exhaust gas of a gasoline-fuelled engine is significantly higher than that of an ethanol-fuelled engine.

The Market

The interest in fuel ethanol on a global scale has been growing in the past few years due to a combination of factors including environmental, social and energy security issues. Currently, world production and consumption are dominated by Brazil and the USA, which are responsible for 70 per cent of world production with 15.3 and 12.9 billion litres (GL), respectively (Rosillo-Calle and Walter, 2006). In addition, more than 30 countries have already introduced, or are interested in introducing, programmes for fuel ethanol (*e.g.*, Australia, Canada, Colombia, China, India, Mexico and Thailand).

Brazil produces ethanol from sugarcane and has used as a fuel since 1975, when Brazilian Alcohol Program (PROALCOOL) started with the purpose of using ethanol for blending with gasoline. Furthermore, after the second oil crisis, the production was expanded to include hydrated ethanol to be used as neat fuel in modified engines. It resulted in a rapid expansion of sugarcane production from 50 MT/year in 1970 to 380 MT/year in 2004 along with improving productivity from 4,200 L/ha/year to 6,350 L/ha/year respectively (Rosiilo-Calle and Walter, 2006).

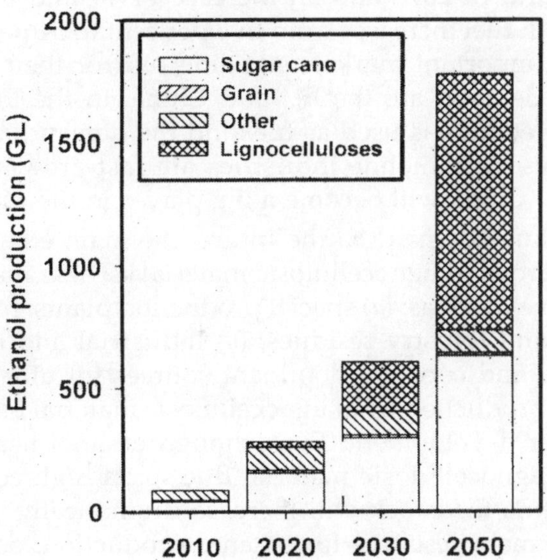

Fig. 11.2. Ethanol potential production from different feedstocks

The USA is the world's fastest-growing fuel ethanol market, representing a two-fold increase in the last 4 years*. The main producers are the states of Iowa, Illinois, Nebraska, South Dakota and Minnesota with 82 per cent of the national production in 2004. The main feedstock for ethanol production

* Adopted from 'Ethanol Industry, *Outlook, 2005*' from http://www.ethanolrfa.org

is corn and ethanol is sold as octane enhancer or oxygenated blended with gasoline and currently represents about 2 per cent of the US fuel market.**

Within the European Union (EU) countries, the community produces more than 2 billion liters of ethanol annually, dominated by France, Germany and United Kingdom, but less than 5 per cent is.used as fuel***. The EU has a long-term goal of achieving a 12 per cent-share for renewable resources by 2010; thus the Commission decided in 1994 to allow tax concessions for pilot plants producing biofuels. As a result, new biofuel projects have been announced in the Netherlands, Sweden and Spain.

In Sweden, cellulosic ethanol is produced in connection with a sulphite pulp mill at Domsjo, Ornskoldsvik, with a capacity of 13,000 cubic metres, while the Agroethanol company at Norrkoping produces about 50,000 cubic metres from barley and wheat****. Ethanol is used in Sweden as an oxygenated high-octane additive (up to 5%) or as E85 (85% ethanol and 15% gasoline).

The market for ethanol is predicted to increase greatly in the future due to the rise of energy demand in transportation; the rising price of oil due to its slower production; and global concerns about environmental and energy security issues. Fulton (2004) (cited by Rosillo-Calle (2006)) predicted a doubled demand in 2010 and an increase of 44-fold in 2050, where the share of ethanol in fuel increases from five per cent to 54 per cent respectively (Fig. 11.2). Two important markets standing out for their potential impacts on fuel ethanol demand are the EU and China. In the EU recently, only a small fraction of ethanol is used as fuel and the demand is growing rapidly. Moreover, Chinese automobile industries are fast-growing and hence it is quite certain that China will become a big player in the fuel ethanol market.

Given such huge demand ia the future, the main ethanol feedstock will be shifted from crops to lignocellulosic materials. These materials are largely abundant resources such as: (*a*) special production plants: timber, switchgrass; (*b*) agricultural and forestry residues; (*c*) industrial and municipal wastes. While sugarcane and corn are dominant sources for ethanol production at present, ethanol production from lignocellulosic material has not been proven and is still under development. Even though ethanol has not been largely produced from lignocellulosic material due to its high cost, it is predicted that the use of this feedstock will increase dramatically in the near future and became the main resource for ethanol production, occupying as much as two-thirds of total ethanol production in 2050 (Rosillo-Calle and Walter, 2006).

** Adopted from presentation slide of Fulton, L. entitled "Biofuel for Transport: An International Perspective", available at International Energy Agnecy website: http://www.iea.org.

*** Adopted from http://www.distill.com/berg/

**** Adopted from http://www.etek.se

Lignocellulosic Materials

Lgnocellulose presents as a building block of plant cell wall structure. The main constituents of lignocellulose are cellulose along with hemicellulose and lignin. The compositions of these constituents may vary from one plant species to another. For example, hardwood has more cellulose-constituent while wheat straw and leaves have more hemicellulose constituent (Table 2.2). In addition, the composition within a single plant varies with age, stage of growth and other conditions (Perez *et al.*, 2002).

Table 11.2 : The Lignocellulose Constituents of Common Agricultural Residues and Wastes

Lignocellulosie material	Cellulose (%)	Hemicellulose (%)	Lignin (%)
Hardwood stems	40-55	24-40	18-25
Softwood stems	45-50	25-35	25-35
Corn cobs	45	35	15
Rice straw	32.1	24	18
Fresh bagasse	33.4	30	18.9
Wheat straw	30	50	15
Leaves	15-20	80-85	0
Switch grass	45	31.4	12.0

Adopted from: Howard *et al.*, (2003), Sun and Cheng (2002)

Cellulose is the main structural polymer in plant cell walls and is found in a very organized fibrous structure. This linear polymer consists of D-glucose subunits linked to each other by β-(1,4)-glycosidic bond (*cf. Fig. 11.3*). Due to this linkage, cellobiose is established as the repeat unit for cellulose chains. The long-chain polymers (called elemental fibril) linked together by hydrogen and van der Waals bonds result in a packed micro fibril. Hemicelluloses and lignin cover the micro fibril. The degree of polymerization (DP) of native cellulose is in the range of 7,000-15,000. Fermentable D-glucose can be produced from cellulose by breaking the β-(1,4)-glycosidic linkages by the action of acid or enzymes.

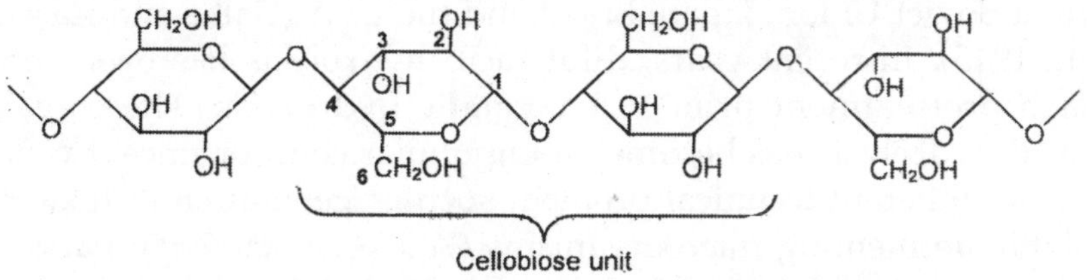

Fig. 2.3 : Schematic illustration of the cellulose chain

Unlike cellulose, hemicelluloses consist of different monosaccharide units such as pentoses (xylose, rhamnose and arabmose), hexoses (glucose, mannose and galactose) and unonic acid (*e.g.*, 4-o-methyl-glucuronic, D-glucuronic and D-galactouronic acids). The backbone of hemicellulose can be either a homo-polymcr or hetero-polymer with short branches at *e.g.*, β-(1, 4) and occasionally β-(1, 3)-glycosidic bonds. In addition, hemicelluloses contain some degree of acetylation *e.g.*, in heteroxylan. The principal component of hardwood hemicellulose is glucuronoxylan whereas glucomannan is predominant in softwood, hi contrast to cellulose hemicellulose an easy hydrolyzable polymer due to its branched nature and does not forming aggregates even when they are co-crystallized with cellulose chains.

Lignin is a complex, cross-linked polymer of phenolic compound monomers that form a large molecule Structure. It is present in the cellular cell wall, conferring structural support, impermeability arid resistance against microbial attack and oxidative stress (Perez *et al.*, 2002). There are three plienyl propionic alcohols as monomers of lignin: coniferyl alcohol (guaiacyl propahol), coumaryl alcohol (*p*-hydroxyphenyl propanol) and sinapyl alcohol (syringyl alcohols). Guaiacyl units are dominant in the softwood while syringyl units are dominant in hardwood.

Hydrolysis

As described, cellulose and hemicellulose are polymers of sugar monomers, and therefore hydrolysis of these polymers results in sugar monomers some of which are fermentable by ordinary yeast. However, producing monomer sugars from cellulose and hemicellulose at high yields is far more difficult than deriving sugars from crop products such as sugarcane or starch. To make cellulose and hemicellulose accessible for hydrolysis, a number of pre-treatments should be carried out. These pre-treatments are summarized in Table 11.3.

Now-a-days, there are at least two hydrolysis methods which; are still of interest to many researchers in the development of ethanol production: dilute-acid hydrolysis and enzymatic hydrolysis. Dilute-acid hydrolysis is an old method (1819) and was operated during World War II in Germany, the former Soviet Union, Japan, Brazil and the USA (Galbe and Zacchi, 2002; Saeman, 1945). In recent years, dilute-acid hydrolysis has been commonly used as a pretreatment prior to enzymatic hydrolysis. The conventional dilute-acid hydrolysis has become an unpopular concept since it was known to poses, an inherent technical problem such as generation of toxic material that inhibits fermenting microorganisms (Klinke; *et al.*, 2003; Larsson *et al.*, 1999a: Leonard and Hajny, 1945; Luo *et al.*, 2002; Taherzadeh *et al.*, 1999b).

Table 11.3 : Pre-treatment Method for Lignocelluloses

Method	Operation (factor) causing changes in the substrate structure	Kind of changes
Physical	Millind and grinding (ball, vibro energy, pressure, hammer); irradiation (electron beam, γ-rays, microwaves); high temperature (pyrolysis, steam explosion);	Increase in specific surface and size of pore, decrease of the degrees of polymerization and crystallinity of cellulose, hydrolysis of hemicellulose, partial depolymerization of lignin.
Chemical	Alkalis, acids, gases, oxidizers, reducers, organic solvents.	Delignification, decrease of the degree of polymerization and crystallinity of cellulose associated with its swelling, prorosity growth.
Biological	White-rot fungi (*Pleurotus, Pycnoporus, Ischnoderma, Phlebia*, etc.)	Delignification and reduction in degree of polymerization of cellulose and hemicellulose.
Combined	Alkali-pulping associated with steam explosion, grinding followed by alkaline or acid treatment.	Degradation of hemicellulose, delignification, increase of the surface area and size of pores.

Adopted from: (Szczodrak and Fiedurek, 1996)

In contrast, enzymatic hydrolysis has hot faced this problem. Cellulases and hemicellulases (glycosylhydrolases) are used for enzymatic hydrolysis and produced by fungi such as *Trichoderma, Penicillum* and *Aspergillus* (Galbe and Zacchi, 2002). Cellulases consist of three classes of enzymes: 1,4-β-D-glucan cellobiohydrolases, endo-1,4-β-D-glucanases, and 1,4-β-D-glucosidase (Jorgerisen *et al.*, 2003). These enzymes attack cellulose and lignin and produce sugar monomers. Despite the advantages of enzymatic pretreatment including mild-energy requirements, high selectivity and low environmental conditions, the rate of hydrolysis in most enzymatic pretreatment processes is very slow. In addition, so far the enzyme price makes the enzymatic process economically not favourable.

Dilute-acid Hydrolysis

While awaiting improvement of the enzymatic process, *i.e.*, improvement of process rate and economically feasible enzyme production, the developments of dilute-acid hydrolysis are still continued (Lee *et al.*, 1999b), Investigations in different kinds of reactor include plug-flow reactors, percolation reactors, progressive batch/percolation reactors, counter-current and co-current reactors have been carried out, in addition to new developments in kinetic investigation which explore a broader range of reaction conditions in term of the temperature and acid concentration. Moreover, intensive research to overcome the technical difficulties has been carried out, *e.g.* research on detoxification of toxic material liberated during dilute-racid hydrolysis. Furthermore, a combination of etnanol production with thermo-generation (a bio-refinery concept) can also solve the problem of low utilization of feedstock, since non-hydrolyzed materials can be compacted into pellets and used as a fuel for heat and electricity generation.

The dilute-acid hydrolysis process occurs in two stages to accommodate the differences between hemicellulose and cellulose (Aguilar *et al.*, 2002; Choi and Mathews, 1996; Larsson *et al.*, 1999a; Lavarack *et al.*, 2000; Saeman, 1945), The first stage is operated under milder conditions which yield more hydrolyzed hemicellulose products such as manno.se and xyldse monomers. The second stage is optimized for hydrolysis of the more resistant cellulose fraction to produce mainly glucose monomers. The liquid hydrolyzates are recovered from each stage, separated from solid material and lignin, neutralized (and detoxified) prior to cultivation. Residual cellulose and Hgnin left over in the solid from the hydrolysis reactors serve as boiler fuel for electricity or steam.production (*Fig. 11.4*).

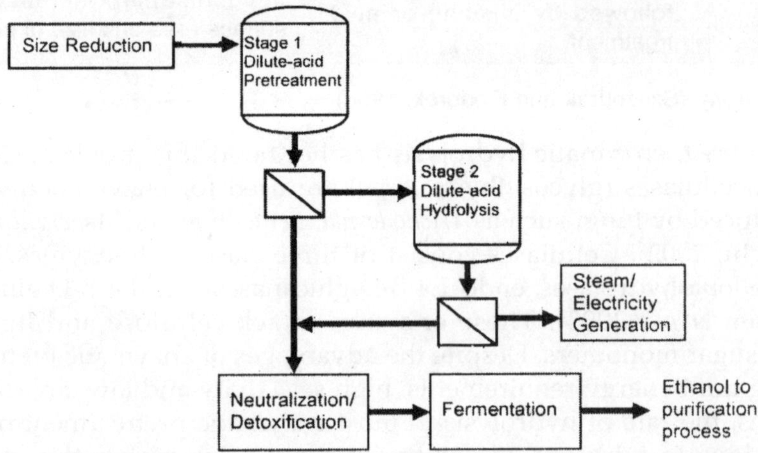

Fig. 11.4 : Schematic diagram of two-stage dilute-acid hydrolysis process

By-products of Dilute-acid Hydrolysis

Dilute-acid hydrolysis is a cheap and fast process to obtain sugar from lignocellulosic materials. However, a significant drawback of dilute-acid hydrolysis is the generation of several by products during the process (Saernan, 1945). Some of them are toxic to the fermenting microorganism, including yeast (Leonard and Hajny, 1945; Olsson and Hahn-Hagerdal, 1996; Palmqvist and Hahn-Hagerdal, 2000). Inhibition by these compounds decrease yield and productivity as well as disturbing cell growth. Many investigations have been dedicated to avoiding this inhibition problem, *e.g.*, by converting the toxic materials to another compound that is less or non-toxic to the yeast, in addition to increase the tolerance of yeast against these toxic materials.

Cellulose, hemicellulose and lignin are broken down to mainly glucose, mannose or xylose, and phenolic compounds during acid hydrolysis, respectively (Fig. 11.5). As soon as the monomers are produced, further decompositions occur during these process conditions yielding other unexpected compounds such as 5-hydroxymethyl furfural (HMF) from hexoses, and furfural from pentoses. HMF and furfural are also decomposed into imainly leyulinic acid and formic acid. Moreover, aliphatic acids, mainly acetic acid, are released from acetyl groups contained in hemicelluloses, while lignin is decomposed and releases phenolic compounds.

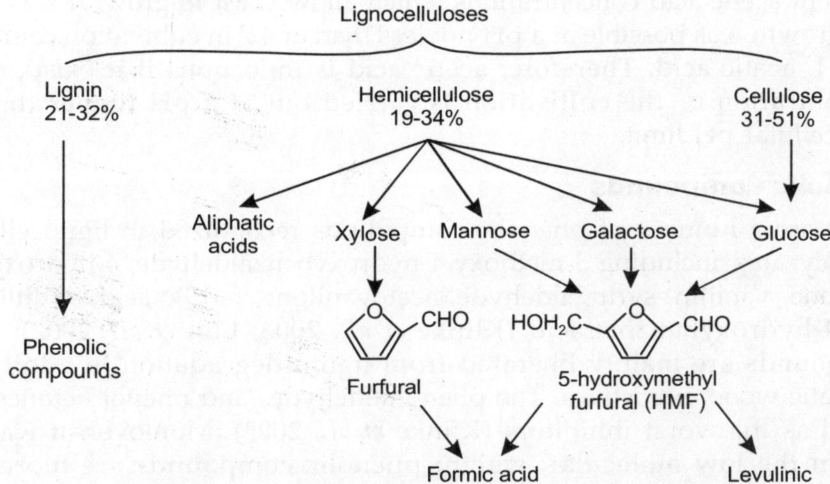

Fig. 11.5 : Some reactions occurred during hydrolysis of lignocelluloses

Organic Acids

A large number of aliphatic acids are present in dilute-acid hydrolyzates originated from wood extractives, lignin degradation and sugar degradation (Luo *et al.*, 2002). Acetic acid is a major acid constituent in hydrolyzates and is mainly produced from degradation of the acetyl group in the polysaccharides whereas levulinic acid and formic acid are products of sugar degradation (*cf. Fig. 11.5*). There are several kinds of fatty acids such as hexadecanoic, 9,12-octadecadienoic, oleic and octadecanoic that most likely are unmodified wood extractives, in addition to short-chain and branched aliphatic acids such as 2-methyl-2-hydroxybutanoic acid, methyl propanedionic acid and methyl botanedioic acid (Luo *at al.*, 2002). These last acids are not important in terms of concentration, and thus result insignificant effects to the yeast.

The undissociated acids are harmful to the cells and inhibit cell growth. They are liposoluble and thus can diffuse across the plasma membrane into cytosol and may dissociate intracellularly (Taherzadetv *et al.*, 1997b). In order to maintain intracellular pH, protons must be transported across the membrane by the action of plasma membrane ATPase. This results in an increase of ATP consumption, and thereby causes lower biomass yield (Verduyn *et al.*, 1990a). In anaerobic conditions, ATP generation is achieved by the ethanolproduction pathway, resulting in higher ethanol yield at the expense of biomass formation (Palmqvist and Hahn-Hagerdal, 2000). However, above critical extracellular concentration, of undissociated acid, the diffusion rate of undissociated acid can exceed the transport capacity of the plasma membrane ATPase and intracellular acidification occurs (Verduyn *et al.*, 1990b). Taherzadeh (1997b) shows the limit of extracellular pH at different acetic acid concentrations which allow yeast to grow: It was found that growth was possible at a pH not less than of 4.7 in cultivation containing 10 g/L acetic acid. Therefore, acetic acid is innocuous if it exists in low concentration or the cultivation is carried out at a pH higher than the extracellular pH limit.

Phenolic Compounds

There are a number of phenolic compounds recognized in lignocellulosic hydrolyzates, including 3-methoxy-4-hydroxybenzaldehyde, 4-hydroxyaceto phenone, vanillin, syringaldehyde, acetovanilone, ferulic acid, vanillic acid and 4-hydroxybenzoic acid (Klinke *et al.*, 2003; Luo *et al.*, 2002). These compounds are mainly liberated from lignin degradation in addition to aromatic wood extractives. The phenol aldehydes and phenol ketones were found as the worst inhibitors (Klinke *et al.*, 2003). Moreover, it was also shown the low molecular: weight phenolic compounds are more toxic (Palmqvist and Hahn-Hagerdal, 2000).

Phenolic compounds are considered to be important inhibitors due to their inhibitory effect in fermentation of lignocellulosic hydrolyzates. These compounds partition biological membranes and cause loss of integrity, hence disturb their ability to serve as selective barriers and enzyme matrices (Palmqvist and Hahn-Hagerdal, 2000). The inhibition mechanism of phenolic compounds has not been elucidated yet. Furthermore; studies in inhibitory action of phenolic compounds have been carried out using higher concentrations than are actually present in the hydrolyzates (Delgenes *et al.*, 1996; Palmqvist and Hahn-Hagerdal, 2000). The water solubility of phenolic compounds is limited and depends on the composition of the liquid, which is different in hydrolyzates and the defined medium; therefore it is possible that the concentration at which the microorganism suffered has been lower. In addition, *S. cerevisiae,* assimilates vanillin, hydroxybenzaldehyde, and syringaldehyde during fermentation (Delgenes *et al.*, 1996), while growth has been reported on cathecol, recorcinol, salicylic acid, and *p*-hydroxybenzoic acid (Palmqvist and/Hahn-Hägerdal, 2000).

Furan Compounds

Furfural and 5-hydroxymethyl furfural (HMF) have been found as further hydrolysis products of pentoses and hexoses respectively (cf. Fig. 11.5). Pentoses form furfural in high yield; but if the furfural is not removed as formed, it partially condenses into high-molecular-weight materials. By an analogous process, hexoses yield HMF which, on continued heating, yields levuliriic acid and formic acid (Saeman, 1945).

Furfural has been reported to be a strong inhibitor for *S. cerevisiae.* The furfural concentration above 1g/L was found to decrease significantly the CO_2 evolution rate, the cell multiplication and the total viable cell number in the early phase of fermentation (Palmqvist *et al.*, 1999; Taherzadeh *et al.*, 1999a). During anaerobic fermentation, reduction of furfural, to furfiiryl alcohol occurs with high yields, while furoic acid is produced from oxidation of furfural during aerobic cultivation (Palmqvist *et al.*, 1999; Taherzadeh *et al.*, 1999a). In both cases, NADH-dependent alcohol dehydrogenase (ADH) is believed to be responsible for furfural conversion in yeasts (Modig *et al.*, 2002).

HMF is chemically related to furfural and thus has similar inhibitory effects as furfural, except that it has a lower conversion rate which might be due to lower membrane permeability (Larsson *et al.*, 1999a). Taherzadeh (2000a) showed that an addition of 4 g/L of HMF decreased the CO_2 evolution rate (32%), ethanol production rate (40%), and specific growth rate (70%). However, these inhibitory effects were less than those caused by the same amount of furfural, and thus HMF cannot be considered as acutely toxic as furfural for growth and fermentation of *S. cerevisiae.* On the other hand, the conversion rate of furfural is much faster than the conversion rate of HMF (Taherzadeh *et al.*, 2000a) (Papers II-IV). Furthermore, HMF is converted to 5-hydroxymethyl furfuryl alcohol (Taherzadeh *et al.*, 1999a) with a similar mechanism as it was shown in the case of furfural conversion. Later, Liu (2004) proposed that the product of HMF conversion is 2,5-bis-hydroxymethylfuran.

12 Solar Fuel

The Sun

The sun is a blazing globe of hot gases fuelled by nuclear fusion—where small atoms are squeezed together at great pressure to make heavier atoms with the release of massive amounts of energy.

The energy from the sun is radiated out in all directions as light. Much of the energy striking the earth is reflected back into space by the atmosphere, but a staggering 90,000 TW of power arrives at the earth's surface, 6,000 times more power than the entire human race uses.

Using Sunlight

Although most forms of energy have the sun as their ultimate source, the term solar energy is generally used to refer to methods of collecting light and turning it directly into a useful form of energy. Available technologies are:

1. Passive Solar Gain: This form of energy is often taken for granted, sunlight enters through windows, and warms the house. In an average house in the UK, passive solar gain contributes 14 per cent of the heating demand.

Thoughtful design can improve this figure further with very little, if any, increase in the cost of building the property:

- Orienting the house so that the more often used rooms face south;
- larger windows on the south side, smaller on the north;
- using building materials that store heat by adding 'thermal mass' to the house; and

- laying out housing so that buildings do not overshadow each other.

2. *Solar Thermal Collectors:* This technology uses a solar panel that is specifically designed to collect light and heat up. Some, more carefully insulated panels, do not require direct sunshine, and will work even on a cloudy day. Typical working temperatures are below 100°C, and the energy is normally used to provide either space heating or hot water for washing. There are many different designs, but two types have found favour in cooler climates—the flat panel and the evacuated tube.

The flat panel solar collectors are generally cheaper systems per unit area. Their common feature is a flat plate with a black surface which absorbs sunlight. This surface may be of a selective coating which absorbs almost all light, but doesn't radiate heat so well.

The heat is transferred to water which is pumped through pipes that are connected to the flat plate. A glazing material insulates the hot plate while letting the sunlight through. Layers of insulation behind the hot plate reduce heat loss to the rear.

Evacuated tube collectors benefit from the extremely high insulation of a vacuum (like in a vacuum flask), which totally eliminates losses by conduction and convection.

The vacuum is maintained inside a sealed glass tube. Sunlight is absorbed by a selective coating on a collector plate inside the tube (right). Heat may be removed by direct circulation of the water or by a 'heat pipe' that contains a refrigerant. The refrigerant evaporates in the tube, and condenses at the cold end, transferring heat into water circulating there.

Evacuated tube collectors are said to be more efficient due to lower losses, and consequently to perform better on cold or cloudy days. Solar thermal systems typically achieve efficiencies over 80 per cent.

3. Photovoltaic Cells: Photovoltaic (PV) cells, which convert light directly into electricity, have become commonplace on devices such as calculators and watches. There are a number of technologies in development with the aim of making PV more economic for electrical power generation. All use semiconductor materials like those used in silicon chips.

The heart of a PV cell is the interface between two different types of semi-conductor. When a light photon hits a silicon atom in this region, it throws out an electron. The electron can travel through the n-type semiconductor to metal contacts on the surface. The hole left by the absence of the electron travels in the opposite direction. Once at the metal contact the electron flows through an electrical circuit back to meet up with a hole at the other contact.

As it flows through the external circuit, the electron does useful work, like charging a battery, or operating an electrical appliance. Photovoltaic systems have been reducing in cost, and increasing in efficiency in recent years. The most efficient commercially available systems can convert up to 16 per cent of the light energy that strikes them into electrical energy.

4. Solar Concentrators: If the sun's rays are concentrated using mirrors, much higher temperatures can be created—enough to make steam to drive a turbine and generate electricity. The light is focused onto a central collector with oil flowing through it. The oil heats up to 400°C, and then moves on to heat water and make high pressure steam.

Solar concentrators only work in direct sunshine, with the collector aimed right at the sun. The mirror is held on a support that can turn to follow the sun as it moves throughout the day, adding to complexity and cost. Because of this, they are only used in areas benefiting from a sunny climate, with more clear days.

An Introduction to Solar Energy

In today's climate of growing energy needs and increasing environmental concern, alternatives to the use of non-renewable and polluting fossil fuels have to be investigated. One such alternative is solar energy.

Solar energy is quite simply the energy produced directly by the sun and collected elsewhere, normally the Earth. The sun creates its energy through a thermo-nuclear process that converts about 650,000,000 tons of hydrogen to helium every second. The process creates heat and electro-magnetic radiation. The heat remains in the sun and is instrumental in maintaining the thermo-nuclear reaction. The electro-magnetic radiation (including visible light, infra-red light, and ultra-violet radiation) streams out into space in all directions.

Only a very small fraction of the total radiation produced reaches the Earth. The radiation that does reach the Earth is the indirect source of nearly every type of energy used today. The exceptions are geothermal energy, and nuclear fission and fusion. Even fossil fuels owe their origins to the sun; they were once living plants and animals whose life was dependent upon the sun.

Much of the world's required energy can be supplied directly by solar power. More still can be provided indirectly. The practicality of doing so will be examined, as well as the benefits and drawbacks. In addition, the uses solar energy is currently applied to will be noted.

Due to the nature of solar energy, two components are required to have a functional solar energy generator. These two components are a collector and a storage unit. The collector simply collects the radiation that falls on it and converts a fraction of it to other forms of energy (either electricity and heat or heat alone). The storage unit is required because of the non-constant nature of solar energy; at certain times only a very small amount of radiation will be received. At night or during heavy cloud cover, for example, the amount of energy produced by the collector will be quite small. The storage unit can hold the excess energy produced during the periods of maximum productivity, and release it when the productivity drops. In practice, a backup power supply is usually added, too, for the situations when the amount of energy required is greater than both what is being produced and what is stored in the container.

Methods of collecting and storing solar energy vary depending on the uses planned for the solar generator. In general, there are three types of collectors and many forms of storage units.

The three types of collectors are flat-plate collectors, focussing collectors, and passive collectors.

Flat-plate collectors are the more commonly used type of collector today. They are arrays of solar panels arranged in a simple plane. They can be of nearly any size, and have an output that is directly related to a few variables including size, facing, and cleanliness. These variables all affect the amount of radiation that falls on the collector. Often these collector panels have automated machinery that keeps them facing the sun. The additional energy they take in due to the correction of facing more than compensates for the energy needed to drive the extra machinery.

Focussing collectors are essentially flat-plane collectors with optical devices arranged to maximize the radiation falling on the focus of the collector. These are currently used only in a few scattered areas. Solar furnaces are examples of this type of collector. Although they can produce far greater amounts of energy at a single point than the flat-plane collectors can, they lose some of the radiation that the flat-plane panels do not. Radiation reflected off the ground will be used by flat-plane panels but usually will be ignored by focussing collectors (in snow covered regions, this reflected radiation can be significant). One other problem with focussing collectors in general is due to temperature. The fragile silicon components that absorb the incoming radiation lose efficiency at high temperatures, and if they get too hot they can even be permanently damaged. The focussing collectors by their very nature can create much higher temperatures and need more safeguards to protect their silicon components.

Passive collectors are completely different from the other two types of collectors. The passive collectors absorb radiation and convert it to heat naturally, without being designed and built to do so. All objects have this property to some extent, but only some objects (like walls) will be able to produce enough heat to make it worthwhile. Often their natural ability to convert radiation to heat is enhanced in some way or another (by being painted black, for example) and a system for transferring the heat to a different location is generally added.

People use energy for many things, but a few general tasks consume most of the energy. These tasks include transportation, heating, cooling, and the generation of electricity. Solar energy can be applied to all four of these tasks with different levels of success.

Heating is the business for which solar energy is best suited. Solar heating requires almost no energy transformation, so it has a very high efficiency. Heat energy can be stored in a liquid, such as water, or in a packed bed. A packed bed is a container filled with small objects that can hold heat (such as stones) with air space between them. Heat energy is also often stored in phase-changer or heat-of-fusion units. These devices will utilize a chemical that changes phase from solid to liquid at a temperature that can be produced by the solar collector. The energy of the collector is used to change the chemical to its liquid phase, and is as a result stored in the chemical itself. It can be tapped later by allowing the chemical to revert to its solid form. Solar energy is frequently used in residential homes to heat water. This is an easy application, as the desired end result (hot water) is the storage facility, A hot water tank is filled with hot water during the day, and drained as needed. This application is a very simple adjustment from the normal fossil fuel water heaters.

Swimming pools are often heated by solar power. Sometimes the pool itself functions as the storage unit, and sometimes a packed bed is added to store the heat. Whether or not a packed bed is used, some method of keeping the pool's heat for longer than normal periods (like a cover) is generally employed to help keep the water at a warm temperature when it is not in use.

Solar energy is often used to directly heat a house or building. Heating a building requires much more energy than heating a building's water, so much larger panels are necessary. Generally a building that is heated by solar power will have its water heated by solar power as well. The type of storage facility most often used for such large solar heaters is the heat-of-fusion storage unit, but other kinds (such as the packed bed or hot water tank) can be used as well. This application of solar power is less common than the two mentioned above, because of the cost of the large panels and storage system required to make it work. Often if an entire building is heated by solar power, passive collectors are used in addition to one of the other two types. Passive collectors will generally be an integral part of the building itself, so buildings taking advantage of passive collectors must be created with solar heating in mind.

These passive collectors can take a few different forms. The most basic type is the incidental heat trap. The idea behind the heat trap is fairly simple. Allow the maximum amount of light possible inside through a window (The window should be facing towards the equator for this to be achieved) and allow it to fall on a floor made of stone or another heat holding material. During the day, the area will stay cool as the floor absorbs most of the heat, and at night, the area will stay warm as the stone re-emits the heat it absorbed during the day.

Another major form of passive collector is thermosyphoning walls and/or roof. With this passive collector, the heat normally absorbed and wasted in the walls and roof is re-routed into the area that needs to be heated.

The last major form of passive collector is the solar pond. This is very similar to the solar heated pool described above, but the emphasis is different. With swimming pools, the desired result is a warm pool. With the solar pond, the whole purpose of the pond is to serve as an energy regulator for a building. The pond is placed either adjacent to or on the building, and it will absorb solar energy and convert it to heat during the day. This heat can be taken into the building, or if the building has more than enough heat already, heat can be dumped from the building into the pond.

Solar energy can be used for other things besides heating. It may seem strange, but one of the most common uses of solar energy today is cooling. Solar cooling is far more expensive than solar heating, so it is almost never seen in private homes. Solar energy is used to cool things by phase changing a liquid to gas through heat, and then forcing the gas into a lower pressure chamber. The temperature of a gas is related to the pressure containing it, and all other things being held equal, the same gas under a lower pressure will have a lower temperature. This cool gas will be used to absorb heat from the area of interest and then be forced into a region of higher pressure where the excess heat will be lost to the outside world. The net effect is that of a pump moving heat from one area into another, and the first is accordingly cooled.

Besides being used for heating and cooling, solar energy can be directly converted to electricity. Most of our tools are designed to be driven by electricity, so if you can create electricity through solar power, you can run almost anything with solar power. The solar collectors that convert radiation into electricity can be either flat-plane collectors or focussing collectors, and the silicon components of these collectors are photovoltaic cells.

Photovoltaic cells, by their very nature, convert radiation to electricity. This phenomenon has been known for well over half a century, but until recently the amounts of electricity generated were good for little more than measuring radiation intensity. Most of the photovoltaic cells on the market today operate at an efficiency of less than 15 per cent; that is, of all the radiation that falls upon them, less than 15 per cent of it is converted to electricity. The maximum theoretical efficiency for a photovoltaic cell is only 32.3 per cent, but at this efficiency, solar electricity is very economical. Most of our other forms of electricity generation are at a lower efficiency than this. Unfortunately, reality still lags behind theory and a 15 per cent efficiency is not usually considered economical by most power companies, even if it is fine for toys and pocket calculators. Hope for bulk solar electricity should not be abandoned, however, for recent scientific advances have created a solar cell with an efficiency of 28.2 per cent efficiency in the laboratory. This type of cell has yet to be field tested. If it maintains its efficiency in the uncontrolled environment of the outside world, and if it does not have a tendency to break down, it will be economical for power companies to build solar power facilities after all.

Of the main types of energy usage, the least suited to solar power is transportation. While large, relatively slow vehicles like ships could power themselves with large onboard solar panels, small constantly turning vehicles like cars could not. The only possible way a car could be completely solar powered would be through the use of battery that was charged by solar power at some stationary point and then later loaded into the car. Electric cars that are partially powered by solar energy are available now, but it is unlikely that solar power will provide the world's transportation costs in the near future.

Solar power has two big advantages over fossil fuels. The first is in the fact that it is renewable; it is never going to run out. The second is its effect on the environment.

While the burning of fossil fuels introduces many harmful pollutants into the atmosphere and contributes to environmental problems like global warming and acid rain, solar energy is completely non-polluting. While many acres of land must be destroyed to feed a fossil fuel energy plant its required fuel, the only land that must be destroyed for a solar energy plant is the land that it stands on. Indeed, if a solar energy system were incorporated into every business and dwelling, no land would have to be destroyed in the name of energy. This ability to decentralize solar energy is something that fossil fuel burning cannot match.

As the primary element of construction of solar panels, silicon, is the second most common element on the planet, there is very little environmental disturbance caused by the creation of solar panels. In fact, solar energy only causes environmental disruption if it is centralized and produced on a gigantic scale. Solar power certainly can be produced on a gigantic scale, too.

Among the renewable resources, only in solar power do we find the potential for an energy source capable of supplying more energy than is used.

Suppose that of the 4.5×10^{17} kWh per annum that is used by the earth to evaporate water from the oceans we were to acquire just 0.1 per cent or 4.5×10^{14} kWh per annum. Dividing by the hours in the year gives a continuous yield of 2.90×10^{10} kW. This would supply 2.4 kW to 12.1 billion people.[6]

This translates to roughly the amount of energy used today by the average American available to over twelve billion people. Since this is greater than the estimated carrying capacity of the Earth, this would be enough energy to supply the entire planet regardless of the population.

Unfortunately, at this scale, the production of solar energy would have some unpredictable negative environmental effects. If all the solar collectors were placed in one or just a few areas, they would probably have large effects on the local environment, and possibly have large effects on the world environment. Everything from changes in local rain conditions to another Ice Age has been predicted as a result of producing solar energy on this scale. The problem lies in the change of temperature and humidity near a solar panel; if the energy producing panels are kept non-centralized, they should not create the same local, mass temperature change that could have such bad effects on the environment.

Of all the energy sources available, solar has perhaps the most promise. Numerically, it is capable of producing the raw power required to satisfy the entire planet's energy needs. Environmentally, it is one of the least destructive of all the sources of energy. Practically, it can be adjusted to power nearly everything except transportation with very little adjustment, and even transportation with some modest modifications to the current general system of travel. Clearly, solar energy is a resource of the future.

About Solar Power Applications

Depending upon your needs and where you live, there are a variety of solar power systems that could work for you.

Solar Power Systems—Grid-Tied (On Grid)

Most people install grid-tied solar power systems-most often in cities, suburbs and industrial areas where access to utility-generated power is available. You can supplement your solar powered electricity with utility-generated energy if you use more electricity than the solar power system supplies.

When your solar power system produces more electricity you need, you can sell the excess to the PG&E, who delivers the clean, renewable energy to other customers. Consequently, the good you do for the environment doesn't stop at your home or office. Even neighbours without solar power can draw upon the renewable energy of the sun-while you bank credit to offset the utility-generated power you use at night.

Solar Power Systems—Grid-Tied with Battery Backup

Solar energy panels combined with batteries and generators for grid-tie applications couple the clean, power supplied by solar panels with the assurance that you will have electricity even during power outages that last for extended periods. During the day, the solar panels generate electricity as needed and charges batteries. If more power is required, or the batteries begin to run low, the natural gas or propane generator kicks in to recharge the batteries. It automatically shuts off when the batteries are fully charged.

Solar Power Systems—Off-Grid

Standalone, or off-grid, solar power systems consist of solar panels and a battery bank. They are typically used in rural areas and regions where there is no access to the utility grid. They may also be appropriate where the grid is somewhat close to the site, but expensive to bring in—for example, across a neighbour's property. We have installed a number of systems with battery back-up where the grid is available but where the homeowner has experienced unreliable power in the past or believes that he/she will be subject to power outages in the future. We have seen a number of property owners install battery back-up system just for philosophical reasons, for the desire to be independent of the grid and the 'gaming' to which utility companies and their power suppliers have subjected customers in the past.

It may cost you as high as $50 per foot to bring utility power to your property, after which you'll continue to pay for power forever. It's often less expensive to add a solar energy system from the start and be your own power company. You can add the solar power system cost to your mortgage, reducing the combined costs of mortgage and utility bills.

When your off-grid solar power system produces excess electricity during the day, it is used to charge the batteries. When the sun's not shining, electricity is drawn from the batteries to power the home or business. The advantage is greater independence for you. The disadvantage is greater complexity and cost.

Solar Power System—Direct DC

Simple, direct DC solar power systems produce energy where and when it's needed. Common uses include powering water pumps and fans. There is no complex wiring, so storage and control systems aren't required. Small systems are easy to transport and install.

Hybrid Power Systems

Hybrid power systems combine various sources of electrical generation, and are well suited for electrification. Solar and wind technologies are modular, and seasonal variations of sun and wind often complement each other.

Advantages of Solar Power

The first commercial use of photovoltaic cells nearly 50 years ago was powering communications satellites in near-earth orbit. Today, the declining cost and increasing efficiency of solar energy technology has given rise to practical applications on earth-from powering personal electronic devices, homes and factories to generating utility-scale power.

Solar energy provides a huge advantage for satellites because they can be launched into orbit without the added weight of a fuel supply. But the advantages on earth are even greater: Solar-generated energy provides abundant and pollution-free energy that's not dependent on fuel-delivery infrastructures, foreign relations or the price machinations of energy brokers and big business.

Moreover, solar power generation provides energy when and where you need it, and is highly scalable to match your electrical demand. Since solar energy cells have no moving parts, they are reliable and easy to maintain.

Solar power has become increasing practical over the last several years. It has gone from a relatively expensive source of electricity to a reasonably economical one. But even beyond the money it can save you on your electrical bill, solar power has tremendous advantages for your home.

Of course, the amount of power you can generate is limited by the amount of sunlight you get. But even in areas with a lot of clouds it is possible to generate some electricity.

Perhaps the greatest advantage of solar power is quite simply the inexhaustable supply. You don't need to worry that the sun is going anywhere! There may be times that you generate less electricity than you need, and thus still need to rely on the power grid, but other times you may be able to sell your excess.

Another advantage is that the generation of solar power does not cause pollution. Once the solar panels are created they generate electricity without any emissions. There is even work being done toward making the recycling of solar panels more effective.

Solar power is quite flexible. You can have an array of solar panels on your roof to generate power for your home, and also have smaller solar cells on garden lights or anything else outside that only needs a small amount of electricity. Not having to run wiring can be a huge timesaver!

Solar power can be used for an impressive array of devices. It is perfect for satellites (not that this helps the average homeowner, other than to encourage solar panel research). There is work being done on producing an effective solar powered car. And, of course, you can use solar power at home.

The technology of solar power generation is steadily advancing, making it more and more practical as time goes by.

Of course, you cannot forget to note that many states are now offering rebates for installing solar power in your home. This has brought the cost down to where it is more reasonable for more families to install solar power.

Solar power is perfect for power generation in remote areas. It costs far less to install solar panels in some areas than it would to run power lines out.

Finally, a properly constructed solar power system requires very little maintenance. This can be a huge advantage when compared to other forms of power generation for those who must rely on their own systems.

There are many advantages worth considering when it comes to solar energy and everything that it offers. There are many advantages that solar energy has over oil energy. Not only does solar energy benefit your pocketbook, but it also benefits the environment as well. However, there are two sides to everything, and there is a list of solar power disadvantages to accompany the list of advantages.

Advantages

- Solar energy is a completely renewable resource. This means that even when we cannot make use of the sun's power because of nighttime or cloudy and stormy days, we can always rely on the sun showing up the very next day as a constant and consistent power source.
- Oil, which is what most people currently use to power their homes, is not a renewable resource. This means that as soon as the oil is gone, it is gone forever and we will no longer have power or energy.
- Solar cells make absolutely no noise at all. They do not make a single peep while extracting useful energy from the sun. On the other hand, the giant machines utilized for pumping oil are extremely noisy and therefore very impractical.
- Solar energy creates absolutely no pollution. This is perhaps the most important advantage that makes solar energy so much more practical than oil. Oil burning releases harmful greenhouses gases, carcinogens and carbon dioxide into our precious air.
- Very little maintenance is required to keep solar cells running. There are no moving parts in a solar cell, which makes it impossible to really hurt them. Solar cells tend to last a good long time with only an annual cleaning to worry about.
- Solar panels and solar lighting may seem quite expensive when you first purchase it, but in the long run you will find yourself saving quite a great deal of money. After all, it does not cost anything to harness the power of the sun. Unfortunately, paying for oil is an expensive prospect and the cost is still rising consistently. Why pay for expensive energy when you can harness it freely?
- Solar powered panels and products are typically extremely easy to install. Wires, cords and power sources are not needed at all, making this an easy prospect to employ.
- Solar power technology is improving consistently over time, as people begin to understand all of the benefits offered by this incredible technology. As our oil reserves decline, it is important for us to turn to alternative sources for energy.

Disadvantages

- The Solar Cells and Solar Panels that are needed to harness solar energy tend to be very expensive when you first purchase them.
- Solar power cannot be harnessed during a storm, on a cloudy day or at night. This limits how much power can be saved for future days. Some days you may still need to rely on oil to power your home.

Relation Between Environment

Energy services can provide cross-cutting influences on both social and economic development, thereby influencing a nation's ability to achieving Millennium Development Goals (MDGs). For the 2 billion people in the world who have no regular access to reliable energy services, electrification or the availability of clean cooking fuels could reduce poverty, improve health conditions, and increase standards of living.

Solar Energy and the Environment

Solar energy is the radiant light and sun's heat. This free accessible energy has been harnessed by humans for thousands of years using a selection of ever-evolving technologies. Still today, only an infinitesimal fraction of the available solar energy is used. Solar power provides electrical generation through heat engines or photovoltaic. Solar applications includes space cooling and heating through solar architecture, potable water via distillation and disinfection, day lighting, hot water, thermal energy for cooking, and high temperature process heat for industrial purposes.

Energy obtained from solar energy is clean. Clean the sun's energy can replace power sources that pollute the environment. The few emissions of greenhouse gases or air pollutants generated by solar energy technologies occur mostly during the manufacturing process. A 100-megawatt solar thermal electric power plant, over its 20-year life, will avoid more than 3 million tons of carbon dioxide (CO_2) emissions when compared to the cleanest conventional fossil fuel-powered electric plants available today.

Many countries through several national and international institutes and agencies have started taking actions to reduce (or eliminate) the pollutant emissions and to attain a sustainable supply of energy. One method to achieve this is to apply solar energy whenever you can. This is in compliance with the agreement signed in the December 1997 in International Kyoto Conference on climate change, where a directory of fifteen concrete proposals emerged for the reduction of global greenhouse gas emissions. The list includes, among others, using solar energy.

Energy is considered a prime agent in the generation of wealth and a significant factor in economic development. The significance of energy in economic development is recognized universally, and historical data verify that you've a strong relationship between the availability of energy and economic activity. Increase in economic activity also increases environmental problems. The growing evidence of environmental problems is because combining several factors, since the environmental impact of human activities has grown dramatically. This is a result of the increase on the planet population, energy consumption and industrial activities.

The most crucial benefit of renewable energy systems is the decrease of environmental pollution, clean energy with no emissions or noise pollution, low operating and maintenance costs, emissions from manufacturing and construction are quickly offset, reliable systems, useful for grid connected and remote applications, modular systems that could be constructed to any size, and creation of new jobs.

The negative environmental impact of solar energy systems includes land displacement and possible air and water pollution resulting from manufacturing, normal maintenance operations and demolition of the systems. However, land use is no issue when collectors.

Solar Power

Introduction

We've used the Sun for drying clothes and food for thousands of years, but only recently have we been able to use it for generating power. The Sun is 150 million kilometres away, and amazingly powerful. Just the tiny fraction of the Sun's energy that hits the Earth (around a hundredth of a millionth of a per cent) is enough to meet all our power needs many times over. In fact, every minute, enough energy arrives at the Earth to meet our demands for a whole year—if only we could harness it properly. Currently in the UK there are grants available to help you install solar power in your home.

California Energy Commission (Sacramento, Calif.) has started the review of the proposed 'Hidden Hills' concentrating solar power project (CSP) in Inyo County. At a regular business meeting on October 5th, 2011, the Energy Commission voted to accept the application for certification for the 500-megawatt solar thermal power project as data adequate.

Data adequacy means the Energy Commission received enough information from the applicant. Hidden Hills Solar Holdings, L.L.C, to begin the discovery analysis phase of the certification process. Hidden Hills Solar Holdings, LLC is a wholly owned subsidiary of Bright Energy, Inc.

Two separate 250-MW CSP plants, each with a solar field of about 85,000 heliostats.

The project will be located on 3,277 acres of privately owned land leased in Inyo Count next to the Nevada border. The project site about 18 miles south of Pahrump, Nevada and about 45 miles west of Las Vegas.

Transmission and natural gas pipeline alignments will be located in Nevada, primarily on land managed by the U.S. Bureau of Land Management.

The applicant will be constructing two separate 250-megawatt solar thermal power plants, each with its own solar field of about 85,000 heliostats and a 750-foot tall solar power tower.

The plant will use heliostats, which are elevated mirrors guided by a tracking system mounted on a pylon, to focus the sun's rays on a solar receiver steam generator atop a power near the center of the solar field.

The Commission named Energy Commissioner Karen Douglas as the presiding member of the committee reviewing the project. Commissioner Carla Peterman is the associate committee member. The committee will ensure that the project meets the Energy Commission's sitting requirements, as well as those of the California Environmental Quality Act (CEQA). The Energy Commission is responsible for reviewing thermal electric power plants that are 50 megawatts and greater in California.

As lead agency under CEQA, the Energy Commission, through its facility certification process, examines public health and safety, environmental impacts, and engineering aspects of proposed power plants and all related facilities, such as electric transmission lines and natural gas and water pipelines.

1,087 jobs at the peak of construction; 120 full-time jobs in operation.

The capital cost for the project is estimated to exceed USD 2.7 billion. The project will create 1,087 jobs at the peak of the 29-month construction period, with another 120 full-time jobs when the project is operational.

If approved by the Energy Commission, construction is expected to be completed by the fourth quarter of 2014 or the first quarter of 2015. Commercial operation of the first solar plant would be in the first quarter of 2015, with the second solar plant operating in the second quarter of 2015.

Solar Water Pump for Irrigation

We supply solar submersible pump with the tanks used in dry area, will include solar pump, solar panels, solar pump controller, storage batteries, level sensors, inverter as requested, flow rate is from 0.20-12m_3/h and head can up to 180m we are now the first factory that could supply exceed 1000 watts of the solar pumps in China, now the maximum power solar pump could up to 4000 watts, and the head can up to 252m with flow rate 2m3/h. we can supply the models as requested, we tested with controllers between Lorentz and ours, found the efficiency ours is higher 10 pre cent than that of Lorentz.

- Suitable for domestic and commercial applications
- Different types available in Submersible well requirements
- Superior Quality Solar Panels

- Available in different capacities
- Protections are provided with control panels
- Suitable for continuous operations
- Trouble free, pollution free, noise free.

No.	Model	Power (*watts*)	Voltage (*V*)	Head (*m*)	Flow Rate (m^3/h)	Outlet Size (*mm*)	Solar Panels (*watts*)
1.	SP120-03	120	24	26	0.3	32	160
2.	SP 150-0.3	150	24	31	0.3	32	200
3.	SP200-0.3	200	36	47	0.3	32	260
4.	SP350-0.5	350	36	51	0.5	50	460
5.	SP500-0.5	500	48	63	0.5	50	660
6.	SP700.07	700	72	93	0.7	50	920
7.	SP1100-1.5	1100	110	90	1.5	50	1400
8.	SP1100-8	1100	110	25	8.0		1440
9.	SP2300-10	2300	220	35	10.0	50	3200
10.	SP3000-12	3000	300	40	12.0	50	4200
11.	SP500-1.0/3	500	48	34	1.0	50	660
12.	SP500-3.0/2	500	48	22	3.0	50	660
13.	SP750-1.5/6	750	72	56	1.5	50	1000
14.	SP750-3.0/4	750	72	36	3.0	50	1000
15.	SP750-5.0/3	750	72	26	5.0	75	1000
16.	SP1100-1.0/11	1100	110	85	1.0	50	1440
17.	SP1100-3.0/8	1100	110	54	3.0	50	1440
18.	SP1100-5.0/6	1100	110	40	5.0	50	1440
19.	SP1100-7.0/4	1100	110	24	7.0	75	1440
20.	SP1500-1.0/17	1500	150	130	1.0	50	2100
21.	SP1500-2.0/16	1500	150	110	2.0	50	2100
22.	SP1500/3.0/12	1500	150	86	3.0	50	2100
23.	SP1500-5.0/8	1500	150	55	5.0	75	2100
24.	SP1500-7.0/6	1500	150	35	7.0	75	2100
25.	SP2200-1.0/23	2200	220	160	1.0	50	3200
26.	SP2200-2.0/20	2200	220	145	2.0	50	3200
27.	SP2200-3.0/18	2200	220	110	3.0	50	3200
28.	SP2200-5.0/10	2200	220	70	5.0	75	3200
29.	SP2200-7.0/7	2200	220	40	7.0	75	3200
30.	SP2200-18.0/3	2200	220	25	18.0	75	3200
31.	SP3000-1.0/26	3000	300	250	1.0	50	4200
32.	SP3000-3.0/22	3000	300	130	3.0	50	4200
33.	SP3000-4.8/14	3000	300	118	4.8	75	4200
34.	SP3000-6.0/11	3000	300	77	6.0	75	4200
35.	SP300-14.0/3	3000	300	36	14.0	75	4200
36.	SP3000-25.0/2	3000	300	25	25.0	75	4200

New Models of Solar Pumps

No.	Model	Power Watt	Flow and Lift	m³/h&m	Outlet (inch)
1.	4PSP2-3-27-48/500	500	1.2m³/h 30m	2.4m³/h 2m³/h 27m 23m	1 1/2
2.	4PSP2-6-50-72/700	700	1.2m³/h 56m	2.4 m³/h 2m³/h 50m. 47m	
3.	4pSP2-11-70-110/1100	1100	1.2m³/h 81m	2.4m³/h 2m³/h 70m 64m	
4.	4PSP2-17-112-150/1500	1500	1.2m³/h 128m	2.4m³/h 2m³/h 112m 104m	
5.	4PSP2-23-140-220/2200	2200	1.2m³/h 160m	2.4m³/h 2m³/h 140m 127m	
6.	4PSP2-26-222-300/3300	3000	1.2m³/h 258m	2.4m³/h 2m³/h 222m 203m	
7.	4PSP3-16-88-150/1500	1500	2.4m³/h 104m	3.6m³/h 3m³/h 88m 71m	
8.	4PSP3-20-107-220/2200	2200	2.4m³/h 37m	3.6m³/h 3m³/h 107m 82m	
9.	4PSP4-2-17-48/500	500	3.6m³/h 19m	4.8m³/h 4m⁴/h 17m 14m	
10.	4PSP4-4-32-72/700	700	3.6m³/h 34m	4.8m³/h 4m³/h 32m 26m	
11.	4PSP4-8-46-110/1100	1100	3.6m³/h 49m	4.8m³/h 4m³/h 46m 37m	
12.	4PSP4-12-72-150/1500	1500	3.6m³/h 77m	4.8m³/h 4m³/h 72m 60m	
13.	4PSP4-18-97-220/2200	2200	3.6m³/h 106m	4.8m³/h 4m³/h 97m 76m	
14.	4PSP4-22-109-300/300	3000	3.6m³/h 120m	4.8m³/h 4m³/h 109m 82m	

...(Contd.)

No.	Model	Power Watt	Flow and Lift	m³/h&m	Outlet (inch)
15.	4PSP6-3-22-72/700	700	4.8m^3/h 27m	6m^3/h 22m 7.2m^3/h 17m	
17.	4PSP-6-8-50-150/1500	1500	4.8m^3/h 59m	6m^3/h 50m 7.2 m^3/h 37m	
18.	4PSP6-10-62-110/1100	1100	4.8m^3/h 72m	6m^3/h 62m 7.2m^3/h 44m	
19.	4PSP6-14-103-300/3000	3000	4.8m^3/h 117m	6m^3/h 103m 7.2m^3/h 83m	
20.	4PSP8-4-21-110/1100	1100	7.2m^3/h 23m	8m^3/h 21m 9.6m^3/h 17m	
21.	4PSP8-6-32-150/1500	1500	7.2m^3/h 35m	8m^3/h 32m 9.6m^3/h 26m	
22.	4PSP8-7-40-220/2200	2200	7.2m^3/h 43m	8m^3/h 40m 9.6m^3/h 31m	
23.	4PSP8-11-68-300/3000	3000	7.2m^3/h 72m	8m^3/h 68m 9.6m^3/h 58m	
24.	6PSP17-3-24-220/2200	2200	14m^3/h 27m	20m^3/h 19m 17m^3/h 24m 20m^3/h	
25.	6PSP17-3-32-300/3000	3000	14m^3/h 36m	17m^3/h 28m^3 32m	
26.	6PSP30-2-22-300/3000	3000	24m^3/h	236 m^3/h 21m30m^3/h 22m 18m	

SOLAR PUMP PERFORMANCE DATA (SCREW TYPE)

No.	Model	Power Watt	Flow & Lift m ^{3}/h Y m		Outlet (inch)
27.	3PS-0.3-28-24/120 120		0.24m^3/h 32m	0.3m^3/h 28m	0.36m^3/h 24m
28.	3PS-0.3-39-24/150-150		0.24m^3/h 44m	0.3m^3/h 39m	0.36m^3/h 33m
29.	4PS-0.3-50-36/200 200		0.24m^3/h 56m	0.3m^3/h 50m	0.36m^3/h 44m

...(Contd.)

No.	Model	Power Watt	Flow & Lift m ^{3}/h Y m		Outlet (inch)
30.	4PS-0.5-53-36/350 350		0.36m^3/h 60m	0.5m^3/h 53m	0.6m^3/h 46m
31.	4PS-0.5-81-48/500 500		0.36m^3/h 88m	0.5m^3/h 81m	0.6m^3/h 76m
32.	4PS-0.7-93-72/700 700		0.6m^3/h 100m	0.7m^3/h 93m	0.84m^3/h 86m

SOLAR PUMP PERFORMANCE DATA (STAINLESS STEEL TYPE)

No.	Model	Power Watt	Flow & Lift m ^{3}/h Y m		Outlet (inch)
33.	4PSSS5-7-38-110/1100	1100	3.6m^3/h 50m	4.8m^3/h 40m	6m^3/h 30m $1^1/_2$
34.	4PSS8-4-24-110/1100	1100	7.2m^3/h 27m	8.4m^3/h 23m	9.6m^3/h 20m
35.	4PSS14-2-110/1100	1100	12m^3/h 48m	414m^3/h 40m	16m^3/h 34m^2
36.	4PSS 14-6-41-300/3000	3000	12m^3/h 14m	14m^3/h 10m	16m^3/h 9m
37.	4PSS17-3-24-220/2200	2200	14m^3/h 35m	16m^3/h 31m	18m^3/h 29m
38.	4PSS17-3-32-300/3000	3000	14m^3/h 26m	16m^3/h 22m	18m^3/h 20m
39.	4PSS30-2-22-300/3000	3000	28m^3/h 24m	24m^3/h 22m	36m^3/h 18m^3
40.	6PSS46-1-13-300/3000	3000	36m^3/h 15m	42m^3/h 14m	48m^3/h 12m
41.	6PSS60-1-10-300/3000	3000	48m^3/h 11m	60 m^3/h 10m	72m^3/h 9m

Photovoltaic Technology

Photovltaic Technology (Singapore) started in 2002 and is to date, one of Singapore's most established designers and producers of solar energy products. PVTECH, caters specifically to the needs of its users, providing clients with reduced environmental impact on their property and lower operational costs. PVTECH strives to offer a comprehensive array of renewal energy and eco-friendly products that will enhance your quality of life while, at the same time contributing positively to the community by setting the standard for affordable clean electricity with solar technology of distinctly superior cost efficiency, versatility, and availability.

With a strong commitment to customer service, competitive pricing, and high standards of work quality, PVTECH identifies, develops and commercializes new and emerging technologies and energy systems that promise to play an increasingly important role in the green energy industry.

At PVTECH, our mission is to increase the awareness and promote the use of renewable energy, to accelerate the development and commercialization of renewable energy technologies. We share a common vision of creating a company dedicated to the successful manufacture and sale of innovative, high-quality products based on advanced materials and components.

Solar energy is commonly known as renewable/green energy—energy that is available in nature that can be tapped for use without causing pollution to the environment. Solar Energy has numerous advantageous over conventional energy.

The main benefits of using renewable energy are as follows:

Environmental Benefits

- Reduce dependency on conventional fuel sources, less damage to the environment
- Does not emit green house gases that contribute to global warming
- Infinitely available compared to conventional fuel sources (oil and coal) Energy Security
- Providing a hedge against future electricity price instability
- This will help ensure supply and avoid price fluctuation
- Increasing domestic security through a more diverse fuel mix

Social Benefits

- Creating positive publicity and enhancing public image on the organizational level
- Boosts local economy, renewable energy is produced locally adding to job creation

Product and Services

PVTECH engages in the invention, engineering, development and commercialization of new materials, products and production technology in the field of solar energy technology and we pride ourselves in providing superior solutions to clients trhough understanding and catering to their specific needs.

PVTECH's expertise is based on designing, manufacturing, and installing the most technologically advanced solar electric power systems available today.

Our Specialization is in Providing DC Application Solutions for

- Stand alone lighting system
- Small home system (up to 1 KW)

- Supply of gears required for solar systems
- Designing stand alone, Hybrid, Grid-tie systems

How It Works

There are three main ways that we use the Sun's energy:

1. Solar Cells

(really called 'photovoltaic', 'PV' or 'photoelectric' cells) that convert light directly into electricity. In a sunny climate, you can get enough power to run a 100 W light bulb from just one square metre of solar panel. This was originally developed in order to provide electricity for satellites, but these days many of us own calculators powered by solar cells.

People are increasingly installing PV panels on their roofs. This costs thousands of pounds, but if you have a south facing roof it can help with your electricity bills quite a bit, and the government pays you for any extra energy you produce and feed back into the National Grid (called the 'feed-in tariff').

But what do solar panels cost?

How much might they generate for you?

What's the 'payback time' until the money you've saved on bills is more than the cost of installation?

Find out with the 'solar calculator' at www.talksolarpanel.co.uk

2. Solar Water Heating

Where heat from the Sun is used to heat water in glass panels on your roof.

This means you don't need to use so much gas or electricity to heat your water at home.

Water is pumped through pipes in the panel. The pipes are painted black, so they get hotter when the Sun shines on them. The water is pumped in at the bottom so that convection helps the flow of hot water out of the top. This helps out your central heating system, and cuts your fuel bills. However, with the basic type of panel shown in the diagram you must drain the water out to stop the panels freezing in the winter. Some manufactures have systems that do this automatically water heating is easily worthwhile in places like California and Australia, where you get lots of sunshine. Mind you, as technology improves it's becoming worthwhile in the UK.

Here's a more advanced type of solar water heating panel. The suppliers claim that in the UK it can supply 90 per cent of a typical home's hot water needs from April to November.

This 'Thermomax' panel is made of a set of glass tubes. Each contains a metal plate with a blueish coating to help it absorb solar energy from IR to UV, so that even in diffuse sunlight you get a decent output. The air has been removed from the glass tubes a reduce heat loss, rather like a thermos flask.

Up the back of the metal plate is a 'heat pipe', which looks a copper rod but contains a liquid that transfers heat very quickly to the top of the glass tube. A water pipe runs across the top of the whole thing and picks up the heat from the tubes.

The suppliers claim that in the UK it can supply 90 per cent of a typical home's hot water needs from April to November.

Find out more at www.solarsense-uk.com/thermomax.php

3. Solar Furnace

A solar furnace is a structure that captures sunlight to produce high temperatures, usually for industry. This is done with a curved mirror (or an array of mirrors) that acts as a parabolic reflector, concentrating light (Insolation) onto a focal point. The temperature at the focal point may reach 3,500°C (6,330°F), and this heat can be used to generate electricity melt steel, make hydrogen fuel or nanomaterials.

Term 'solar furnace' has also evolved to refer to solar concentrator heating systems using parabolic mirrors or heliostats where 538°C (1,000 °F) is now commonly achieved. The largest solar furnace is at Odeillo in the Pyrenees-Orientales in France, opened in 1970. It employs an array of plane mirrors to gather sunlight, reflecting it onto a larger curved mirror. The rays are then focussed onto an area the size of a cooking pot and can reach 3,500°C (6,330 °F), depending on the process installed, for example:

- about 1,000°C (1,830°F) for metallic receivers producing hot air for the next generation solar towers as it will be tested at the Themis plant with the Pegase project;
- about 1,400°C (2,550°F) to produce hydrogenby cracking methane molecules;
- up to 2,500°C (4.530°F) to test materials for extreme environment such as nuclear reactor or space vehicle atmospheric recentry;
- up to 3,500°C (6,330°F) to produce nanomaterials by solar induced sublimation and controlled cooling, such as carbon nanotubes or zinc nanoparticles.

Advantages

- Solar energy is free—it needs no fuel and produces no waste or pollution.
- In sunny countries, solar power can be u' ed where there is no easy way to get electricity to a remote place.
- Handy for low-power uses such as solar powered garden lights and battery chargers, or for helping your home energy bills.

Disadvantages

- Doesn't work at night.
- Very expensive to build solar power stations, although the cost is coming down as technology improves. In the meantime, solar cells cost a great deal compared to the amount of electricty they'll produce in their lifetime.
- Can be unreliable unless you're in a very sunny climate. In the United Kingdom, solar power isn't much use for high-power applications, as you need a large area of solar panels to get a decent amount of power. However, technology has now reached the point where it can make a big difference to your home fuel bills.

Renewable and Non-Renewable

Renewable Energy Resources are ones that won't run out. *Example:* Winds will keep on blowing, whether we use the energy or not. So Wind power is a renewable energy resource.

Non-renewable resources will eventually run out. *Example:* When we've extracted all the Earth's oil, there isn't any more. So oil is NOT a renewable energy resource.

As we realise more and more that fossil fuels are going to run out, we're trying harder to develop other means of generating the electricity on which we depend. Renewable sources, such as solar, hydro-electric, tidal and wind power are particularly attractive are mounted on the top of a building, the maintenance required is minimal and the pollution caused by demolition is not greater than the pollution caused from demolition of a conventional system of the identical capacity.

It can, therefore, be concluded that solar energy systems are friendlier to the environment and offer significant protection of the environment. The reduction of greenhouse gases pollution is lower than replacement utilizing solar energy. Therefore, solar energy systems should be employed wherenever possible to get a sustainable future, thus applying the slogan "THINK GLOBALLY—ACT LOCALLY".

Industry and the Environment—Renewable Energy

This web page is a compendium of all the information about renewable energy sources and the relation between industry and the environment. It explains all doubts on this topic.

Renewable energy is often confused with the one obtained from the so-called, sources of non-environmental degradation. However, in most cases, its production is not indifferent to the ecology.

All renewable energy sources (RES) obtain energy from something that already exists, but without, as is the case with traditional power plants, hazardous waste generation and greenhouse gas emissions. The second its most important feature is the renwal, so it does not reach the energy deficits, their source is still working on its production, even if it is not needed.

HYDROGEN AS FUEL

Fuel Source

Hydrogen does not occur free in nature; it can be made by 're-forming' natural gas or another fossil fuel, or by using electricity to split ('electrolyze') water into its comppnents of oxygen and hydrogen. In this sense, hydrogen is like electricity: the energy to generate it can be obtained from sources ranging from the burning of high-sulfur coal to pollution-free photovoltaic cells (solar cells).

Wholesale Availability

There is not currently a bulk hydrogen distribution, infrastructure on anything like the scale of that for fossil fuels, though studies have been undertaken of the possibility of sending it through the existing natural-gas pipeline network (with some substantial modifications). Because hydrogen can be made from natural gas by re-forming or from water by electrolysis, and natural gas, electricity, and water are readily available, it might be simpler to make the hydrogen at the point of sale, rather than ship it there.

Retail Availability

See above; hydrogen is currently available only as an industrial or scientific chemical product, not as a bulk fuel.

Advantages

Hydrogen has been called the 'most alternative' of the alternative fuels: if it is made by electrolysis, of water using electricity from a non-polluting source like wind or solar power, then no pollutants of any kind are generated by burning, it in an internal combustion engine except for trace amounts of nitrogen oxides, and if it is used in a *fuel cell* then even these disappear. Furthermore, no greenhouse gases are generated because there's no *carbon* in the fuel. All that comes out the vehicle's exhaust is drinkable water! Using hydrogen as the 'battery' to store energy from a non-polluting, renewable source would result in a truly unlimited supply of clean fuel. The advantage of using hydrogen to store energy rather than a battery pack is that a hydrogen, tank can be refilled; in minutes rather than recharged in hours, and it takes less space and weight to store enough hydrogen to drive a given distance on a single refueling than it does to carry enough battery capacity to go the same distance on a single recharging. The battery electric drivetrain uses energy more efficiently, and can handle the vast majority of daily commute-and-errands driving that people do, but for long trips hydrogen could prove to be a lot more convenient.

Disadvantages

Hydrogen is currently very expensive not because it is rare (it's the most common element in the universe!) but because it's difficult to generate, handle, and store, requiring bulky and heavy tanks like those for *compressed natural gas* (CNG) or complex insulating bottles if stored as a cryogenic (super-cold) liquid like *liquefied natural gas* (LNG). It can also be stored at moderate temperatures and pressures in a tank containing a metal-hydride absorber or carbon adsorber, though these are currently very-expensive. It is possible to store a hydrogen-bearing fuel like natural gas, methanol, or even gasoline aboard the vehicle and re-form it to get hydrogen as needed; this simplifies storage and refueling, but adds cost and complexity to the drivetrain (and reduces efficiency). It is not a very good fuel for an internal combustion engine, being prone to preignition, though BMW, Mazda, and Ford have done some tests; the most efficient way to use it is in *fuel cell* vehicles, but these are still in the demonstration stage.

Under 'Advantages', above, I discussed the benefits of using Hydrogen generated from renewable, non-polluting power like solar electricity. However, as hydrogen fuel has gained political momentum, concern is growing that the inefficiencies of generating, transporting, and storing hydrogen may make it a poor choice if the energy used to generate the hydrogen comes from fossil fuels (whether via re-forming those fuels directly, or by burning them to generate electricity for. electrolysis of water). It is definitely more efficient to generate electricity from a fossil fuel, transport it via wires, and use it to charge, up a battery-electric vehicle/than it is to burn the same fossil fuel in an interrial-combustion engine aboard a conventional vehicle; however, it is uncertain whether it is more or less efficient to use that fossil fuel to generate hydrogen for use in a vehicle. If the hydrogen is produced at a central plant, there are inefficiencies associated with generating it, transporting it via truck or pipeline, and storing it aboard the vehicle as a compressed gas or cryogenic liquid; if it is generated at the point of sale by electrolysis, you can replace the inefficiency of trucking or piping the hydrogen with the efficient utility-line transportation of electricity, but you still have the other losses, and you add the fact that a smaller-scale hydrogen generator will be less efficient than a largerscale one. The jury is still out on whether it is more energy-efficient to use fossil fuels to make hydrogen than it is to burn them in a *hybrid-electric* vehicle, though on balance it looks likely that use of hydrogen will.cut down on ordinary combustion-engine pollutants like carbon monoxide, soot, and oxides, of nitrogen. Stay tuned...

A fuel is any compound that has stored energy. This energy is captured in chemical bonds through processes such as photosynthesis and respiration. Energy is released during oxidation. The most common form of oxidation is the direct reaction of a fuel with oxygen through combustion. Wood, gasoline, *coal* and any number of other fuels have energy-rich chemical bonds created using the energy from the *Sun,* which is released when the fuel is burned (*i.e.,* the release of chemical energy). Chemical fuels or the fossil fuels are useful reserve of fuels and are therefore used extensively to satisfy the demands of an energy-dependent civilization.

Fossil fuels are principally *hydrocarbons* with minor impurities. They are so named because they originate from the decayed and fossilized remains of plants and animals that lived millions of years ago.

Fossil fuels can be separated into three categories. The first is *petroleum* or oil. This is a mixture of light, simple hydrocarbons dominated by the fractions with 6 to 12 carbons but also containing some light hydrocarbons (*e.g.,* methane, and ethane). Fully half of the energy consumed in the United States is from petroleum used to produce fuels for automobiles, recreational vehicles, home heating, or industrial production.

The principal use of petroleum is the production of gasoline. Over 40 per cent all of all production ends up consumed in automobiles and such. Smaller fractions are turned into fuel oil (27%), jet fuel (7.4%), and other miscellaneous fuels, while the small fraction (about 10%) is used for the synthesis of tile thousands of petrochemicals used in out daily lives. Indeed, many food compounds and pharmaceuticals owe their synthesis to a petrochemical precursor.

The second most ptorminent and naturally most abundant fossil fuel is coal. Coal also originates from decayed vegetative material buried eons ago, but the process is slightly different, being less oxidizing. The resulting material still has some of the original lignin-like structure exhibiting many fused rings and a large fraction of aromatic compounds. Consequently, coal is more of a polymeric substance than petroleum and is found as a solid not a liquid. The *carbon* to hydrogen ratio in coal is close to 1:1 (depending upon the type of coal), whereas the carbon to hydrogen ration in petroleum is closer to the 1:2 value expected for a hydrocarbon chain.

Minable coal is defined as 50 per cent of the coal in a seam of at least 12 in thickness. The proven reserves of minable coal are sufficient to supply the industrial needs of modern society for the next four to five hundred years. Unfortunately, as a fuel source, coal has many disadvantages. It is a very dirty fuel that produces a large amount of unburned hydrocarbon, particulate and—most damaging of all—significant quantities of sulphur dioxide byproducts. Indeed, it is the coal burning power plants of the eastern United States that are responsible for much of the acid rain and environmental damage observed in upstate New York and eastern Canada. The other significant disadvantage of coal is that it is not liquid, making it awkward to transport andstore aridlimiting its use in applications like automobiles. A great deal of research has been done on the liquefaction of coal but with little economically viable success.

The third major fossil fuel is *natural gas*. This is a generic term for the light hydrocarbon fractions found associated with most oil deposits. Natural gas is mostly methane with small quantities of ethane and other gases mixed in. It is hydrogen rich, since methane has a carbon to hydrogen ratio of 1:4. It is also an excellent fuel, burning with a high heat output and little in the way of unwanted pollution. It does produce *carbon dioxide*, which is a greenhouse gas, but all organic compounds also generate Carbon dioxide on combustion. Natural gas is also easy to transport through pressurized pipelines.

All of this would appear to make natural gas the perfect fuel. However, it is not without its drawbacks. This includes the presence of hydrogen sulfide in some gas fields, leading to the term 'sour gas.' Hydrogen sulfide is the smell of rotten eggs, but if smell were the only problem, this would be of little concern. However, hydrogen sulfide is extremely corrosive to the pipes used to transport natural gas and is a very toxic compound being lethal at levels around 1,500 ppm.

In addition, natural gas is potentially explosive as the gas must be maintained under pressure, and any hydrocarbon, in a gaseous state, can explode. This is in contrast to the use of gasoline, which is a much safer fuel. Nevertheless, both the gaseous and liquid forms of hydrocarbons are much more volatile and represent a hazard compared to coal.

It has been suggested that because all of the oxygen in the atmosphere came from the splitting of carbon dioxide via photosynthesis, the total oxygen content may lead to an estimate of the total carbon reserves. However, it is not the total abundance of fuels that is critical—it is the accessibility from both an engineering and economics standpoint that makes near-term global fuel shortages appear probable.

In addition there are serious flaws ill the gross estimate of fuels as a significant amount of the world's carbon reserves are tied up in calcium carbonate *rock* formations. Loosely speaking, calcium carbonate is *limestone* and there is abundance of limestone present throughout the world. Accordingly, most industry analysts place available fossil fuel reserves at much lower levels. It is estimated by a wide variety of sources that we will reach maximum oil production in the next twenty years. After that, production will decline worldwide and we will be forced to wean ourselves from an oil-based society. The estimates for coal provide a slightly better prognosis giving a window of about 500 years for consumption ofall known reserves.

Natural gas also has one significant advantage over the other fossil fuels: it is "renewable." Natural gas is found as a side product of any decaying material. Methanogenic bacteria—literally, methane-making bacteria—exist in the garbage dumps and waste disposal sites of the industrial world, busily producing methane from garbage. Enough that the Fresh Kills garbage dump on Staten Island, New York is capable of heating 16,000 homes.

Various companies have been exploring the use of hydrogen as a fuel. When used in simple combustion, hydrogen has some of the problems associated with natural gas. It must be stored under pressure and is extremely explosive upon ignition in air (*e.g.* the Hindenburg disaster, in which a hydrogen-filled airship explosively burned). The type of explosion—the shape of the detonation—also makes hydrogen unsuitable as an alternative fuel for the conventional automobile. The sharpness of the explosion would quickly rattle pistons to pieces.

However, hydrogen does not need to be burned directly with oxygen to provide energy. Fuel cells combine hydrogen and oxygen at electrodes to produce *electricity,* which can then be used to run an electrics motor or a spacecraft. NASA has been employing hydrogen/oxygen fuel cells for years to provide the electricity for both manned and unmanned spacecraft. In addition, fuel cells have the added bonus of providing crew members with fresh drinking water, as the only product of the reaction is pure water. Using fuel cells, hydrogen could potentially be used for conventional automobiles. Questions about storing hydrogen and long-term viability of the fuel cells need to be addressed, but the future of this technology looks promising. At present, however, our economically viable supply of hydrogen is obtained from fossil fuels because hydrogen is released from hydrocarbons during the refining proces.

Both the use of sunlight and solar panels to create sufficient electricity to electrolyze water and bacteria capable of splitting water to generate hydrogen and oxygen may make hydrogen the chemical fuel of the future. In addition, research is underway into the use of methanol as a potential partner for a fuel cell, eliminating the need for hydrogen and greatly reducing the difficulties with storage and filling the tank.

Nuclear Fuels

An Introduction to Nuclear Energy

Nuclear energy is the energy that comes from the core or the nucleus of an atom. The bonds which hold the atoms together contain a massive amount of energy. This energy must be released in order to make electricity. This energy can be freed in two ways: nuclear fission and nuclear fusion.

Nuclear Fission and Nuclear Fusion

Nuclear fission works by splitting the atoms apart to produce smaller atoms, and as a result energy is released. Nuclear fission is used in nuclear power plants to generate electricity through the splitting of the nuclei of uranium atoms.

On the other hand, when atoms are joined together to form a larger atom is commonly referred to as nuclear fusion. The sun produces energy through nuclear fusion where the nuclei of hydrogen atoms are fused into helium atoms.

Uranium—The Nuclear Fuel

Uranium is the most common fuel used today by nuclear power plants. Uranium is a common metal discovered in rocks all over the world and it is considered as non-renewable. A certain type of uranium known as U-235 is used in nuclear power plants because its atoms are easily split apart.

Using Nuclear Energy to Generate Electricity

Power plants burn fuel to produce heat to generate electricity, however, nuclear power plants use the heat given off during fission as fuel to turn water into steam. Steam is then used to turn huge turbine blades that drive generators to make electricity.

Nuclear Energy and the Environment

Nuclear energy is cleaner than power plants that use fossil fuel such as coal to generate electricity. Nuclear power plants produce no carbon dioxide and air pollution.

Unfortunately, nuclear power generation has by-product wastes. These by-products are spent fuels, radioactive waste and heat. The primary environmental concerns for nuclear power are spent fuels and radioactive wastes. Most nuclear waste is low-level radioactive waste, while spent fuel assemblies are highly radioactive and must be stored initially in specially designed pools or dry storage containers.

While nuclear energy has come under a lot of scrutiny in the last several decades, mainly due to the two most famous incidents, The Three Mile Island accident and the disastrous Chernobyl explosion, nuclear power remains a viable renewable energy source that has minor environmental implications.

Nuclear power isn't a new concept. The very first nuclear fission was achieved in 1934 by an Italian Physicist named Enrico Fermi and the first nuclear power plant to generate electricity for an actual power grid was the USSR's Obninsk Nuclear Power Plant in 1954. The United States wasn't far behind with the construction of the Shippingport Reactor in Pennsylvania by the end of 1957. But even before the United States completed the construction on our first reactor, the US Navy embraced the power of nuclear energy and constructed the very first nuclear powered submarine in 1954 called the USS Nautilus. Since then, the US Navy has used nuclear energy to power more marine transportation than any other organization, powering watercraft like submarines and aircraft carriers.

Since the birth of nuclear power, the US has begun a steady process of developing this renewable energy source, but politics and misinformation about the energy source has somewhat slowed down the overall growth and use of nuclear in our energy consumption. It still stands today, however, that nuclear power is the world's largest source of emission-free energy—a fact that is indisputably hard to ignore.

How Does Nuclear Energy Work?

To really understand nuclear energy firstly you have to understand the general mechanics of the process in creating nuclear power. Nuclear energy occurs during a process called nuclear fission, where the atomic nucleus of an element absorbs a neutron and splits the atom into two or more smaller nuclei and releases a large amount of energy. Nuclear power plants harness this thermal energy to boil water and generate steam, which in turn powers a steam turbine and creates electricity.

Nuclear power can come from the fission of many different kinds of elements including, uranium, plutonium, or thorium. However, almost all of the nuclear power generated today comes from uranium. Today, almost 20 per cent of all the electricity produced in the United States comes from using nuclear power.

The Benefits of Using Nuclear Power

Nuclear power is a clean source of energy that produces no carbon-dioxide emissions or greenhouse gases. That means there is little impact on the environment, and we could actually improve the quality of the air if nuclear were to replace other fossil-burning energy sources such as coal, which produce huge amounts of pollution and waste.

For example, to make the comparison of nuclear power and coal, nuclear power produces only 2,000 tons of solid waste each year. While coal produces more than 100,000,000 tons of solid waste in the form of ash and sludge every year. That ash that is released into our environment contains poisons such as mercury and nitric acid—pollutants that are both harmful to the environment and to our health!

Also nuclear power has another advantage over coal. The fission of just one atom of uranium produces more than 10 million times the energy that comes from burning an atom of carbon from coal.

In terms of safety, nuclear power has been plagued by the myth that the harnessing of this type of clean energy is unsafe, but did you know that there has not been one single fatality from Nuclear power in the United States? During the Three Mile Island incident back in 1979, the reactor was destroyed, but the core itself remained confined and there is no evidence that the public was harmed.

Even more interesting is the infamous Chernobyl accident in 1986. When we really examine the facts of the case, we begin to understand that when compared to.other accidents that happen all over the world in the coal mining industry, the effects of Chernobyl were relatively minor. Only 31 people were killed during the explosion.

In the United States alone, there have been 717 coal mining disasters that resulted in at least 5 or more deaths, and more than 1500 coal miners die a year from black lung—a result of coal dust particles settling in the lungs. On average, about 60 people in the US die from coal mining accidents every year. In China, just from 2000-2008, almost 50,000 people have died due to coal mining.

Thousands of fatalities have occurred due to coal mining in the history of the United States. Compare that to not a single lost life for nuclear power in US history and there really is no comparison. After examining the construction of Chernobyl, it was determined that the design of the power plant was extremely poor and the actual maintenance itself wasn't up to par either. The reactor actually reached 150 times its normal power level before the water pressure was high enough to blow the plant apart.

The Future of Nuclear Power

In 2009, there were 439 nuclear reactors operating in 30 countries, with more than 40 under current construction. The United States has 104 nuclear reactors in operation today, generating 20 per cent of our total electricity production, and 26 new nuclear reactors are on the immediate horizon for the US.

While the construction of nuclear power plants had waned in recent years, the current geopolitical circumstances have revived the US's interest in developing nuclear power. With sufficient nuclear power, the United States could potentially reduce the current dependency on foreign imports for gas and oil and decrease the amount of pollution caused by the burning of these fuels.

Nuclear power is a powerful source of clean energy that can't be ignored. It has vast potential to power our country's energy needs without the dangers of mining and the harmful environmental implications that are produced from fossil-fuel consumption. And, when combined with other renewable clean energy sources such as wind, solar, hydro, and geothermal power, it could eventually lead to the United States being solely powered by clean, efficient energy that originates within our borders, cutting down our reliance on other countries to provide us with sufficient resources to supply our increased demand for energy.

NUCLEAR POWER TECHNOLOGY DEVELOPMENT SECTION

Highlights and Events

New Leadership for Nuclear Power Technology Development

14 September 2011—Mr Thomas Koshy has assumed the position of Section Head of the Nuclear Power Technology Development Section in the Division of Nuclear Power, IAEA Department of Nuclear Energy, effective September 2011.

Non-Electric Applications of Nuclear Energy

9 September 2011—Technical Meeting/Workshop on "Non-Electric Applications of Nuclear Energy" will be held at Nuclear Research Institute Rez, Prague, Czech Republic, 3-6 October 2011. The role of the meeting is to exchange information on current and future non-electric applications as well as assessing safety, economics and technical considerations associated.

IAEA Nuclear Power Newsletter—September 2011

1 September 2011—The latest issue of the *Nuclear Power Newsletter* (Vol. 8, No. 3) highlights results from the IAEA Ministerial Conference on Nuclear Safety. It also offers background articles on side events of the General Conference covering nuclear power issues. An event on establishing a Nuclear Industry Cooperation Forum will be held on 21 September 2011 *(See p. 6 of the Nuclear Power Newsletter and also see p. 10-11 for articles on Technology Development of Nuclear Power Reactors).*

Applications of Nuclear Energy

The most important application of nuclear energy is for electricity generation in thermonuclear plants. Thermonuclear power plants exploit the immense energy released during nuclear fission chain reaction. The chain reaction is controlled within reactors of thermonuclear power plants so that it proceeds at an appropriate speed for converting the heat given off during reaction to generate steam. The steam generated runs the turbine which in turns propels the electric generator.

If the nuclear fission chain reaction is left uncontrolled, it can release enormous amounts of energy resulting in nuclear explosion. This is the principle forming the basis of nuclear weapons such as an atomic bomb.

Benefits of Nuclear Energy

Nuclear energy is clean and efficient. The power plants that are fuelled by enriched uranium are clean as they do not release carbon dioxide in the atmosphere. Since a pound of nuclear fuel has the energy equivalent of 1,500 tons of coal, the saving in fossil fuel is enormous. Thus nuclear energy offers an environment friendly alternative to the dwindling fossil fuels.

Read more at Suite 101: *Applications and Limitations of Nuclear Energy | Suitel01.com http://zeeshan-amin.suitel01.com/applications-and-limitations-of-nuclear-energy-a254725#ixzzlaBNGvwlA*

Limitations of Nuclear Energy

Though conversion of nuclear energy into electricity does not pollute the environment, there are some other negative effects linked with it. Serious accidents resulting from safety failures may entail terrible and long lasting consequences. On the other hand, the solid residues produced by the fission process are radioactive and are stable enough to contaminate the environment for thousands of years.

Nuclear weapons also produce damage that is not experienced with chemical explosives. Much of the energy released during a weapons blast occurs in the form of X-rays, gamma rays, and other forms of radiation that can cause serious harm to plant and animal life.

In addition, the isotopes formed during fission and fusion—called fission products—are all radioactive.

These fission products are carried many miles away and deposited on the ground, on buildings, on plant life, and on animals. As they decay over the weeks, months, and years following a nuclear explosion, the fission products continue to release radiation, causing damage to surrounding organisms.

Nuclear Energy at Work

Nuclear fission chain reactions release energy in huge quantities. If properly exploited, they can be effective in overcoming our energy woes to a great extent. Nuclear energy is being used for *electricity generation*. On the other hand, the disposal of nuclear wastes is a tedious task as it is radioactive. Similarly, the harmful impacts of nuclear weapons are disastrous and long lasting.

Read more at Suite 101: *Applications and Limitations of Nuclear Energy I Suitelol.com http://zeeshan-amin.suitel01.com/applications-and-limitations-of-nuclear-energy-a254725#ixzz1aBNN8 y7d.*

Uses of Nuclear Energy

Nuclear energy in one of the safest energies, that can be used to achieve many desired results, provided it's used safely with due precautions. It can be used in diversified fields for peaceful purposes such as electricity generation, medicinal purposes, reduce pollution, etc.

Nuclear Energy is the energy that is released from the nucleus of an atom, as it is evident from the term nuclear. During the process, mass gets converted into energy. The relation between mass and energy is given by Einstein's famous formula $E = mc^2$, where 'E' is energy, 'm' is mass and 'c' is the constant speed of light. In brief, nuclear energy is the energy that is obtained from the splitting of uranium atoms in a process known as nuclear fission. Although there are three ways from which nuclear reaction is possible–fission, *fusion* and decay, only the energy from the first has been utilized till date.

REASONS TO USE NUCLEAR ENERGY

Environmental Safety

The process to generate nuclear energy is one of the most cleanest, and makes lowest impact on the environment. It is because nuclear plants do not emit any harmful gases like carbon dioxide, nitrogen oxide and sulphur dioxide, produced from the conventional electricity power plants that threaten atmosphere by increasing *global warming*. The energy can hence be termed as 'emission-free energy'. They require little space for the production, thus promoting land and habitat preservation. There is absolutely no effect on land, water and air resources.

Clean Water

The water discharged from nuclear power plants is very safe, free of any *radiation* or harmful pollutants, and meets all regulatory standards. Hence, helps in protecting the aquatic life and *conserving wildlife*.

Reliable

One utmost importance of nuclear energy, is reliability. The energy don't have to depend upon weather conditions, unpredictable costs or foreign supplies. Its a reliable source of energy even during extreme weather changes.

The plants can run for about 500 to 700 days continuously, before they are shut down for refuelling.

Reduces the Dependence on Fossil Fuels

There has been an increase in production and supply of *fossil fuels* like oil and gas, as the world has been using them at an unbelievable pace. Their deposits are emptying. On the other hand, nuclear energy requires very little quantity of fuel to produce large quantities of energy. Consider this, one ton of uranium can produce energy that is more than that of several million tons of coal and oil.

Peaceful Uses

There has been great advances in using nuclear energy for peaceful purposes, such as medicinal use of isotopes and radiation techniques. One major on-going advancement is Sterile Insect Technique (SIT), that helps in large scale food irrigation and biological control of pests. Other various uses are:

Food and Agriculture

The use of isotopes and radiation techniques in agriculture come under this category. Leading organizations have been working on the technology to increase agricultural production, improve food availability and quality, reduce production costs and minimize pollution of food crop.

Human Health

One very common application of nuclear energy, is in the treatment of cancer-radiotherapy. Also, small amounts of radioisotope tracers are used for diagnostic and research purposes. These techniques have helped in monitoring the levels of toxic substances in food, air and water.

Nuclear energy can also be used in industries for processing and sterilization of various products by means of radiation. With so many above mentioned advantages, *nuclear energy* is surely the fuel for the 21st century. To conclude, nuclear energy has enormous benefits but, its up to humans to use it safely, and for peaceful purposes.

Advantages and Disadvantages of Nuclear Energy

Nuclear energy is released from the nucleus of an atom. Nuclear reactions like fusion (when two atomic nuclei combine to form a single heavy nucleus) and fission (when a single heavy nucleus splits into two smaller nuclei), release very high amounts of energy. The mass of an atom gets converted into energy. Einstein's famous equation helps to calculate the amount of energy released during a nuclear reaction. This equation is given as:

$$E = mc^2$$

where, E is energy, m is mass, and c is the speed of light in vacuum

The energy released, is the result of the differences in the total mass of the participating elements, before and after the reaction. The process is a chain reaction and energy is released, until the atom becomes stable.

Nuclear energy, also known as atomic energy, was first discovered by French scientist Henri Becquerel in 1896. Nuclear energy is used as a power source. Nuclear reactors are the devices that initiate and control nuclear chain reactions. They are used as sources for generation of nuclear power. Currently, the fission process is prominently carried out in most of the nuclear reactors to generate energy. Uranium (U-235) is used as fuel for nuclear reactors because it's atoms split very easily. Fission reaction generates heat which helps boiling of water and produces steam. The pressurized steam moves the steam turbines, resulting in the production of electricity.

What are the Advantages of Nuclear Energy?

- Nuclear reactions release a million times more energy, as compared to hydro or wind energy. Hence, a large amount of electricity can be generated. Presently, 12-18 per cent of the world's electricity is generated through nuclear energy.
- The biggest advantage of nuclear energy is that there is no release of greenhouse gases (carbon dioxide, methane, ozone, chlorofluoro-carbon) during nuclear reaction. The greenhouse gases are a major threat in the current scenario, as they cause global warming and climate change. As there is no emission of these gases during nuclear reaction, there is very little effect on the environment.
- The burning of fossil fuels result in emission of the poisonous carbon dioxide. It is a menace to the environment as well as human life. There is no release of carbon di-oxide at the time of nuclear reaction.
- Nuclear reactors make use of uranium as fuel. Fission reaction of a small amount of uranium generates large amount of energy. Currently, the high reserves of uranium found on Earth, are expected to last for another 100 years.
- High amount of energy can be generated from a single nuclear power plant. Also, nuclear fuel is inexpensive and easier to transport.

What are the Disadvantages of Nuclear Energy?

- Nuclear energy can be used for production and proliferation of nuclear weapons. Nuclear weapons make use of fission, fusion or combination of both reactions for destructive purposes. They are a major threat to the world as they can cause a large-scale devastation.
- Though large amount of energy can be produced from a nuclear power plant, it requires large capital cost. Around 15-20 years are required to develop a single plant. Hence, it is not very feasible to build a

nuclear power'plant. The nuclear reactors will work only as long as uranium is available. Its extinction can again result in a grave problem.

- The waste produced after fission reactions contains unstable elements and is highly radioactive. It is very dangerous to the environment as well as human health, and remains so, for thousands of years. It needs professional handling and should be kept isolated from the living environment. The radioactivity of these elements reduces over a period of time, after decaying. Hence, they have to be carefully stored. It is very difficult to store radioactive elements for a long period.
- The Chernobyl disaster that occurred at the Chernobyl Nuclear Power Plant in Ukraine (1986), was the worst nuclear power plant disaster. One of the nuclear reactors of the plant exploded, releasing high amount of radiation in the environment. It resulted in thousands of casualties, mostly due to exposure to harmful radiation. One cannot deny the possibility of repetition of such disasters in future.

There are proponents and opponents of nuclear energy. You can go through the link on *applications of nuclear energy* for further information on the subject. However, only the future will make it clear whether nuclear energy is a boon or a bane!

Many people around the globe are convinced that one of the best solutions on how to free ourselves from being dependent on fossil fuels is using more nuclear power. Nuclear power is by many presented as the clean, reliable energy source, completely on par with renewable energy solutions like wind power, and solar power. Is nuclear energy really clean energy sources, and what about safety risks, are they really as minimal as nuclear plant owners say they are?

The safety of nuclear power is usually referred to some possible events that could lead to unwanted radioactive materials release like that unfortunate event that happened in Chernobyl more than 20 years ago, back in 1986, when one nuclear reactor exploded which resulted in a severe release of radioactivity. When people talk about the nuclear power safety they usually want to know what are the chances of nuclear reactor exploding. From current point of view chances for this are really minimal and almost negligible, and accidents like Three Mile Island and Chernobyl really look very unlikely, especially given today's maximum safety measures that are required in all nuclear power plants around the globe.

Nuclear reactor(s) but there is one issue that is much more important in the nuclear power story, namely the radioactive waste. Radioactive waste is really the biggest disadvantage that nuclear power has. Radioactive waste has a lifespan of 5000-10000 years, and current methods of storing this waste still do not provide total guarantee, since 5000 years time of potential danger is very long time to worry about. The thing you should also know that on average, a nuclear power plant annually generates around 20 metric tons of high-level radioactive waste. When you take into account every nuclear plant on Earth, the combined total Nuclear power is therefore almost completely safe regarding the possible explosion of number climbs to roughly 2,000 metric tons each year. This is whole lot of waste that needs to be safely stored each year.

With nuclear power plants there is also the risk of possible terrorist attack that could even wipe out an entire region in one foul swoop. So nuclear safety issue despite introduction of many new safety measures still remains major hurdle to nuclear power because although risks are extremely low, the consequences of possible nuclear accident could be fatal. Basically, what we are trying to say here is that stakes are simply too high, even with such small safety risks.

Safety therefore still remains the biggest disadvantage of nuclear power plants, though this is not the only disadvantage of nuclear power. The other disadvantage of nuclear power are high operational costs, especially since lot of money has to be spent on safety. Building nuclear power plant also doesn't come cheap.

Nuclear power also has some advantages that need to be mention here. Nuclear power doesn't depend on fossil fuels to produce electricity, and therefore the biggest advantage of nuclear power are minimal CO_2 emissions; in case of nuclear power these emissions are mostly associated with the life cycle of uranium, namely with the emission of gases during mining and transporting uranium.

Also, when it comes down to reliability very few other energy sources are as reliable as nuclear power is. All what it takes for constant generation of electricity is uranium, and there is still plenty of uranium left on our planet. Nuclear power plants also have very high efficiency, even comparable with coal power plants, meaning they can produce lot of electricity.

These two factors, reliability and efficiency, are the two main reasons why in 2007 a respectable 14 per cent of the world's electricity came from nuclear power. The United States produces the most nuclear energy, with nuclear power supplying around 19 per cent of consumed electricity. France, for instance, produces more than three quarters (78%) of its electricity from nuclear power plants.

HOW DOES NUCLEAR ENERGY AFFECT THE ENVIRONMENT?

Introduction

- Nuclear energy has been proposed as an answer to the need for a clean energy source as opposed to CO_2-producing plants. Nuclear energy is not necessarily a clean energy source. The effects nuclear energy have on the environment pose serious concerns that need to be considered, especially before the decision to build additional nuclear power plants is made.

Carbon Dioxide

- Nuclear power has been called a clean source of energy because the power plants do not release carbon dioxide. While this is true, it is deceiving. Nuclear power plants may not emit carbon dioxide during operation, but high amounts of carbon dioxide are emitted in activities related to building and running the plants. Nuclear power plants use uranium as fuel. The process of mining uranium releases high amounts of carbon dioxide into the environment. Carbon dioxide is also released into the environment when new nuclear power plants are built. Finally, the transport of radioactive waste also causes carbon dioxide emissions.

Low Level Radiation

- Nuclear power plants constantly emit low levels of radiation into the environment. There is a differing of opinion among scientists over the effects caused by constant low levels of radiation. Various scientific studies have shown an increased rate of cancer among people who live near nuclear power plants. Long-term exposure to low level radiation has been shown to damage DNA. The degree of damage low levels of radiation cause to wildlife, plants and the ozone layer is not fully understood. More research is being done to determine the magnitude of effects caused by low levels of radiation in the environment.

Radioacative Waste

- Radioactive waste is a huge concern. Waste from nuclear power plants can remain active for hundreds of thousands of years. Currently, much of the radioactive waste from nuclear power plants has been stored at the power plant. Due to space constraints, eventually the radioactive waste will need to be relocated. Plans have been proposed to bury the radioactive waste contained in casks in the Yucca Mountains in Nevada.

  There are several issues with burying the radioactive waste, Waste would be transported in large trucks. In the event of an accident, the radioactive waste could possibly leak. Another issue is uncertainty about whether the casks will leak after the waste is buried. The current amount of radioactive waste requiring long-term storage would fill the Yucca Mountains and new sites would need to be found to bury future radioactive waste. There is no current solution to deal with the issue of radioactive waste. Some scientists feel that the idea of building more nuclear power plants and worrying about dealing with the waste later has the potential of a dangerous outcome.

Cooling Water System

- Cooling systems are used to keep nuclear power plants from overheating. There are two main environmental problems associated with nuclear power plant cooling systems. First, the cooling system pulls water from an ocean or river source. Fish are inadvertently captured in the cooling system intake and killed. Second, after the water is used to cool the power plant, it is returned to the ocean or river. The water that is returned is approximately 25 degrees warmer than the water was originally. The warmer water kills some species offish and plant life.

Nuclear Power Plant Accidents and Terrorism

- According to the Union of Concerned Scientists, regulated safety procedures are not being followed to ensure that nuclear power plants are safe. Even if all safety precautions are followed, it is no guarantee that a nuclear power plant accident will not occur. If a nuclear power plant accident occurs, the environment and surrounding people could be exposed to high levels of radiation. Terrorism threats are another concern that needs to be addressed. A satisfactory plan to protect nuclear power plants from terrorism is not in place.

Conclusion

- There is no disagreement that clean sources of energy are vital to the environment. The disagreement lies in what form that clean energy should be in. Supporters of nuclear energy argue that it is an efficient source of energy that is easy to implement. People against nuclear energy propose using combined methods of solar, wind and geothermal energy. 'Solar, wind and geothermal energy still have environmental issues, but ones that are not as great as nuclear plants or coal-burning power plants.

Read more: *How Does Nuclear Energy Affect the Environment? | eHow.com http://www.ehow.com/how-does 4566966 nuclear-energy-affect-environment. html# ixzzlaBPYmqzi*

Environmental Impact of Nuclear Power

The *environmental impact of nuclear power* results from the *nuclear fuel cycle.* operation, and the effects of nuclear accidents.

The routine health risks and *greenhouse gas emissions* from nuclear fission power are small relative to those associated with coal, but there are 'catastrophic risks': the possibility of over-heated fuel releasing massive quantities of fission products to the environment, and *nuclear weapons* proliferation. The public is sensitive to these risks and there has been considerable *public opposition to nuclear power.* The 1979 *Three Mile Island accident* and 1986 *Chernobvl disaster,* along with high construction costs, ended the rapid growth of global nuclear power capacity.

In March 2011 an earthquake and tsunami caused damage that led to *explosions and partial meltdowns* at the *Fukushima I Nuclear Power Plant* in Japan. Concerns about the possibility of a large scale radiation leak resulted in 20 km exclusion zone being set up around the power plant and people within the 20-30km zone being advised to stay indoors. John Price, a former member of the Safety Policy Unit at the UK's National Nuclear Corporation, has said that it "might be 100 years before melting fuel rods can be safely removed from Japan's Fukushima nuclear plant".

Waste Streams

Nuclear power has at least four waste streams that contaminate and degrade land:

(1) they create *spent nuclear fuel* at the reactor site (including *Plutonium* waste);

(2) they produce tailings at *uranium mines* and mills;

(3) during operation they routinely release small amounts of radioactive isotopes;

(4) during *accidents* they can release large quantities of radioactivity.

The nuclear fuel cycle involves some of the most dangerous elements and isotopes known to humankind, including more than 100 dangerous *radionuclides* and carcinogens such as *strontium-90, iodine 131* and cesium - 137, which are the same toxins found in the fall out of nuclear weapons".

Radioactive Waste

Main article: *Radioactive waste*

High-level Waste

Around 20-30 tons of high-level waste are produced per month per nuclear reactor.The world's nuclear fleet creates about 10,000 metric tons of high-level spent nuclear fuel each year. Several methods have been suggested for final disposal of high-level waste, including deep burial in stable geological structures, transmutation, and removal to space. So far, none of these methods have been implemented.There is an "international consensus on the advisability of storing nuclear waste in deep underground repositories", but no country in the world has yet opened such a site. There are some 65,000 tons of nuclear waste now in temporary storage throughout the U.S., but in 2009, President Obama "halted work on a permanent repository at Yucca Mountain in Nevada, following years of controversy and legal wrangling".

Nuclear reprocessing may reduce the volume of high-level waste, but by itself does not reduce radioactivity or heat generation and therefore does not eliminate the need for a geological waste repository. Reprocessing has been politically controversial because of the potential to contribute to *nuclear proliferation,* the potential vulnerability to *nuclear terrorism*, the political challenges of repository siting (a problem-that applies equally to direct disposal of spent fuel), and because of its high cost compared to the once-through fuel cycle, the Obama administration has disallowed reprocessing of nuclear waste, citing nuclear proliferation concerns. Nine U.S. states have "explicit moratoria on new nuclear power" until a long-term storage solution emerges.

See also: *High-level Radioactive Waste Management* and *Deep Geological Repository.*

Other Waste

Moderate amounts of low-level waste are produced through chemical and volume control system (CVCS). This includes gas, liquid, and solid waste produced through the process of purifying the water through evaporation. Liquid waste is reprocessed continuously, and gas waste is filtered, compressed, stored to allow decay, diluted, and then discharged. The rate at which this is allowed is regulated and studies must prove that such discharge does not violate dose limits to a member of the public (see *radioactive effluent* emissions).

Solid waste can be disposed of simply by placing it where it will not be disturbed for a few years. There are three low-level waste disposal sites in the United States in South Carolina, Utah, and Washington. Solid waste from the CVCS is combined with solid radwaste that comes from handling materials before it is buried off-site.

POWER PLANT EMISSIONS

Radioactive Gases and Effluents

Most commercial nuclear power plants release gaseous and liquid radiological effluents into the environment as a byproduct of the Chemical Volume Control System, which are monitored in the US by the EPA and the NRC. Civilians living within 50 miles (80 km) of a nuclear power plant typically receive about 0.1 μSv per year. For comparison, the average person living at or above sea level receives at least 260 μSv from *cosmic radiation.*

The total amount of radioactivity released through this method depends on the power plant, the regulatory requirements, and the plant's performance. Atmospheric dispersion models combined with pathway models are employed to accurately approximate the dose to a member of the public from the effluents emitted. *Effluent monitoring* is conducted continuously at the plant.

Limits for the Canadian plants are shown below:

Regulatory limits on Radioactive Gaseous Effluents from Canadian Nuclear Power Plants.

Effluent Units	Tritium (TBqb × 10^4)	Iodine-131 (TBq)	Noble Gases (TBq-MeVe × 10^4)	Parti-culates (TBq)	Carbon-14 (TBq × 10^3)
Point Lepreau Nuclear Generating Station	43.0	9.9	7.3	5.2	3.3
Bruce Nuclear Generatiny Station A	38.0	1.2	25.0	2.7	2.8
Bruce B	47.0	1.3	61.0	4.8	3.0
Darlington	21.0	0.6	21.0	4.4	1.4
Pickering Nuclear Generating Station A	34.0	2.4	8.3	5.0	8.8
Pickering B	34.0	2.4	8.3	5.0	8.8
Gentilly-2	44.0	1.3	17.0	1.9	0.91

Effluent emissions *for Nuclear power in the United States* are regulated by 10 CFR 50.36(a)(2). For detailed information, consult the *Nuclear Regulatory Commission's database.*

Tritium

A leak of radioactive water at *Vermont Yankee* in 2010, along with similar incidents at more than 20 other US nuclear plants in recent years, has kindled doubts about the reliability, durability, and maintenance of aging nuclear installations in the United States.

Tritium is a radioactive isotope of hydrogen that emits a low-energy beta particle and is usually measured in *becquerels* (*i.e.,* atoms decaying per second) per litre (Bq/L). Tritium becomes dissolved in ordinary water when released from a nuclear plant. The primary concern for tritium release is the presence in drinking water, in addition to biological magnification leading to tritium in crops and animals consumed for food.

Legal concentration limits have differed greatly to place to place (*see para below*). For example, in June 2009 the Ontario Drinking Water Advisory Council recommended lowering the limit from 7,000 Bq/L to 20 Bq/L. According to the NRC, tritium is the least dangerous radionuclide because it emits very weak radiation and leaves the body relatively quickly. The typical human body contains roughly 3,700 Bq of *potassium-40*. The amount released by any given plant also varies greatly; the total release for plants in the United States in 2003 was at least counted to be 0 and at most 2,080 curies (77 TBq).

Tritium Effluent Limits Country Limit (Bq/L) Australia 76,103 Finland 30,000 WHO 10,000 Switzerland 10,000 Russia 7,700 Ontario, Canada 7,000 United States 740 European Union 1001 California Public Health Goal 14.8.

Uranium Mining

Uranium mining can use large amounts of water—for example, the Roxby Downs mine in South Australia uses 35,000 m^3 of water each day and plans to increase this to 150,000m^3 per day.

Risk of Cancer

There have been several epidemiological studies that claim to demonstrate increased risk of various diseases, especially cancers, among people who live near nuclear facilities. A widely cited 2007 *meta-analysis* by Baker *et al.*, of 17 research papers was published in the European Journal of Cancer Care. It offered evidence of elevated leukaemia rates among children living near 136 nuclear facilities in the United Kingdom, Canada, France, United States, Germany, Japan, and Spain. However this study has been criticized on several grounds—such as combining heterogeneous data (different age groups, sites that were not nuclear power plants, different zone definitions), arbitrary selection of 17 out of 37 individual studies, exclusion of sites with zero observed cases or deaths, etc. Elevated leukaemia rates among children were also found in a 2008 German study by Kaatsch *et al.* that examined residents living near 16 major nuclear power plants in Germany.This study has also been criticised on several grounds.These 2007 and 2008 results are not consistent with many other studies that have tended not to show such associations. The British Committee on Medical Aspects of Radiation in the Environment issued a study in 2011 of children under five living near 13 nuclear power plants in the UK during the period 1969-2004, The committee found that children living near power plants in Britain are no more likely to develop leukaemia than those living elsewhere.

Comparison to Coal-fired Generation

In terms of net radioactive release, the *National Council on Radiation Protection and Measurements* (NCRP) estimated the average radioactivity per short ton of coal is 17,100 millicuries/4,000,000 tons. With 154 coal plants in the United States, this amounts to emissions of 0.6319 TBq per year for a single plant.

In terms of dose to a human living nearby, it is sometimes cited that coal plants release 100 times the radioactivity of nuclear plants. This comes from NCRP Reports No. 92 and No. 95 which estimated the dose to the population from 1000 MWe coal and nuclear plants at 4.9 man-Sv/year and 0.048 man-Sv/year respectively (a typical *Chest x-ray* gives a dose of about 0.06 mSv for comparison). The *Environmental Protection Agency* estimates an added dose of 0.3 u-Sv per year for living within 50 miles (80 km) of a coal plant and 0.009 milli-rem for a nuclear plant for yearly radiation dose estimation. Nuclear power plants in normal operation emit less radioactivity than coal power plants.

Unlike coal-fired or oil-fired generation, nuclear power generation does not directly produce any sulfur dioxide, nitrogen oxides, or mercury (pollution from fossil fuels is blamed for 24,000 early deaths each year in the U.S. alone). However, as with all energy sources, there is some pollution associated with support activities such as manufacturing and transportation.

Waste Heat

As with some *thermal power stations,* nuclear plants exchange 60 to 70 per cent of their thermal energy by cycling with a body of water or by evaporating water through a *cooling tower.* This thermal efficiency is somewhat lower than that of coal fired power plants, thus creating more *waste heat.*

The cooling options are typically once-through cooling with river or sea water, pond cooling, or cooling towers. Many plants have an *artificial lake* like the *Shearon Harris Nuclear Power Plant* or the *South Texas Nuclear Generating Station.* Shearon Harris uses a cooling tower but South Texas does not and discharges back into the lake. The *North Anna Nuclear Generating Station* uses a cooling pond or artificial lake, which at the plant discharge canal is often about 30°F warmer than in the other parts of the lake or in normal lakes (this is cited as an attraction of the area by some residents). The environmental effects on the artificial lakes are often weighted in arguments against construction of new plants, and during droughts have drawn media attention.

The *Turkey Point Nuclear Generating Station* is credited with helping the consenvation status of the *American Crocodile,* largely an effect of the waste heat produced.

The *Indian Point* nuclear power plant in *New York* is in a hearing process to determine if a cooling system other than river water will be necessary (conditional upon the plants extending their operating licences).

It is possible to use waste heat in *cogeneration* applications such as *district heating.* The principles of cogeneration and district heating with nuclear power are the same as any other form of thermal power production. One use of nuclear heat generation was with the *Agesta Nuclear Power Plant* in Sweden. In Switzerland, the *Beznau Nuclear Power Plant* provides heat to about 20,000 people. However, district heating with nuclear power plants is less common than with other modes of waste heat generation: because of either *siting regulations* and/or the *NIMBY* effect, nuclear stations are generally not built in densely populated areas. Waste heat is more commonly used in industrial applications.

During Europe's *2003* and *2006 heat waves.* French, Spanish and German utilities had to secure exemptions from regulations in order to discharge overheated water into the environment. Some nuclear reactors shut down.

Glossary
Refinery-related Terms

ABSORPTION The disappearance of one substance into another into another so that the absorbed substance loses its identifying characteristics, while the absorbing substance retains most of its original physical aspects. Used in refining to selectively remove specific components from process streams.

ACID TREATMENT A process in which unfinished petroleum products such as gasoline, kerosene and lubricating oil stocks are treated with sulphuric acid to improve colour, odour, and other properties.

ADDITIVE Chemicals added to petroleum products in small amounts to improve quality or add special characteristics.

ADSORPTION Adhesion of the molecules of gases or liquids to the surface of solid materials.

AIR FIN COOLERS A radiator-like device used to cool or condense hot hydrocarbons; also called fin fans.

ALICYCLIC HYDROCARBONS Cyclic (ringed) hydrocarbons in which the rings are made up only of carbon atoms.

ALIPHATIC HYDROCARBONS Hydrocarbons characterized by open-chain structures: ethane, butane, butane, acetylene, etc.

ALKYLATION A process using sulphuric or hydro-fluoric acid as a catalyst to combine olefins (usually butylene) and isobutene to produce a high-octane product known as alkylate.

API GRAVITY An arbitrary scale expressing the density of petroleum products.

AROMATIC Organic compounds with one or more benzene rings.

ASPHALTENES The asphalt compounds soluble in carbon disulfide but insoluble in paraffin naphthas.

ATMOSPHERIC TOWER A distillation unit operated at atmospheric pressure.

BENZENE An unsaturated, six-carbon ring, basic aromatic compounds.

BLEEDER VALVE A small-flow valve connected to a fluid process vessel or line for the purpose of bleeding off small quantities of contained fluid. It is installed with a block valve to determine if the block valve is closed tightly.

BLENDING The process of mixing two or more petroleum products with different properties to produce a finished product with desired characteristics.

BLOCK VALVE A valve used to isolate equipment.

BLOWDOWN The removal of hydrocarbons from a process unit, vessel, or line on a scheduled or emergency basis by the use of pressure through special piping and drums provided for this purpose.

BLOWER Equipment for moving large volumes of gas against low-pressure heads.

BOILING RANGE The range of temperature (usually at atmospheric pressure) at which the boiling (or distillation) of a hydrocarbon liquid commences, proceeds, and finishes.

BOTTOMS Tower bottoms are residue remaining in a distillation unit after the highest boiling-point material to be distilled has been removed. Tank bottoms are the heavy materials that accumulate in the bottom of storage tanks, usually comprised of oil, water, and foreign matter.

BUBBLE TOWER A fractionating (distillation) tower in which the rising vapours pass through layers of condensate, bubbling under caps on a series of plates.

CATALSYST A Material that aids or promotes a chemical reaction between other substances does not react itself. Catalysts increase reaction speeds and can provide control by increasing desirable reactions and decreasing undesirable reactions.

CATALYTIC CRACKING The process of breaking up heavier hydrocarbon molecules into lighter hydrocarbon fractions by use of heat and catalysts.

CAUSTIC WASH A Process in which distillate is treated with sodium hydroxide to remove acidic contaminants that contribute to poor odour and stability.

CHD UNIT See Hydrodesulphurization.

COKE A high carbon-content residue remaining from the destructive distillation of petroleum residue.

COKING A process for thermally converting and upgrading heavy residual into lighter product and by product petroleum coke. Coking also is the removal of all lighter distillable hydrocarbons that leaves a residue of carbon in the bottom of units or as buildup or deposits on equipment and catalysts.

CONDENSATE The liquid hydrocarbon resulting from cooling vapours.

CONDENSER A heat-transfer device that cools and condenses vapour by removing heat via a cooler medium such as water or lower-temperature hydrocarbons streams.

CONDENSER REFLUX Condensate that is returned to the original unit to assist in giving increased conversion or recovery.

COOLER A heat exchanger in which hot liquid hydrocarbon is passed through pipes immersed in cool water to lower its temperature.

CRACKING The breaking up of heavy molecular weight hydrocarbons into lighter hydrocarbon molecules by the application of heat and pressure, with or without the use of catalysts.

CRUDE ASSAY A procedure for determining the general distillation and quality characteristics of crude oil.

CRUDE OIL A naturally occurring mixture of hydrocarbons that usually includes small quantities of sulphur, nitrogen, and oxygen derivatives of hydrocarbons as well as trace metals.

CYCLE GAS OIL Cracked gas oil returned to a cracking unit.

DEASPHALTING Process of removing asphaltic materials from reduced crude using liquid propane to dissolve no asphaltic compounds.

DEBUTANIZER A fractionating column used to remove butane and lighter components from liquid streams.

DE-ETHANIZER A fractionating column designed to remove ethane and gases from heavier hydrocarbons.

DEHYDROGENATION A reaction in which hydrogen atoms are eliminated from a molecule. Dehydrogenation is used to convert ethane, propane, and butane into olefins (ethylene, propylene, and butanes).

DEPENTANIZER A fractionating column used to remove pentane and lighter fractions from hydrocarbon streams.

DEPROPANIZER A fractionating column for removing propane and lighter components from liquid streams.

DESALTING Removal of mineral salts (most chlorides, *e.g.*, magnesium chloride and sodium chloride) from crude oil.

DESULPHURIZATION A chemical treatment to remove sulphur or sulphur compounds from hydrocarbons.

DEWAXING The removal of wax from petroleum products (usually lubricating oils and distillate fuels) by solvent absorption, chilling and filtering.

DEWAXING The removal of wax from petroleum products (usually lubricating oils and distillate fuels) by solvent absorption, chilling, and filtering.

DIETHANOLAMINE A chemical $C_4H_{11}O_2N$ used to remove H_2S from gas streams.

DISTILLATE The products of distillation formed by condensing vapours.

DOWNFLOW Process in which the hydrocarbon stream flows top to bottom.

DRY GAS Natural gas with so little natural gas liquids that it is nearly all methane with some ethane.

FEEDSTOCK Stock from which material is taken to be fed (charged) into a processing unit.

FLASHING The process in which a heated oil under pressure is suddenly vapourized in a tower by reducing pressure.

FLASH POINT Lowest temperature at which a petroleum will give off sufficient vapour so that the vapour-air mixture above the surface of the liquid will propagate a flame away from the source of ignition.

FLUX Lighter petroleum used to fluidize heavier residual so that it can be pumped.

FOULING Accumulation of deposits in condensers, exchangers, etc.

FRACTION One of the portions of fractional distillation having are restricted boiling range.

FRACTIONATING COLUMN Process unit that separates various fractions of petroleum by simple distillation, with the column tapped at various levels to separate and remove fractions according to their boiling ranges.

FUEL GAS Refinery gas used for heating.

GAS OIL Middle-distillate petroleum fraction with a boiling range of about 350°-750° F, usually includes diesel fuel, kerosene, heating oil, and light fuel oil.

GASOLINE A blend of naphthas and other refinery products with sufficiently high octane and other desirable characteristics to be suitable for use as fuel in internal combustion engines.

HEADER A manifold that distributes fluid from a series of smaller pipes or conduits.

HEAT As used in the Health Considerations paragraphs of this document, heat refers to thermal burns for contact with hot surfaces, hot liquids and vapours, steam, etc.

HEAT EXCHANGER Equipment to transfer heat between two flowing streams of different temperatures. Heat is transferred liquids or liquids and gases through a tubular wall.

HIGH-LINE OR HIGH-PRESSURE GAS High-pressure (100 psi) gas from cracking unit distillate drums that is compressed and combined with low-line gas as gas absorption feedstock.

HYDROCRACKING A Process used to convert heavier feedstock into lower-boiling, higher-value products. The process employs high pressure, high temperature, a catalyst, and hydrogen.

HYDRODESULPHURIZATION A catalytic process in which the principal purpose is to remove sulphur from petroleum fractions in the presence of hydrogen.

HYDROFINISHING A catalytic treating process carried out in the presence of hydrogen to improve the properties of low viscosity-index naphthenic and medium viscosity naphthenic oils. It is also applied to paraffin waxes and microcrystalline waxes for the removal of undesirable components. This process consumes hydrogen and is used in lieu of acid treating.

HYDROFORMING Catalytic reforming of naphtha at elevated temperatures and moderate pressures in the presence of hydrogen to from high-octane BTX aromatics for motor fuel or chemical manufacture. This process results in a net production of hydrogen and has rendered thermal reforming somewhat obsolete. It represents the total effect of numerous simultaneous reactions such as cracking polymerization, dehydrogenation, and isomerization.

HYDROGENATION The chemical addition of hydrogen to a material in the presence of a catalyst.

INHIBITOR Additive used to prevent or retard undesirable changes in the quality of the product, or in the condition of the equipment in which the product is used.

ISOMERIZATION A reaction that cataiytically converts straight-chain hydrocarbon molecules into branched-chain molecules of substantially higher octane number. The reaction rearranges the carbon skeleton of a molecule without adding or removing anything from the original material.

ISO-OCTANE A hydrocarbon molecule (2,2,4- trimethylpentane) with excellent antiknock characteristics on which the octane number of 100 is based.

KNOCKOUT DRUM A vessel wherein suspended liquid is separated from gas or vapour.

LEAN OIL Absorbent oil fed to absorption towers in which gas is to be stripped. After absorbing the heavy ends from the gas, it becomes fat oil. When the heavy ends are subsequently stripped again becomes lean oil.

LOW-LINE or LOW-PRESSURE GAS Low pressure (5 psi) gas from atmospheric and vacuum distillation recovery systems that is collected in the gas plant for compression to higher pressures.

NAPTHA A general term used for low boiling hydrocarbon fraction that are a major component of gasoline. Aliphatic refers to those naphthas containing less than 0.1 per cent benzene and with carbon numbers from C3 and contain significant quantities of aromatics hydrocarbons such as benzene (>0.1%), toluene, and xylene.

NAPHTHENES Hydrocarbon (cycloalkanes) with the general formula CnH_2n, in which the carbon atoms are arranged to from a ring.

OCYANE NUMER A number indicating the relative antiknock characteristics of gasoline.

OLEFINS A Family of unsaturated hydrocarbons with one carbon-carbon double bond and the general formula CnH_2n.

PARAFFINS A Family of saturated aliphatic hydrocarbons (alkanes) with the general formula CnH_{2n+2}.

POLYFORMING The thermal conversion of naphtha and gas oils into high-quality gasoline at high temperature and pressure in the presence of recalculated hydrocarbon gases.

POLYMERIZATION The process of combining two or more unsaturated organic molecules to from a single (heavier) molecule with the same elements in the same proportions as in the original molecule.

PREHEATER Exchanger used to heat hydrocarbons before they are fed to a unit.

PRESSURE-REGULATING VALVE A valve that releases or holds process-system pressure (that is, opens or closes) either by preset spring tension or by actuation by a valve controller to assume any desired position between fully open and fully closed.

PYROLYSIS GASOLINE A by product from the manufacture ethylene by steam cracking of hydrocarbon fractions such as naphtha or gas oil.

PYROPHORIC IRON SULPHIDE A substance typically formed inside tanks and processing unit by the corrosive interaction of sulphur compounds in the hydrocarbons and the iron and steel in the equipment. On exposure to air (oxygen).

QUENCH OIL Oil injected into a product leaving a cracking or reforming heater to lower the temperature and stop the cracking process.

RAFFINATE The product resulting from a solvent extraction process and consisting mainly of those components that are least soluble in the solvent. The product recovered from an extraction process is relatively free of aromatics, naphthenes, and other constituents that adversely affects physical parameters.

REACTOR The vessel in which chemical reactions take place during a chemical conversion type portion of the tower.

REBOILER An auxiliary unit of a fractionating tower designed to supply additional heat to the lower portion of the tower.

RECYCLE GAS High hydrogen-content gas returned to a unit for reprocessing.

REDUCED CRUDE A residual product remaining after the removal by distillation of an appreciable quantity of the more volatile components of crude oil.

REFLUX The portion of the distillate returned to the fractionating column to assist in attaining better separation into desired fractions.

REFORMATE A graded naphtha resulting from catalytic or thermal reforming.

REFORMING The thermal or catalytic conversion of petroleum naphtha into more volatile products of higher octane number. It represents the total effect of numerous simultaneous reactions such as cracking, polymerization, dehydrogenation and isomerization.

REGENERATION In a catalytic process the reactivation of the catalyst, sometimes done by burning off the coke deposits under care fully controlled conditions of temperature and oxygen content of the regeneration gas stream.

SCRUBBING Purification of a gas or liquid by washing it in a tower.

SOLVENT EXTRACTION The separation of materials of different chemical types and solubility's by selective solvent action.

SOUR GAS Natural gas that contains, sulphur-bearing compounds such as hydrogen sulphide and mercaptans.

STABILIZATION A process for separating the gaseous and more volatile liquid hydrocarbons from crude petroleum or gasoline and leaving a stable (less-volatile) liquid so that it can be handled or stored with less change in composition.

STRAIGHT-RUN GASOLINE Gasoline produced by the primary distillation of crude oil. It contains no cracked, polymerized, alkylated, reformed, or visbroken stock.

STRIPPING The removal (by steam-induced vapourization or flash evaporation) of the more volatile components from a cut or fraction.

SULPHURIC ACID TREATING A refining process in which unfinished petroleum products such as gasoline, kerosene, and lubricating oil stocks are treated with sulphuric acid to improve their colour, odour, and other characteristics.

SULPHURIZATION Combining sulphur compounds with petroleum lubricants.

SWEETENING Processes that either remove obnoxious sulphur compounds (primarily hydrogen sulphide, mercaptans, and thiophens) from petroleum fractions or streams, or convert them as in the case of mercaptans, to odourless disulphides to improve odour, colour, and oxidation stability.

SWITCH LOADING The loading of a high static-charge retaining hydrocarbon (*i.e.,* diesel fuel) into a tank truck, tank car or other vessel that has previously contained a low-flash hydrocarbon (gasoline) and may contain a flammable mixture of vapour and air.

TAIL GAS The lightest hydrocarbon gas released from a refining process.

THERMAL CRAKINH The breaking up of heavy oil molecules into lighter fractions by the use of high temperature without the aid of catalysts.

TURNAROUND A planned complete shutdown of an entire process or section of a refinery, or of an entire refinery to perform major maintenance, overhaul, and repair operations and to inspect, test and replace process materials and equipment.

VACUUM DISTILLATION The distillation of petroleum under vaccum which reduces the boiling temperature sufficiently to prevent cracking or decomposition of the feedstock.

VAPOUR The gaseous phase of a substance that is a liquid at normal temperature and pressure.

VISBREAKING Viscosity breaking is a low-temperature cracking process used to reduce the viscosity or pour point of straight-run residuum.

WET GAS A gas containing a relatively high proportion of hydrocarbons that are recoverable as liquids.

Index

A

Advantages of ethanol fuel, 146-155
- additive compativity, 148-149
- corrosion, 149
- deposits, 148
- E10 blending and handling issues, 149
- E10 performance issues fuel properties, 148
- equipment compativibility, 149
- ethanol challenges in a current scenario and technical tips, 148
- ethanol fuel
  - ease of access, 146
  - if hydrogen producer, 147
  - is cost-effective, 147
  - is environment friendly, 147
  - promotes agriculture, 147
  - reduces GHG gases, 147
- ethanol fuel advantage of
  - employability, 147
  - independency, 146-147
- ethanol fuel as
  - organic fuel, 146
  - source of renewable energy, 146
- fuel economy, 149
- tech tips, 150-151
- what are the key issues related to E10 ethanol use, 148

Alternative Fuels Data Center, 10
American Crocodile, 214
American Petroleum Institute (API), 83
American Society for Testing and Materials, 27
Andhra Pradesh, 138
Aspergillus, 165
ASTM, 58
Aviation gasoline, 27
Aviation Turbine fuel, 5

B

Biodiesel, 58-64
- biodiesel and air pollution, 62
- biodiesel cost, 62-63
- engine studies, 60-61
- engine warranties, 64
- mixing and storage of biodiesel, 62
- potential fuel from oil crops, 63

Bioethanol from lignocellulose, 156-169
- bioethanol, 156-157
- by-products of dilute-acid hydrolysis, 166-167
- dilute-acid hydrolysis, 165-166
- environmental impact, 159-160
- eth..nol as fuel, 157-158
- furan compounds, 169
- hydrolysis, 164-165

lignocellulosic materials, 163-164
market, 161-162
organic acids, 167-168
phenolic compounds, 168-169
Bioethanol, 151
bioethanol production, 153
concentrated acid hydrolysis process, 154
dilute acid hydrolysis, 154
dry milling process, 154
enzymatic hydrolysis, 154
fractional distillation process, 155
introduction, 151-153
sugar fermentation process, 155
wet milling processes, 154
what are the benefits of bioethanol, 153
British Committee on Medical Aspects of Radiation, 213
Bureau of Indian Standard Act, 1986, 39

C

Calculated Cetane Index, 55
California Energy Commission, 183
California Environmental Quality Act, 184
Chernobyl disaster, 210
Chernobyl Nuclear Power Plant in Ukraine, 206
China, 162
Clostridium acetobutlium, 24
CNG, 22, 35
CWS, 15
Czech Republic, 201

D

Description of petroleum refining processes and related health and safety considerations, 88
alkylation, 109-110
amine plants, 114-115
analytic cracking, 99-100
asphalt production, 115-116
atmospheric distillation tower, 92-93
blending, 118
catalytic hydrotreating, 105-106
catalytic reforming, 104-105
crude oil distillation, 92
crude oil pretreatment, 88-91
fluid catalytic cracking, 100-101
health and safety consideration, 91, 93-95, 96, 98-99, 101-102, 103-104
hydrocracking process, 103
hydrocracking, 102-103
hydrogen production, 117
isomerization, 107-108
lubricant, wax and grease manufacturing processes, 118-120
other hydrotreating processes, 106-107
polymerization, 108-109
saturate gas plants, 115
solvent dewaxing, 96
solvent extraction, 95-96
and dewaxing, 95
sulphuric acid alkylation process, 110-112
sweetening and treating processes, 112-113
thermal cracking, 96-98
unsaturated gas plants, 113-114
Diesel, 53-57
gas liquid chromatograpyh for quantitative determination of adulteration in diesel with kerosene, 56
introduction, 53
light diesel oil, 57
observations and calculations, 56
test method, 53-55
DNA, 208

E

Earth, 177
Engine lubricating oil, 65-78
calculation, 67, 70
introduction, 65
method, 67
neutralisation value, 69

procedure for acid number, 69-70
procedure for base number, 70-71
reagents, 71
standardisation of acid, 71
summary of test method, 69
test methods and their significance, 66-67
total base number of new and used lubricating oils, 71
total base umber, 71-72
viscosity index, 68-69
Environmental Protection Agency, 213
ETBE, 87
Ethanol fuel, 131-145, 146-155
advantages of the system, 137
alcohol production, 141
anhydrous ethanol potential for gasoley blending, 138-139
availability, 140
cost, 140-141
demand supply for ethanol, 137-138
ethanol and health, 145
ethanol and your car, 144
ethanol as a fuel, 132-133
ethanol world-wide, 133-134
exhaust versus evaporative emission, 144-145
introduction, 131-132
molecular sieve ethanol dehydration technology for fuel ethanol, 136-137
molecular-sieve-dehydration, 135-136
process-description, 137
process-of-manufacture, 135
sugar industry perspective and ethanol production, 139
why ethanol blended petrol, 143-144
EU, 162
European General of Cancer Care, 213

F

Fuel oil, 5
Fuel uses, 44
heating and lighting, 44-45
Furnace oil/black oil, 75
introduction, 75
test methods and their significance, 76-77

G

Gasohol Programme, 137
Gazette of India, 134-134
Global warming, 203
GoM, 143
Good Business, 35
Green house effect, 20

H

Health and safety considerations, 88
Hidden Hills, 183
High speed diesel, 5
How does nuclear energy affect the environment, 207
carbon dioxide, 208
cooling water system, 209
environmental impact of nuclear power, 209-210
high-level waste, 210-211
introduction, 207-208
low level radiation, 208
MKVI spareswww.gasturbinecontrols.com, 209
nuclear power plant accidents and terrorism, 209
other waste, 211
radioactive waste, 208
radioactive waste, 210
waste streams, 210
Hydrogen as fuel, 193
advantages, 193
disadvantages, 194-197
fuel source, 193
retail availability, 193
wholesale availability, 193

I

Indian standard, 37
- anhydrous ethanol for use in automotive fuel-specification, 37-38
- BIS certification marking, 39
- marking, 39
- packing and marking, 39
- quality of reagents, 40
- requirements, 38-39

Institute of Defence Studies and Analyses, 143
International Kyoto Conference on Climate Change, 181
Introduction, 1-10
- advantages, 10
- alternative fuel types, 9
- avoiding carbon dioxide emissions entirely, 8-9
- bulk petroleum products, 4-5
- carbon content, 8
- disadvantages, 10
- fuel chemistry, 5-6
- fuel source, 9
- general nature of petroleum and bulk petroleum products, 1
- hydrocarbons, 1-2
- incomplete combustion, 6-7
- molecular size, 6
- other types of compounds in petroleum, 3
- oxygen content, 7-8
- retail availability, 10
- types of crude oil, 3-4
- wholesale availability, 10

K

Karnataka, 138
Kerosene, 42-52
- cooking, 47
- entertainment, 47
- history, 43-44
- other uses, 47-48
- properties, 42-43
- toxicity, 49
- transportation, 46-47

Kerosene/superior kerosene oil, 49
- introduction, 49
- test methods as per IS 1459/1974, 49-51
- thin layer chromatographic methods for the detection of oil soluble dyes, 51

Kingston Fossil Plant, 20

L

Light diesel oil, 5, 53
Lignocellulose, 156-169
Liquid fuels, adulteration and environmental impact, 22-41
- adulteration and emissions, 30
- adulteration detection, 31-32
- common forms of fuel adulterants, 28-29
- common fuel additives, 27-28
- consumers front, 35-36
- fuel adulteration and environmental effect, 29-30
- fuel impurities, 25-26
- general properties of the liquid fuel, 24-25
- green fuel, 36-37
- impacts due to gasoline adulteration, 30-31
- impacts due to diesel adulteration, 31
- introduction, 22-24
- limitations of marker system, 34
- properties of markers, 33-34
- selected parameters for gasoline testing, 32
- selected parameters for diesel testing, 32-33
- some important measures to control fuel adulteration, 34-35

LPG, 4, 22, 35, 99
Lubricating greases, 72
- acidity and alkalinity of greases, 73
- block penetration, 75

classification of greases, 73
cone penetration, 75
corrosion ASTM D 4048: P 51 IS 1448 methods of tests, 74
drop point, 73
evaporation loss, 74
introduction, 72
oil separation from lubricating gases during storage, 74
oxidation stability, 74
prolonged worked penetration, 75
thermal stability, 75
worked penetration, 75

M

MDGs, 181
Mile Island, 206
Ministry of Petroleum and Natural Gas Resolution, 134
Molecular Sieve Beds, 137
MPNG, 139

N

NASA, 197
National Council on Radiation Protection and Measurements, 213
New York Mercantile exchange, 16
NGOs, 35
NIMBY, 214
Nuclear fuels, 198-214
benefits of using nuclear power, 200
future of nuclear power, 201
how does nuclear energy work, 199-200
introduction to nuclear energy, 197
nuclear energy and the environment, 199
nuclear fission and nuclear fusion, 197
uranium, 197
using nuclear energy to generate electricity, 197
Nuclear power technology development section, 201
applications of nuclear energy, 202
benefits of nuclear energy, 202
highlights and events, 201
IAEA nuclear power newsletter, 201
limitations of nuclear energy, 202
new leadership for nuclear power technology development, 201
non-electric applications of nuclear energy, 201
nuclear energy at work, 202-203
uses of nuclear energy, 203
NYMEX, 16

O

Obama, 210
Ontario Drinking Water Advisory Council, 212
Other refinery operations, 120
cooling towers, 125-126
electrical power, 126-127
feedwater, 122-123
gas and air compressors, 127-128
heat exchangers, coolers and process heaters, 120-121
heater fuel, 121-122
marine, tank car, and tank truck loading and unloading, 128
pressure relief health and safety considerations, 123-124
pressure-relief and flare systems, 123
pumps, piping and valves, 129-130
steam generation, 121
tank storage, 130
turbines, 128-129
wastewater treatment, 124-125

P

Penicillium, 165
Pennyslvania Main Line Canal, 44
Petroleum refining operations, 87
introduction, 87
refining operations, 87-88
Petroleum, 79-130
basic refinery process, 80-81

basics of crude oil, 81-83
basics of hydrocarbon chemistry, 83-85
common refinery chemicals, 87
introduction, 79-80
major refinery products, 86-87
non-hydrocarbons, 85-86
Planning Commission, 140
Power plant emissions, 211
comparison to coal-fired generation, 213-214
radioactive gases and effluents, 211-212
risk of cancer, 213
tritium, 212-213
uranium mining, 213
waste heat, 214
Project Lapponia, 46
PVTECH, 189

R

Reasons to use nuclear energy, 203
advantages and disadvantages of nuclear energy, 204-205
clean water, 203
environmental safety, 203
food an agriculture, 204
human health, 204
peaceful uses, 204
reduces the dependence on fossil fuels, 204
reliable, 203-204
what are the advantages of nuclear energy, 205
what are the disadvantages of nuclear energy, 205-207

S

Saccharomyces cerevisiae, 156, 169
Safety Policy Unit, 210
Solar fuel, 170-182
about solar power applications, 177
advantages of solar power, 178-180
advantages, 180
direct DC, 178
disadvantages, 181
grid tied with battery backup, 177-178
hybrid power systems, 178
introduction to solar energy, 172-177
off-grid, 178
relation between environment, 181
solar energy and the environment, 181-182
solar power systems, 177
sun, 170
using sunlight, 170-172
Solar power, 183-197
advantages, 191
disadvantages, 192
how it works, 190-191
industry and the environment, 192-193
introduction, 183-184
new models of solar pumps, 186
our specialization is in providing DC application solutions for, 189-190
photovolatic technology, 188-189
product and services, 189
renewable and non-renewable, 192
solar pump performance data, 187
solar water pump for irrigation, 184-188
Solid fuels and environment, 11-21
South Texas Nuclear Generating Station, 214
Sterile Insect Technique (SIT), 204
Superior Kerosene Oil, 35

T

TAME, 87
TEL, 87
Trichoderma, 165
Types of solid fuels, 11
advantages and disadvantages, 18
advantages, 20
bagasse, 18
charcoal, 16-17

coal, 11-12
    as fuel, 14-15
    as traded commodity, 15-16
coke burning, 17
cultural usage, 16
disadvantages, 20
dung cakes, 19
economic aspects, 19
environmental effects, 19-20
hexamine fuel tablets, 17-18
refined coal, 15
types of coal, 12-14
wood pellets, 18-19

U

UK National Nuclear Corporation, 210
USA, 7
USS Nautilus, 199
USSR Obninsk Nuclear Power Plant in 1954, 199

V

VOC, 160

W

West Texas Crudes, 83

Y

Yucca Mountains, 208